BEFORE YOU GO

BEFORE YOU GO

LOWER LEAGUE LIFE AND LOVE AT THE LAMEX

JOHN AIZLEWOOD

First published by Pitch Publishing, 2025

Pitch Publishing
9 Donnington Park,
85 Birdham Road,
Chichester, West Sussex,
PO20 7AJ
www.pitchpublishing.co.uk
info@pitchpublishing.co.uk

© 2025, John Aizlewood

Every effort has been made to trace the copyright.
Any oversight will be rectified in future editions at the
earliest opportunity by the publisher.

All rights reserved. No part of this book may be reproduced,
sold or utilised in any form or transmitted in any form or by
any means, electronic or mechanical, including photocopying,
recording or by any information storage and retrieval system,
without prior permission in writing from the publisher.

A CIP catalogue record is available for this book
from the British Library.

ISBN 978 1 83680 022 4

Printed and bound on FSC® certified paper in line with
our continuing commitment to ethical business practices,
sustainability and the environment.

Typesetting and origination by Pitch Publishing
Printed and bound in India by Replika Press Pvt. Ltd.

Contents

Introduction 9

July – Anticipation 23

August – On Our Way, Sort Of 34

September – Quinn the Eskimo's Here. 59

October – Kwame Poku, We'll Never Forget You 75

November – Our Unhappy Home Life. 109

December – The Most Footballistic Month 129

January – Includes the Best Night of Our Lives 155

February – Is That Really You, Vadaine Oliver? 187

March – 'Why Are All Our Strikers Awful?' 224

April – The Things We Do for Love and a Free Pie. . 262

May – Is That All There Is? Yes 295

Appendix 1: Best and Worst Moments. 304

Appendix 2: The Players 306

Acknowledgements. 315

Bibliography 316

For the accidental gang

Introduction

The First Photograph

There we are. That's us. I'm looking at the photograph on Stevenage FC's website meant to seduce potential season ticket purchasers for the 2024/25 season. It's probably from April 2024's calamitous late-season home loss to Burton Albion, the defeat that formally ended hopes of a spin on the play-offs merry-go-round. It was a deflating ending, but one we'd seen coming for months. Nevertheless, 2023/24 was rewarding for little Stevenage, a year of enhanced consolidation, where one of League One's smallest clubs with one of the entire Football League's smallest budgets more than held their own after a swashbuckling promotion from League Two.

The photograph is certainly of the East Terrace, the Lamex Stadium's pitch-length standing area, where 2024/25 season tickets will cost £360 for adults and £190 for 12–18s. Cup ties extra, even those in whatever the EFL Trophy is calling itself. The photograph shows a motley crew of fired-up, mostly corpulent, overwhelmingly white and overwhelmingly male Stevenage supporters. I can see the sweet guy with long, long, long ginger hair and glasses we'd clung to during last season's breath-holding but victorious Carabao Cup penalty shoot-out against a nearly full-strength Watford. More importantly, I can see us, right in the centre.

I'm wearing a T-shirt that makes me look – what's the word? – fat. Oscar is sporting his Boro top (Stevenage used to be called Stevenage Borough and now Boro is the shortcut used by all). My left arm is raised and mercifully covering some of my face. My mouth is wide open, mid-chant. There's no sign of Oscar's arms, but his *Eraserhead* hair is piled high and his mouth is even more wide open than mine. A closer examination would perhaps reveal spittle somewhere on our fronts. Presumably we're chanting in sync with those around us, but we are oblivious to them all. We look intense, we look deranged, we look ludicrous.

Is this who me and my then-12-year-old son are? Is this who we've become? Why, yes it is. Excellent.

What Happened?

I can tell you exactly when it happened for him. It is 16 November. The year is 2021. The clock is approaching 10pm. League Two Stevenage are hosting League One MK Dons in an FA Cup first-round replay, two days after manager Alex 'Revs' Revell has been sacked. Stevenage had been a goal down, but by the last minute of added time they had hauled themselves level. In front of the North Stand, closed for the evening by lack of interest, Elliott 'Listy' List wriggled his way into the penalty area, where he was felled by the otherwise too-good-for-this Harry Darling. We're sat in the Lamex's West Stand and, as Luke 'Nozzer' Norris steps up to take the penalty, it feels very much as though my forearm is being knifed. It's Oscar's 11-year-old nails digging in.

INTRODUCTION

I have been taking him intermittently to the Lamex for a few months now. Inverse snob that I am, I can't bear the thought of him supporting Tottenham Hotspur or Arsenal (he has a Spurs soft spot, but I can live with that) and we're fast approaching the dying days of me being able to impose my will on him.

My grooming was gentle, for addicts only become addicts when they want to. Oscar moved at his own pace until he began to ask to go to games. On this November night, he's beginning to fret that Boro might – as looks likely – slip out of the Football League entirely, but this is FA Cup time and the planets are about to align. He's desperate for Norris to score and his tiny claws are hurting my arm. He's almost piercing my flesh. I too want Nozzer Norris to score. For him.

Norris – ice in veins and other clichés – sends Andy Fisher the wrong way and Boro are through. As the ball hits the net, Oscar is on his feet, pumping his fists, dancing his little boy's dance and going 'yeah!' while pulling me to and fro. He gets it. He's in. And next round Boro are out, losing at non-league Yeovil Town, an early reminder for Oscar of how the world works.

Anyway, by the end of the month, the distractingly dapper Paul Tisdale had filled the vacant manager's post, but the undeniably undapper football sunk Boro further still. By March, Tisdale was sacked after winning just three games, a footnote in the big scheme of things. Oscar, though, had found his first football hero, the mighty Scott Cuthbert, a bald, bearded Scottish centre-half hewn from some sort of indestructible material, a leader with admirably little tolerance for the failings of those around him. 'Coooothbert', Oscar calls him. Or Roy Kent from *Ted Lasso*.

Just when National League tundra looks imminent, enter Steve Evans, the roly-poly convicted tax fraudster and, bafflingly, one of the game's less loved figures. This is the panda of a man Oscar and I will fall in love with, the man who will give us the very best of times and the man who was gracious and humble when a nervous Oscar asked him for selfies at Gateshead and King's Lynn, grounds league teams only visit in the early rounds of the FA Cup.

With the concern of a new zealot and not really knowing who Steve Evans is yet, little Oscar is worried about the future. 'Will me and you still go if we're non-league?' he asks anxiously, already at the 'we' stage. And he wants to go to away games to help halt the plummet. I don't tell him this, but if it is to be the National League in 2022/23, I can't see an immediate return for Boro.

First, we go to doomed, tragic Scunthorpe on a Bank Holiday Monday, where we play football in a basketball court beforehand and where the actual match ends in a mutually incompetent draw. On the way home he calls his friends in faux-casual mood: 'Yeah, just coming back from seeing Boro at Scunthorpe ... that's Stevenage at Scunthorpe United ... they're in League Two ... no it's the proper league.'

Taking advantage of his mother not knowing where Mansfield is, we go there on a school night. Boro lose 2-0 and a super-kind steward gives Oscar a poster that says 'thank you for travelling 118 miles to support your club'. It still adorns his bedroom wall. Mansfield's stadium has three sides, Boro's 78 travellers are sprawled at one end and, as the teams enter the arena, 5,013 Mansfield fans unite to abuse their former manager Steve Evans at ear-splitting volume: 'You fat bastard, you fat bastard!' Evans gives them a cheery wave.

Boro stay up. 'It's the Evans Way,' says Steve Evans many moons later. The actual Evans Way turns out to be him selecting the team and his admirable, hard-working deputy Paul Raynor working out the finer points in training. We buy season tickets for 2022/23. Scott Cuthbert is released and Oscar finds another hero: big, bearded Michael 'Bozzie' Bostwick, a veteran who hits the ball harder than any man alive (n.b. this may not actually be true). Oscar makes it clear he doesn't want to sit in the West Stand any more. He wants to stand on the East Terrace, where all the noise comes from. He wants to shout until he's hoarse. It's Oscar's masterstroke, the decision that will bind us closer to each other and to the club. Oh, and he wants to wear the Boro shirt all kiddie season ticket holders are given. It's the one he's sporting on the photograph I was mulling over. And 2022/23 is an amazing season: Boro are automatically promoted, knock Aston Villa out of the FA Cup at Villa Park and Bozzie is released to sign for Boston.

My Best Moments of 2022/23

1. Being two of the 38 who travelled to a freezing Portsmouth for a Pizza Cup (i.e. the Papa Johns EFL Trophy) tie. We parked right outside the ground. The steward told us we were two of the six who'd bought advance tickets.

2. Being one down at Premier League Aston Villa in the 88th minute of an FA Cup third-round tie and winning. Oscar had to explain to me at some

length that life and football aren't really like that. I didn't listen.

3. The header by our lovely Danny Rose – we sat next to his early-departing father at Doncaster and Bradford – at Swindon from within the six yard box that went back the way the cross had come for a throw-in. The most tense game of the season and for a moment every Boro fan was laughing. I swear his team-mate Alex 'Gilbinho' Gilbey laughed too.

Oscar's Best Moments of 2022/23

1. The whey-faced, portly teenager who came up to him and whispered 'wanker' at Bradford. Ever the diligent parent, I didn't notice.

2. Being one down at Premier League Aston Villa in the 88th minute of an FA Cup third-round tie and winning. I had to explain to Oscar at some length that life and football aren't really like that. He didn't listen.

3. Sutton United are losing at the Lamex. They win a throw-in. The ball bounces to Oscar. Sutton's Joe Kizzi sprints over to take it from him. Oscar throws the ball over his head back into the crowd. Kizzi shakes his head, very slowly, very sadly.

In truth, 2023/24 wasn't bad either. We renewed our season tickets without even talking about it, Boro signed three players called Thompson (although only two of them are related) and we told ourselves that staying in League One was enough. In the event, Boro were in the play-off positions for most of the season, before being scuppered by a late-season goal freeze and the dubious recruitment that would see Vadaine Oliver arrive on loan after being unable to get into League Two strugglers Bradford City's team. He would depart having achieved what is surely a record for a striker after seven starts and seven substitute cameos: more own goals (1) than actual goals (0) to his name. He tried hard though.

Steve Evans complained about referees almost every week ('Championship? My knackers,' he spluttered when it was put to him that Boro were getting higher-grade referees) but, more often than not, he was right and, while it was nonsense, his 'they don't want little Stevenage in the Championship' mantra bound us tighter. Ninth place (eight points ahead of tenth) was about right.

When Rotherham United sacked Matt Taylor in November, there was careless talk about them pinching Evans, who'd taken them to promotion twice. Rotherham chairman Tony Stewart attended the wedding of one of Evans's daughters. But Stevenage offered him an upgraded contract and that was that, seemingly forever. In hindsight, the Evans magic evaporated at that moment. On 17 April, four days after the Burton defeat, with two games remaining and the play-offs out of reach for Boro, Rotherham sacked Leam Richardson and appointed Evans in one press release. We always knew he'd leave us, but it would have been nice if he'd said goodbye, if he'd admitted the Boro slump had followed Rotherham's initial approach and if he'd acknowledged that Boro did almost as much for his moribund career as he did for Boro. Had he lost interest, knowing Rotherham would return? Possibly. A fine season, nevertheless.

Evans's number three, Revs (remember him?), took over for those two remaining games, an enjoyable purloining of a point at Oxford, which Sky must have sorely regretted covering, and a victory over Cheltenham that sent them down. Cheltenham's grisly fate reminded Boro fans of the worst-case scenario before the season, one that had never looked remotely likely during it.

My Best Moments of 2023/24

1. Nathan Thompson scoring right in front of the 77 of us at Port Vale in the FA Cup. Boro's other two goals were right in front of us too, as was the penalty shoot-out. The Port Vale fans afterwards who stopped us to tell us how great Boro were.

2. The nice people at Exeter who gave the 96 of us a free cup of coffee on a chilly Carabao night.

3. Bolton on a school night. School finishes at 3.45. We agree to turn back if traffic defeats us. Somehow, it doesn't. M25, M6, M6 toll, M6 again, M62, M60, M61. We make kick-off. Sometimes, Oscar, you have to do something that's completely off-kilter. 'So sometimes it's okay to miss school?' Well, no, and you didn't actually miss school. 'I see ...'

Oscar's Best Moments of 2023/24

1. The fan who sidled up to him after Boro fluked a draw at Carlisle and hissed 'cunt'. 'Shall I tell

Mum, Dad?' Best not Oscar, best not. I missed that one, too.

2. Added time at home to Cambridge. Boro were clinging on at 1-0. At the very moment Cambridge were about to equalise, one of their fans lobbed a smoke bomb on to the pitch and the referee stopped the game. How we laughed.

3. Port Vale away on a school night. 'Mum doesn't know where Port Vale is, does she Dad?' I wouldn't think so. 'We can go then?' We can. We did.

Oh, and we sample cuisine at every ground to provide a pie chart. See what we've done there? This may be the moment to mention that while Florence Nightingale did not invent the pie chart, she popularised it. He's the ultimate arbiter here, not least since I'd mark down clubs who don't take cash ('you're so old-fashioned, Dad'). Here's 2023/24's, but not every club is here because he forgot to mark sometimes – an error that won't be repeated – and we didn't go to every game.

1. Portsmouth. The pie as art form. Delicious art form.

2. Northampton Town. A piping-hot pie for a piping-hot opening day. Deep-filled, but worth the care and effort it took to eat.

3. Lincoln City. Expensive, looked a little sad. All forgiven after the tasting.

4. Derby County. Tasty sanity in the maddest of away afternoons. There were over 1,000 of us and Boro didn't deserve defeat.

5. Exeter City. Not overly filling, but hey it was lovely.

6. Cambridge United. Massive queues, massive portions.

7. Bolton Wanderers. Bog-standard, but since we'd made it in time to sneak one, it was a pie of victory.

8. Stevenage. A little bit unlicensed burger van on the A602, but the servers are sweet and brisk. We don't indulge often.

9. Port Vale. Ruined by a rogue, unidentifiable spice.

10. Bristol Rovers. A pie made by people who don't know how to make pies. The texture of hemp.

11. Carlisle United. A Scotch pie. Ooh, a local delicacy at a football ground? We had to sample. Slippery, greasy meat of mystery surrounded by clag-central pastry. Vile.

Boro wouldn't give Revs the manager's job permanently in the close season, would they? Surely not. After his sacking, Revs went away, studied psychology to augment his sports science degree and acquired a car with a personalised number plate. He qualified as a personal trainer, but was sufficiently self-aware to accept demotion and work under Tisdale (with the kids, as part-time academy manager) and then as Evans's full-time number three. He could have fled to Rotherham – one of his former clubs – with Evans and Rayner, but he chose not to. Paul Warne contends that Revs has the finest teeth in English football, and we unequivocally love him.

But we can't forget Revs had been deposed as number one before the MK Dons tie after winning one of his last 14 league games. And he's one of around 20 people (that figure's inexact, since success is in the eye of the beholder and Graham Westley had four goes at it) who've empirically proved they're not up to this particular job. Yet maybe, just maybe, Revs hadn't had a fair crack of anyone's whip as Boro manager. COVID didn't help and nor did being unable to recruit properly in the summer of 2020 as Boro waited on a Macclesfield points deduction to discover whether they would retain their EFL place.

I explain to a not-that-interested Oscar what a shame it is that we'll never know whether Darrell Clarke (who has the same agent as Steve Evans, who has the same agent as Alex Revell) would work for Boro, since he's joined Barnsley. Maybe Pete Wild, who'd done such a sterling job at Barrow (our least enjoyable away trip, for the drenching, for our squabbling, for the grasping family who took so many of the Boro players' shirts that I couldn't get one for Oscar) could do another sterling job at Boro. Perhaps Scott Lindsey, who'd done a Stevenage with Crawley, would come, although his Swindon were pretty wretched two seasons ago at the Lamex. Ryan Mason, sometime interim Tottenham manager, might fancy a first step in management. Maybe even Mark Bonner would blossom again after mysteriously losing his way at Cambridge. They give it to Revs, this season's unpublicised requirement being that Boro are at least two places above the relegation slots throughout the campaign. If that happens, his job is safe. I'm unsure how I feel. Oscar isn't happy: 'No ambition.'

Still, Scott Cuthbert returned as number three, taking on Revs's most recent role and the chance to pursue further coaching qualifications. They're great friends, which makes me a little wary. Brand-new number two Neil Banfield, first-team coach at Arsenal during some of Arsène Wenger's glory years, should add old-boy wisdom. Is Revs's return like asking Liz Truss to become Prime Minister again? I hope not.

Oscar's ambivalent, although he's thrilled by the re-emergence of the man we must no longer call Coooothbert, whose departure from a coaching position at Woking seemed suspiciously abrupt. We'd loved seeing Raynor give the on-field pre-match pep talks before leading the players to applaud us, home and away. Our hearts swelled with love. It was something else that brought everyone together. 'Will they still do it?' Oscar asks. I don't know, I really don't know. In the event, Boro will settle on a group circle in front of wherever the fans are, as we applaud. It's different but just as good. That ring of players binds us all.

Before You Go

We were fooled. Jessica, Oscar's older sister, came into the world like a chapter from the *Mills & Boon Book of Fairytale Births*. A blooming beautiful mother, and a swift mid-morning arrival to candlelight and music. At one time, I'd have had the birth soundtracked by Enya, both because births are surely better with Enya and because she's lush and magical and maverick. Then I took tea and cake with her in a stately home south of Dublin and put my Enya Theory to Enya, the one about how lush and magical and maverick she was, rather than births going better when they're accompanied by her music. Not one to take a compliment, she wasn't having any of it. I've never felt the same about her since. No Enya at the birth then. 'Sail away, sail away, sail away ...'

Oscar was different and difficult. His birth began with a lovely smiley midwife telling me about life in Lagos and ended many, many hours later with his wardrobe-sized mother – still beautiful to me, etc. – drugged to the gunwales with whatever they give birthing mothers when said birth isn't working out. She was whisked into some operating theatre as a handful of men in shirts and ties gathered round. The now less-jolly midwife barred me from the room, but not before, to paraphrase Charlene in 'I've Never Been to Me', I'd seen some things a man ain't supposed to see.

I loved Oscar straight away, of course. I've never been bored of him (not once), he's never failed to make me laugh, he has such kindness in his heart, he's as pertinacious as boys of his age ought to be and he's made me appreciate both Formula 1 and expensive male fragrance. The feeling isn't always reciprocated. For some reason he doesn't like me improving his haircuts, he doesn't like his picture being taken (and put on Twitter [now known as X]: we fell out over that one) and he does get bored of me: 'I really don't like spending time with you ... why do you talk so much, all the time?' But we've bonded over his goalkeeping, the gym (although he won't go with me now), *The Simpsons*, Eminem, Sade (who he somehow discovered himself) and sushi. But most of all we've bonded over Boro.

Next school year he takes his GCSEs so we'll have to be careful how much Boro we see and, anyway 15/16-year-old boys don't want to spend almost every Saturday and many Tuesdays with their dads. Significantly, he went to the final game of last season against Cheltenham without me, but with his friends. He had too good a time for my liking, but if things get tricky this season, or if he remembers to ask, we'll take his friends with us. Whyever not? After the 2025/26 season, it's probably two years of A levels, two more years of growing up too quickly, maybe university and then who knows? We'll attend every Boro game home and away this season. It's now or never. Before he goes.

He says in passing that he wants to live abroad at some point. He must, of course, if that's how his life goes, but it'll break my heart. And there's me. I'm fretting. I'm not immortal, in fact I feel very mortal indeed. Already I'm not remembering other people's names as I once did. And if I keel over tomorrow, what happens to my James Patterson-level advance? If I spend it on heroin and prostitutes (I'm tempted, every day I'm tempted) and end up manuscript-free in a ditch in some surreal metaphor for Boro, I assume there may be legal ramifications. But if I die midway through the season, the car breaks down on the way to Shrewsbury or I'm seriously injured – knowing my luck it'll be after we've trekked to Peterborough twice in three October days – do they insist on recouping the money? The contract isn't clear. I must cross the road carefully until 3 May.

So we're doing *Before You Go*, before he goes. And, in a very different way, before I go. Not that I can tell him any of this.

July – Anticipation

2 July 2024

Speaking Truth to Power (1)

The close season trundles along. All Boro's main players are retained, which is a relief. Some so-so signings arrive and the morning after Ollie Watkins scores for England against the Netherlands, Boro post a tweet saying 'morning all' above a picture of Boro's grinning Jamie 'Reidy' Reid, Dean Campbell and Jake 'League Two Pirlo' Reeves hurtling past a disconsolate Watkins after Campbell's FA Cup winner at Villa Park. I laugh a lot, as does Oscar. Fans of other clubs don't. 'Weird … tinpot … strange' are the most used words. There are calls for Boro's Twitter posse to be sacked. I'd promote them or, since there's probably nowhere for the administrators of Stevenage FCs Twitter to be promoted, give them a pay rise. I couldn't be more proud, unless Boro started printing a programme again.

With the season looming, Phil Wallace hosts a fans' forum. He has been Stevenage's owner, or at least 91 per cent of it, since 1999. He runs a tight ship, so tight that Stevenage don't run at a loss and do run in the real world, which lets us all sleep at night. He's in remarkably fine fettle for a 75-year-old, and being CEO and majority shareholder of the multinational Lamex Food Group ('one of the world's largest privately owned frozen and chilled food exporters and importers. 25 offices based on 6 continents, providing 24-hour coverage for the entire world', trills their awkwardly worded company statement) means he's very wealthy indeed. Even so, in 2019 he wasn't wealthy enough to refrain from seeking further investment so Boro could become 'a bigger spending club, attracting new supporters and aiming for the Championship. To do that, we need additional funding.' Nothing came of it, but I like that too, as it means (or at least implies) he's open to power-sharing.

Better still, the childhood Leyton Orient supporter is not a Boro fan (self-evidently, fans shouldn't run their clubs) and in fact spent most of the '90s as chairman of Boreham Wood 20 miles down the A1. In 1999, the club then called Stevenage Borough were in danger of going out of business or, worse, being merged with Barnet. 'If they were to shut down, then they could join with us to preserve their name. But it would not be a takeover,' said Barnet chairman Tony Kleanthous, defining the word 'disingenuous' before it fell through.

Frustrated by Boreham Wood's lack of support, Wallace sold his shares, bought Stevenage and the rest is history. Obviously it's history, that's how linear time works.

Cannily, Wallace's first target at Boro was the training facilities – always a winning strategy with players, since it's where they do nearly all their work – and he oversaw the building of a 42-acre complex at Bragbury End, way out Ware way. Then he changed the name of the ground from Broadhall Way to the Lamex and the name of the team from Stevenage Borough to Stevenage. And this evening at 5.30pm he's holding court.

JULY – ANTICIPATION

There are (about) 70 people present at the Lamex's '76 Lounge, so called because it resembles a Czechoslovakian regional Communist Party headquarters circa 1976. Coincidentally, it's also the year Boro were formed. Oscar and I are (about) the 69th and 70th people to arrive, so we have to stand, rather too visibly for my liking. Jay 'Drackers' Drackford is compering. He does the pre-match and half-time MCing on the Lamex pitch and he's a wry joy. Not a match goes by without me and Oscar chuckling, whether he's interviewing monosyllabic mascots, benevolently teasing away fans, taunting Boro Bear (of whom much more later) or just spreading a little more togetherness.

Phil Wallace sits at a table alone. Drackers and his microphone roam in search of questioners. There are early questions about Steve Evans, about putting nets up so fans don't get hit during the pre-match shooting drills and (I think) about erecting some kind of railings to help older people mount the stairs. It's hardly *Frost/Nixon*. Somebody has to be the bastard. Hi everyone, here I am.

Drackers smiles and hands me the microphone. First of all, I thank Phil Wallace for doing it – he really doesn't have to put himself through this – and then I nod to Oscar (we'd discussed this beforehand), who nods back in assent. At some length, I complain about the new signings and by implication the recruitment policy, which partly resulted in last season's play-offs slipping out of reach. Immediately the atmosphere changes. Drackers sighs loudly, someone actually hisses and collective morale dips as heads shake. Mr Buzzkill is in the house. I don't help myself by delivering all this in a slightly sulky monotone. I've left my sing-song voice that's charmed, ooh, dozens of viewers and listeners on television and radio at home.

I go for facts. Louis Appéré is a striker who scored six goals last season and couldn't get in Northampton's team, a team who finished below Boro. Lewis Freestone could get in Cheltenham's team, but they were relegated from League One. Dan Kemp couldn't make League Two MK Dons' starting line-up and scored three goals after New Year, albeit after an undeniably successful loan spell at League Two Swindon Town. And I conclude by asking whether these arrivals signify lack of ambition and/or Revs's lack of sway. I don't even mention Vadaine Oliver. It's not the moment to ask if the printed programme can be restored. Oscar won't ask anything because he's too shy to speak and, shamefully, he doesn't care about printed programmes.

Phil Wallace isn't happy. In fact, he's offended: 'I'm offended by that question,' he says. Then he takes each signing one by one and justifies them. He also insists they weren't 'cast-offs' (tellingly, I hadn't used those words); that Boro had been chasing them all for months and that they were swayed by a presentation Revs made to them, although if Boro had been chasing them for months, Revs wouldn't have been involved in the early courting. In short, if there was one reason these non-cast-offs came, it was Alex Revell. Drackers won't come within 20 metres of me for the rest of the forum, so I can't counter. Oscar shakes his head. Later he says, 'You were right, but couldn't you have said how much you hoped you were going to be proved wrong? Really?' I forgot.

The exchange doesn't make Boro's official Twitter feed, but it doesn't escape everyone. An attending fan tweets at length: 'Some guy not impressed by our signings.' He ignores my facts and quotes – selectively quotes – only Phil Wallace's replies, so, 'Kemp is a ridiculous signing for us, an incredible signing, we've been trying for six months', omitting Phil Wallace's admission that Kemp had fallen out with MK Dons. Freestone is 'a warrior with Stevenage DNA, the only reason Cheltenham didn't go down earlier' and Appéré 'chose us over multiple League One clubs and the geography was right'.

Phil Wallace also batted hard for his recruitment team. 'He cannot emphasise enough how much work goes into signing these players,' continues my Twitter chum. 'We know exactly what we are and what we want.'

After that, it's all 'Can we have a bar on the East Terrace?' From my killjoy's point of view, hopefully not, and it would be tricky to adhere to the no-alcohol-in-view-of-the-pitch rule, but I guess it would make financial sense. There are more adroit questions vis-à-vis playing style. Phil Wallace contends that getting the ball forwards quickly is another part of Stevenage's DNA and it was too often lacking at the end of last season. Managerial restlessness isn't mentioned.

In 2019, Phil Wallace looked to the Championship. Where he might be looking now is less clear. For this season, it seems his aim is to be in loose contention for the League One play-offs. That's fair, but there were moments last term – outplaying Derby County at home and winning; outplaying Portsmouth away and somehow losing – where it wasn't unreasonable to dream of more.

Oscar's right, I should have stressed to Phil Wallace how much I wanted to be wrong, but I'd envisaged a lengthier discussion. Like everyone in that room, I desperately want me to be wrong. I want to shout, 'We've got super Alex Revell,' as Boro career upwards. I want us to be there when Dan Kemp scores his 20th goal of the season and Louis Appéré matches that in assists, and I want Lewis Freestone to attract attention from half the Championship. I'd just love to tell you how wrong I was. I'm repeating myself now. Sorry.

'I expected more,' shrugs Oscar as we shuffle towards the subway with its genuinely inspiring street art mural featuring a host of Boro greats, including current captain Carl 'Pidge' Piergianni. Nobody is making eye contact with us. 'I wanted to believe a bit more.'

Phil Wallace had promised a fourth signing. Next day, good as his word, one arrives. Dan Phillips helped St Johnstone survive in the Scottish Premier League and didn't get a full summer of rest because he was playing for Trinidad & Tobago. I like the look of him and his giant thighs. He'll help maintain the unsavoury tradition of Boro having more black players than supporters, although, for the record, I've never heard a racist comment, let alone a racist chant, at the Lamex, unless the anti-Luton one, 'We hate the fucking Luton', counts. Phillips is a midfield hardman (11 yellow cards last season, no goals) and it's a gap that needs filling. That's better. Let's go.

13 July 2024
Stevenage 2 Watford 2 –
pre-season friendly

My prediction: don't care
His prediction: don't care

I don't want to go. He doesn't want to go. I accept this might not be the expected tsunami of enthusiasm a new season should bring, but it's a pre-season friendly, an extended training workout without tackles, which Boro used to include as part of the season ticket. Now, the season tickets aren't ready and they have the brazen cheek to charge.

We had a massive argument last summer when I attempted to entice Oscar to take in an away friendly. The boy who abandons everything to see Boro home and away, freezing and baking, top of the league and bottom of the league, simply refused. In fact, he cried at the prospect. I was furious with him, but he was right. I shouldn't have pushed him to attend a phony war. After we reconciled days later, I promised that some walking-pace encounter against West Bromwich Albion two years ago would be our last friendly. Even there he wasn't as impressed as I was by seeing Steve Evans and Steve Bruce deep in pre-match conversation in the seats behind us.

But here we are. It's surreally early in the year. His school year hasn't finished yet, nor have the Euros. But on balance I feel we should go to this friendly. I play the 'for the book' card much, much earlier than I'd hoped, I've bribed him with a Nando's and we've abandoned all our routines to turn up at the last minute, admire the Watford team coach – a functional Stewarts, as used by Reading – and go home. He's still not happy, he refuses to wear his Boro shirt ('not a proper game'), but once the gnashing of teeth is complete, he acquiesces. I'm not happy either: I've broken a promise and you can't do that with children. They remember.

Speaking of promises, I promised Oscar too that mighty Watford, recently a Premier League team and the only other league club in Hertfordshire, would sell out their away end. There's 813 of them, but that's no sell out, although Watford's line-up is strong. Serendipitously, I don't actually pay to go in: a sweet man gives me a free ticket as we queue.

Half the ground is closed. Boro launch their new home kit (shirts £50 for adults, £40 for kids) and while it doesn't quite exude the amateur darts player aura that the Twitter pictures suggested, it's no design marvel. I don't do replica kits, thanks, but Oscar's had his for two seasons and myriad growth spurts now. The purple away one looks good, but he'll see how it looks on Jordan 'Robbo' Roberts before making a decision. He's not a greedy boy. The game's not that bad, I suppose, especially if you don't insist on football being a contact sport. It's all the better for having no added time.

There's a goalkeeping situation. Burton Albion came in for Boro's Taye Ashby-Hammond, fluttering their eyelashes rather seductively and bearing more money than you might think Burton are capable of bearing. Instead, Taye accepted Boro's offer of a 'new, improved and extended contract' (i.e. the club don't want us to know for how long and for how much) in the week, but he's not around today.

At the forum, Phil Wallace had explained that they're looking for a back-up keeper, a change in Steve Evans's policy of having more experienced competition. Rylee Mitchell is only 18, so it's a big hello to Triallist A (probably not his real name).

Phillips loses possession and gives away a goal, Boro score with the last kick of each half and somewhere in between is a Watford penalty, although I was looking at the sky and weeping softly, so I miss it. There's even some on-field aggro when Dan 'Sweens' Sweeney wades into a sea of yellow shirts as Watford's crafty foxes try to intimidate some of the chicken-coop kids (Boro have a 15-year-old, Ryan Doherty, out there). Unhelpfully, centre-forward Aaron Pressley ('Press', rather than Elvis or Reg) injures himself after half an hour. He'll have to have an ankle operation.

I sort of like Pressley. At the Northampton opener last season, as Oscar and I grappled with the piping pies. Pressley was all Bambi legs, eager running and absence of goal threat. Oscar wasn't enamoured. 'He'll never score for us.'

An older bloke behind us spoke up: 'Mark my words, he'll get goals.' I add my vast weight of football knowledge and weigh in on the older bloke's side. Pressley scored one goal from open play all season and the conversation at Northampton is another Oscar never forgets. Pressley was publicly berated by Evans for the concession of Derby's late, late winner at Pride Park and by the end of the season we're singing 'let Pressley score' because we can all see what he's going through, still all Bambi legs, still all eager running and still all absence of goal threat.

What have we learned from today Oscar?

'Nothing, Dad.'

We make a joint decision. No more friendlies.

So when Boro win in Jersey (Phil Wallace lives there), I'm watching athletics and Oscar is watching the Hungarian Grand Prix qualifying (Lando Norris on pole, that went well) and playing computer games with his friends.

When Boro lose at home to Coventry, I'm in the bath. Oscar is playing computer games with his friends.

When Boro win at Braintree, I spend the evening working at my second job, unpaid taxi driver to a stroppy teenage girl. Oscar is playing computer games with his friends.

When Boro beat Chelsea (that's Chelsea Under-21s), I'm wading through the Smashing Pumpkins catalogue and Oscar is playing computer games with his friends. We don't talk about any of those games. We don't care.

We have much to talk about, though. This summer break isn't going at all well for Boro. Bad news keeps rolling in like a sewage-topped tidal wave. Jamie 'Reidy' Reid – 22 goals last season, although just the two after January – has returned late after playing for Northern Ireland, for whom he made his international debut in March, four months shy of his 30th birthday, 11 years after he last played for their Under-21s. It's a maternal grandmother thing. That's fine, of course, but, more pressingly, he's returned with some condition the club aren't sharing and he'll miss August. The goalkeeping situation I mentioned takes another dark turn, for it turns out Taye has done his finger in. (Is 'done his finger in' a medical term? I believe it is.) Cultured midfielder Jake 'JFC' Forster-Caskey, who limped out of last season's culinary ill-fated Carlisle game early on, isn't even close to being ready.

And there's Terence 'TVC' Vancooten, who's been here for seven years. Unlike Taye, he turned down a new Boro deal and allowed himself to be seduced by mighty Burton Albion for an 'undisclosed' fee (why 'undisclosed'? He's a lower league footballer, not *The Haywain*) that seems to be £500,000. I never knew the Guyana international's best position. Full-back? Centre-back? Chaperone of the defence? But he'll be sorely missed and he played Oscar at some computer game when TVC and a few players turned up at a computer shop in Stevenage town centre a couple of years ago to meet their adoring public. TVC triumphed. But only because 'I let him win; didn't want him to be upset during the next game.' Oscar is still pursuing this line two years later, so it must be true.

There was more: every time we picked our way through the Lamex car park pre-match. We'd seek out TVC's Mercedes – 'Very expensive,' speculates Oscar, who knows the value of such things – with its personalised number plate and we would touch it for luck. Another pleasure gone forever.

Striker Tyreece Simpson arrived for, yes, an undisclosed fee. On the one hand, he's only 22, although, self-evidently, experience and leadership are essential to either escape League One or keep a club in it. On the other hand, Simpson looks like a beast. On the third hand, he signed a biggish deal for Huddersfield Town in 2022; ten appearances and no goals later he was loaned out to Northampton, thus becoming Boro's second summer signing who couldn't get in Northampton's starting XI. Just the three Northampton league goals for Simpson, half as many as Louis Appéré, but three more than Vadaine Oliver. Simpson's first tweet as a Boro player, 'reset, restart, refocus', could have come from the instructions to my mobile phone, but it's followed by a reference from St Paul's 1 Thessalonians, 'give thanks in all circumstance'. None of which feels like a ringing endorsement of his reduced status. 'He was shite,' tweets a Huddersfield fan.

Meanwhile, a former manager, Mark Stimson, is fined £1,052 and convicted of assault, while the goalkeeping situation is partly resolved when Murphy Cooper arrives on a season's loan from Queens Park Rangers. Pre-season passes without Taye playing a minute.

August – On Our Way, Sort Of

There's a final signing just before opening day. It's Charlie Goode, another centre-back. He isn't a kid and he even played a few Premier League games for Brentford in 2021, but he looks injury-prone and 2021/22's loan spell at Sheffield United was cut short after he was sent off in his second game, while last season's loan at Wigan Athletic was ended for whatever 'personal reasons' might be. But we'll see. Either way, Boro won't be numerically short of centre-backs. It could be three in a 5-3-2 or a 3-5-2, but Revs tends to favour 4-3-3 or 4-2-3-1.

Am I being too downbeat seeing a certain amount of struggle ahead? Please no. Let's look on the bright side. With two days to go, Revs does an 'exclusive' interview for Sky (who on earth could they have possibly fought off for said exclusive?) as part of their Pretending to Care About the EFL campaign, where they'll mess around with kick-off times, as if Boro were Barça and there's a viewership eagerly awaiting Burton Albion host Stevenage.

Revs does well, admitting to messing up first time around and that he hadn't been ready to manage anyway: 'It was nobody else's fault. I did not lead well enough. It got too much for me.' He's aiming for higher than ninth, acknowledges goals are a problem and, while my doubts aren't wholly assuaged, I see light, although Taye's finger condition has now spread to the rest of his hands. The day before the season begins, I dispense another Nando's bribe to Oscar. Over some overpriced chicken, I set out my terms for the season and invite his.

We can't fall out. This might be problematic. I still annoy him, not least since I like to be early everywhere I go, while he reminds me 'you never apologise properly'. Our remit may exclude friendlies, but it encompasses all the cups home and away, including the Pizza Cup, which we're now hilariously calling the Second-Hand Car Cup since Papa Johns was usurped by Bristol Street Motors last season.

'We've been drawn against Crystal Palace Under-21s in the Second-Hand Car Cup group, I'm not bothered about that,' he explains, reasonably enough.

That's okay, I'll write about us being underwhelmed.

'And what when there's a League One evening game a long way away on a school night?'

You might have a headache that day. This he likes. Rather too much.

He points out that since he plays football on Sunday (of which much more later), Saturday is the peak of his social life, the day a young man and his friends go to shopping centres to test fragrances. I hadn't thought of that. I feel awful. Sorry.

'Hmmm. Every Saturday, Dad?'

Well not when Boro are playing teams who have call-ups in international break weeks. Or have been knocked out of the FA Cup. Or when the fixture list turns peculiar, as it did for that Friday night we spent at Oxford last season.

'Oh ...' Did I mention I feel awful? He has another demand.

'No photos.'

I hadn't thought of that either.

10 August 2024
Stevenage 1 Shrewsbury Town 0

My prediction: 2-0
His prediction: 3-0

As we're prising ourselves out of the Lamex, a man thumps me on the shoulder, quite hard and points at Oscar. 'What did he say? Did I hear that right?'

Oscar had been loudly relating the news from Exeter, where Steve Evans's Rotherham have lost. We subsequently learn he'd refused to shake hands with home manager Gary Caldwell post-match and acquired yet another FA misconduct charge. Our new friend had, indeed, heard right.

'A good day for Stevenage,' he chuckles. He thumps me on the shoulder again and fist-pumps. I respond with a rather more non-committal fist-shrug, but my grin is wide. He's right: this has been a fine day.

For us it began around midnight, when we flew over the Lamex as we returned from holiday. Croatia, since you ask, the place where the actual Nazis asked, 'Could you tone down the Nazi stuff a little, guys? Cheers!' We couldn't see the Lamex, mind, but we knew it was there. We felt it. That was enough.

Anyway, Sky's Pretending to Care About the EFL campaign means that today every League One game kicks off at 5.30pm and is on television, apparently, although

I'd wager they won't be releasing the viewing figures for Stevenage vs Shrewsbury Town. The stupid start time means our routine is out of whack. We can't even park at Fairlands over the road from the Lamex for free because there's some kind of event – I hear the throb of poor-quality music all evening – and they're charging for the limited spaces that are available. We find somewhere in the estate just east of the ground.

It's a blinding game, chiefly because it's summer and 5.30pm, so the sinking sun dazzles all of us on the East Terrace. Wisely I'd anticipated this and purchased some sunglasses in Croatia for this very moment. I forget to bring them.

Oscar's quite excited before the game. 'We'll finish sixth,' he asserts. 'Look at our squad.'

But you said you wanted Revs to resign on the plane last night.

'I do.'

It's a mark of mature thinking to simultaneously hold seemingly conflicting opinions, so he generously agrees to give Revs a chance unless Boro lose the first five games. We pick up our season tickets, buy some away tickets and gaze upon the Shrewsbury Town team coach, a handsome (and local) Longmynd. The offer for Oscar to acquire a Boro shirt still stands, but he's happy to continue to sport his old one. It looks great and it still fits, growth spurts or not.

We don't usually eat at the ground but – routine busted – we share some so-so chicken goujons, some not-that-bad-actually chips and a bottle of lukewarm Fanta from which, mercifully, they don't bother to take the cap off. The players no longer warm up in front of us and there's no mutual applause until the new-fangled huddle, but hey, new era ... I take an occasional note. I thought he'd be embarrassed, but Oscar doesn't mind. Bless him, and when I offer to WhatsApp every note to him, he's delighted.

Shrewsbury was last season's opener too. A crowd of 3,962 including 412 away fans attended. Today it's 3,357 with 437 away fans. That's not good: a mixture of Sky and new regime apathy.

Revs gives debuts to starters Murphy Cooper, Dan Kemp, Tyreece Simpson, Lewis Freestone and Dan Phillips, while Louis Appéré is on the bench. As he always does, Drackers reads out the visiting team against the backdrop of the *Hawaii Five-O* theme and the Boro team to Bill Conti's *Rocky* theme, 'Gonna Fly Now'. As a kid, I knew every second of the *Hawaii Five-O* credits and I've even fallen in love with Sammy Davis Jr's vocal version, 'You Can Count On Me', with its slightly out of natural sequence lyric 'I'll be there to catch you and I won't let you fall'. I've never seen a *Rocky* film, I can't abide 'Eye of the Tiger', but 'Gonna Fly Now', with its parping horns, slightly wistful tone and sense of occasion is an inspired choice. These pieces of music have become the soundtrack to our lives. The wonderful Boro Bear mascot hurtles on to the pitch and pumps his furry heart, the teams enter just after him. We're off.

'Simpson reminds me of Adebayo Akinfenwa,' says Oscar. He's loved Akinfenwa, ever since inadvertently entering the room when myself and Akinfenwa were on Zoom.

'What's your name?' asked Akinfenwa, loveliness itself.

'Oscar.'

'Do you want to be a footballer, Oscar?'

'Yes, but how do I do it?'

'If you believe, you can achieve. If someone gives you their opinion, that doesn't make it so. Nobody can be you better than you, Oscar. Your individual source is your greatest power. As early as possible, feel comfortable in your own skin, your own aura and your own energy. That's when you'll progress.'

It's a cagey first half. Murphy Cooper makes a makes-himself-big save from Tom Bloxham, but 0-0 is about right. In his Sky interview, Revs had suggested training had focused on set pieces. It doesn't look like it. According to Phil Wallace, Neil Banfield was brought in for his in-game tactical acumen and things are indeed very different after the restart. Boro stick to 4-2-3-1, but the older hands, Elliott 'Listy' List and dainty midfielder Harvey White, look different (and better) players than they did under Evans. Just before the hour, Louis Thompson breezes forwards and finds Listy, who cuts in from the left and curls home the winner past erstwhile Boro loanee Toby Savin.

Apart from the mercurial Tommi O'Reilly and a banner from their travellers begging MAKE US DREAM AGAIN, Shrewsbury are poor. They're one of the few teams widely predicted to finish below Boro. They probably will.

It's the week following the Far-Right Riots and this afternoon there's a 'protest' scheduled in Shrewsbury involving Town's long-standing, ahem, firm, the English Border Front. It's also the day of the Shrewsbury Flower Show, so in Shrewsbury the far right are massively outnumbered by old dears buying alstroemerias. Here, midway through the second period, there's a demand that people cease their racist and/or homophobic chanting.

We're too far away to hear properly, but the announcement seems to be aimed at the away support.

There's even a penalty when Dan Kemp takes a tumble. He strokes it wide and his confidence crumbles. Like Pressley, Simpson doesn't look much of a goal threat, but there's a lot of good here. Freestone and Phillips could be players to fall in love with and, channelling his inner Evans, Revs acquires a yellow card when Appéré takes another, rather more theatrical, tumble and, rightly, isn't awarded a penalty. And what really excited me are the ones who were injured: Taye, Pressley, Dan Butler, JFC and Reidy. Plus Charlie Goode. With Rotherham defeated, it really couldn't have gone better.

Then it could have gone very much better. Oscar decides there's a shortcut to the car and takes it. He's wrong, of course, but I'm the one who gets hopelessly lost. I have to call him so he can guide me back to the car he'd found easily. He's delighted. 'Shall I tell mum and Jess?' he gloats. I'd rather you didn't. God, I feel old.

13 August 2024
Norwich City 4 Stevenage 3 –
Carabao Cup

My prediction: 1-1
His prediction: 1-2

For me (and probably me alone), if you're driving north, Norwich begins just south of Thetford when the Elveden War Memorial hoves into view on the western side of the A11. It's a magnificent 39-metre 1921 obelisk, a deliciously overblown tribute to the locals of three parishes who perished in the First World War. With many a metre to spare, they even added some Second World War victims a few years later. Even Oscar's impressed, albeit momentarily.

Steam further up the A11 and you'll pass Wymondham, from where the last peasants' revolt began in 1549 when wealthy farmer, Robert Kett, objected to some kind of grazing rights outrage. He marched to Norwich with 15,000 men, captured it – some swam across the River Wensum, evading a fusillade of arrows – held it for a few weeks, refused a pardon and was finally defeated by the rather brutal Earl of Warwick, who, unsportingly, hired some merciless, turbo-charged German mercenaries. Kett was hanged from the walls of Norwich Castle. Many of the peasants were massacred, but there's a primary school named after him in Wymondham, with the motto 'achieving together', so it was worth it.

Tonight, in a no-way hopelessly contrived segue, Norwich will be invaded again, this time by 516 Stevenage fans, delighted that it's only £10 for adults and £1 for under-17s. Taye's injury has taken a turn for the even worse, so a new back-up goalkeeper, Dean Bouzanis, has joined until January. We're in super-high spirits: a night away game at a Championship club on a balmy non-school night, no travel issues (until we reach Norwich, where it's roadworks everywhere, with nobody working on them) and one of my favourite grounds. We suck on mints, evaluate Tyler the Creator's love triangle *Igor* album track by track (I'm quite taken by 'Are We Still Friends?', he's more of a 'Gone, Gone/Thank You' type) and investigate the delights of Mango Tango.

More pertinently, we haven't established a swearing policy this season. It's been straightforward for two seasons. He was allowed two swears per game – no 'cunt' of course, under any circumstances; the thought of him saying it crushes me – but every time I swear, that gives him a free hit. That two swears restriction is abandoned if it's as tense as it was at Cambridge last year or if Sean Clare's playing for the opposition. It doesn't always work: a Boro-supporting woman told him off at King's Lynn while staring at me, the world's worst parent. On balance, it's gone reasonably well.

This season, it may not go so well since 'I'm taller than you now, so I can swear as much as I want.' For the triggered record, he is not taller than me. I know this because he insists on going shoulder-to-shoulder, back-to-back most weeks, just to check. I reckon I've got until the end of the season. There has to be discipline, though, even if it's of a laissez-faire variety. This means he's not swearing as much as he wishes – in my mind, he's still the smiley five-year-old little fella who dressed as Sportacus from *LazyTown* – but I'll have to compromise.

I guide him to Carrow Road, where the ground is almost invisible until you're actually upon it, having crossed over the Wensum, at a point where Kett's men probably didn't swim. Oscar seethes when a kindly steward says 'the little one that way', so we enter via separate turnstiles. Norwich owner Delia Smith has just announced that she'll be stepping down from her Norwich duties later in the season, but she surely retired from their catering a long time ago, if she was ever part of it. We both try a 'gastro' steak-and-ale pie plus a carton of water for the price of a house in Middlesbrough. The pie's hot and peppery, but it's not claggy and it tastes better with each lip-scorching bite. A fair start, although Oscar thinks about putting it below Boro in his inchoate pie chart, before changing his mind next morning. There's a programme too, which doesn't trouble itself with notes from spectacularly inexperienced new boss, the worryingly sockless Johannes Hoff Thorup, an appointment so leftfield it'll be duetting with John Lydon any moment now. But it's a programme.

It's a funny atmosphere. Few Norwich fans over school age seems to have turned up, so we're heckled by a gaggle of nine-year-olds ('who are ya, who are ya'), a row of non-threatening teenagers and a cheery, too-tall bald man who does a rather impressive clockwork dance when Norwich score. He looks ready to end it all when Boro reply and pretends to comb his non-existent hair when it's suggested that he resembles a boiled egg. I'm a fan. There's a woman wearing a signed Vadaine Oliver shirt in front of us. 'Must have won it in a raffle,' mutters Oscar.

The game's a cracker. Inspired by the Cuban, Onel Hernández, Norwich are better, as they should be, but Boro, who've made seven changes, recover from 1-0 and 2-1 down and pull a third back at 4-2. The set pieces do seem to have been worked on – Harvey White sets up one goal with a free kick and another with a corner – and the returning full-back Dan Butler, as he usually does, spends half-time in kickabout with the substitutes, although he's replaced on the hour.

That said, two of the Boro goals are flukes, three of Norwich's are preventable and Revs's substitutions are worryingly naïve, although he may have had one eye on Saturday's trip to Huddersfield. Dan Kemp fluffs an early sitter and, as with Saturday's penalty miss, it shatters his confidence. Charlie Goode looked robust for his 45-minute cameo, White's blossoming apace and we're falling in love with Lewis Freestone. 'First half great, second half not good enough,' muses an overly disgruntled Oscar on the walk back. True, the second half wasn't great, so I can see where he's coming from, but he's being harsh. Revs will make better substitutions and there's more to come, especially when there's a full squad to select from.

To celebrate defenestrating Stevenage from the Carabao Cup at the first-round stage, Norwich do a lap of honour. They look sheepish, the crowd look confused. We stay behind to laugh at the lot of them.

17 August 2024
Huddersfield Town 2 Stevenage 1

My prediction: 0-0
His prediction: 2-3

We're on our way home. Do you want to talk about it?

'Not really.'

Me neither, but we have to at some point.

'I know.'

Go on then …

Oscar puts down his phone – an event so rare as to be worth noting – and lets rip at volume.

'What happened? What was he thinking? How could he do that? It's the worst miss I've ever seen. I could have scored it and I'm not exaggerating.'

'He' is Elliott List. And 'that' is the chance Listy somehow screwed wide 48 minutes into a game in which Boro had struggled from the moment Revs picked the wrong team. Eleven yards out. Goalkeeper prostrate after Appéré had brilliantly left his man flailing and crossed low. No defenders near. It took some missing. Listy managed it.

Had List scored, Huddersfield might still have rallied. We'll never know, but it would have been nice to find out. Harvey White – creator of two at Norwich, lest we forget – and Lewis Freestone have been Boro's best performers this season. In his post-match interview at Norwich, Revs had noted things were better when Freestone replaced Dan Butler. So he dropped White and kept Freestone on the bench.

And he deploys three centre-backs in a back five. The left-sided one, Carl 'Pidge' Piergianni, is too close to left-back Butler, while right-back Luther James-Wildin is overrun. Huddersfield feed the wings and Lasse Sørensen and Mickel Miller run riot.

After a wretched first half (Huddersfield have eight shots; eight more than Boro), Revs switches to a back four, but White doesn't appear until the 75th minute and Freestone not at all. Still, Dan Kemp (rightly dropped) causes problems and Appéré really ought to be starting a league game now. 'We're going down,' reckons Oscar, master of the wildly swinging opinion. He's wrong. At least I think he's wrong.

It's been a tricky few days. We weren't speaking for most of them because I was rude when he helped me set the new television up after the old one exploded (fact check: it didn't 'explode'; it died peacefully during a Cold War documentary, but I'm attention-seeking). Worse, for me Huddersfield is a treat. It's not for him though. 'If the best they can do is the Yorkshire Sculpture Park and the National Coal Mining Museum they can't have much going for them,' snarls my young philistine.

We make good time despite five needlessly lengthy stretches of roadworks on the M1, which, boom boom, is the total amount of workers we saw loitering around them. This is my first and (probably) last roadworks rant: why do they need to erect them for ten miles? Where are the workers (I'm all for the dignity of the working man, I saw Test Dept but …)? Why, having 'won' a contract, can the companies take as long as they please? Etc, etc.

Since we're early into the former wool town, we wander around the ground, passing a mascot dressed in a *Transformers* outfit and watch the Boro players arrive. Boro use the apostrophe-unfriendly Greys of Ely, who haul Cambridge United and Peterborough United too. Either Greys are not the expensive option or there are no coach firms in Hertfordshire, but it's functional enough. We give the squad a clap, wonder why there are so few of them on board and I chat to a Huddersfield fan who asks how we're coping without Steve Evans ('wouldn't want him here') and amble inside the John Smith's Stadium, perhaps the most beautiful football stadium in England. It's 30 years old next week.

Huddersfield's new American owners have embarked upon what the *Yorkshire Post* describes as 'a multi-million-pound re-brand' alongside something that thinks it's called Fantastic Media. Since they'll always be Huddersfield Town, we know how this one will end, although the venerable but struggling *Huddersfield Examiner*, with sales under 3,000 and their Town correspondent made redundant, may not be there to report it. For now, this means dozens of kids with flags loitering non-committally on the halfway line and some flames welcoming the teams.

There's a proper, 60-page programme, but they could start with rebranding the catering. We both chance a tiny steak-and-ale pie (just the £4.50, although its effluvia is free) and it's the worst offering since Carlisle: greasy pastry, surrounding some kind of clagfest filling that bears no relation to a) steak or b) ale.

The Town fans pump up the volume and their team is pumped up too. Charlie Goode leaves Josh Koroma free to score the first and is hooked at the break, while Sweens is slumbering soundly when Ben Wiles whips in number two, post-List's miss. We away hordes, all 328 of us, are frustrated and, by the end – White scores an added-time penalty that nobody bothers cheering too loudly – we're singing 'how shit must you be, you've got to play us' at the relative aristocrats. This early in the season, the air of resignation is almost palpable.

Afterwards, we're quiet and grumpy as we head down the A629 towards the M1. We're hungry, too, after that pie so, just as Huddersfield turns from urban to rural, we stop at a fish'n'chips shack with tables outside. Oscar has not had hardcore northern fish'n'chips for years. They're cooked in beef dripping, a chirpy woman sprinkles bits over them and we're in food heaven. We touch plastic forks and watch the early evening traffic rumble by. Perhaps the world isn't as sad as it seems.

20 August 2024
Stevenage 1 Crystal Palace Under-21s
0 – Bristol Street Motors EFL Trophy

My prediction: 2-0
His prediction: 3-0

Ah, the Second-Hand Car Cup. As we already know, Oscar's not impressed, but he's getting pompous in his old age: 'I do not come to games where they've closed half the stadium.' He needs bribing again, but this time it's only a lemon Fanta. I'm quite up for this. It's a free hit, a nice evening where I can still wear shorts and we're perched behind the dugouts in the West Stand, a fist-bump from Palace insider Mark Bright. There are 903 of us, including 99 from Palace, presumably family members. Drackers is here, announcing that names can be printed on replica shirts now ('No thanks,' announces Oscar), Boro Bear is not, so it's not the same. How could it be?

They play Secret Affair's 'Time for Action' and the *Pirates of the Caribbean* soundtrack before kick-off. The electronic scoreboard says 'Crystal Palace' rather than 'Crystal Palace Under-21s' and, while the atmosphere is supportive, it's muted, so we can hear Scott Cuthbert barking instructions, mostly based around 'feeding it wide'.

Revs has picked a strongish team and this time his selection is spot on. To our right, there's a clutch of Boro players who aren't playing: Pidge, Robbo Roberts, Dan Phillips and, best of all, a fit-looking Jamie 'Reidy' Reid. I'd like to think they're here out of solidarity rather than contractual obligation, but while they're surely keen to progress in this daft cup, equally surely nobody wants anyone in their position to play especially well. Dean Bouzanis plays in goal but he won't have a shot to save. Dan Kemp and Tyreece Simpson start with a view to notching confidence-building goals. It partly pays off when Simpson does indeed score, impressively volleying home Lewis Freestone's flick after the Palace kids couldn't deal with Charlie Goode's long throw and subsequent header. Simpson doesn't celebrate too wildly. Elliott List misses another sitter, while Kemp does some deft things but still doesn't look like scoring. And a big hello to Goode, who heads out of the ground from almost under the bar. There are three Thompsons on the pitch for the first time this season, but missing chances is becoming a problem again. Boro drift off towards the end of a game they should have long put to bed and the situation becomes so perilous that the untried kids on the bench aren't unveiled.

Being boys in search of Premier League contracts, Palace try hard, but they aren't great (Justin Devenny sends a free kick out of the ground), and when they do break out towards the end, they're thwarted by their prodigal finishing. Having the kids travel on an upmarket Ellisons rather than a decrepit charabanc surely sends the wrong message, but if you want a future Premier League player, try Franco Umeh. If he's asking if you'd like an extra topping with your pizza three years from now, I was joking.

Boro get £20,000 for taking part. There are two more Southern Group D games (£10,000 per win, £5,000 per draw) to go. Then the last 32 (£20,000 per win), then the last 16 (£40,000 per win), then the last eight (£50,000 per win), then the semi, then Wembley (£100,000 for a win, £50,000 for losing finalists). 'Do we have to go to all the group games?' Oscar asks, forgetting how anxious he'd been during Palace's late rally.

We do.

'Okay then.'

24 August 2024
Burton Albion 0 Stevenage 0

My prediction: 1-2
His prediction: 0-1

I have been asked by a lot of people* how close I am to visiting all 92 current league grounds (*actual number of people who've asked: 0). I had it once, briefly, but now I'm missing Rotherham, Shrewsbury, Bromley, Chesterfield, Fleetwood, Harrogate, Salford, Morecambe and, guess where, Burton-Upon-Trent.

Oscar's excited about the Pirelli Stadium, chiefly because he thinks Formula 1 tyres may be made at the Pirelli tyre factory (they're not: it's Romania and Turkey). He doesn't know the Football Association and its elite training facility, St George's Park, are in Burton, or that there's a brewing tradition, or that it was mentioned in the *Domesday Book*, or that Oswald Mosley was raised at the now-demolished Rolleston Hall just up the road or that Kane Hemmings, last season's fairly successful Boro loanee, was born here, as was DJ Nathan Dawe, who still lives here, although he has a box at Aston Villa. 'When Burton came to Villa Park in the Championship,' he told me, 'the whole away end started pointing at me and singing "you're just a shit Calvin Harris". I couldn't help but laugh.' Today, though, the Burton fans are silent.

Me? I'm happy to be at a new ground. Opened in 2005 on Pirelli land (the naming rights were part of the deal), it's a typical newish build with three sides standing and advertisements eulogising one Don Amott, the self-crowned King Of Caravans: 'At Don Amott Leisure Kingdom, our story is one of passion, dedication and a profound love for the world of caravans and motorhomes.'

The toilets are festival-level disgusting, but there's a programme with a three-page tribute to Tea Bar Sue, who met her husband at Burton's old ground Eton Park (we park on Eton Road) in 1966. Oh, Tea Bar Sue, we love you … The food menu is on the suspiciously long side (just the £5.50 for a baked potato with either beans or cheese). So I go safe with a Pukka steak pie. Oscar tries a hot dog. It's not a frankfurter, but he gets to apply his own ketchup and the roll isn't stale. He's easily impressed sometimes.

The Sky-induced lunchtime kick-off, part of their Pretending to Care About the EFL campaign, guarantees a soporific game, viewing figures in the dozens with Brighton & Hove Albion against Manchester United on another channel (I cannot see what's in this idiocy for Sky, beyond tax assistance), an early start for the 197 of us who make the trek, a McDonald's breakfast (oh, the phone's ringing: 'Hello, this is the Britain's Worst Parent Awards. Would you be interested in entering?'), me somehow missing the M1 turning and, hurrah! Terence Vancooten.

We try to uphold an old tradition and seek TVC's Mercedes in the players' car park, but we fail. He might have acquired a new vehicle with his Burton booty, of course. Either way, it's lovely to see him again. Midway through the second half, right in front of us, he takes a waist-high cross in what, since we're in coy mood, we may describe as his gentleman's area. I feel sick on his behalf. After some time, TVC staggers to his feet. 'How's the bollocks Terence?' someone shouts. He laughs, but he looks very, very pale indeed. There's a disappointing chant of 'fuck off Vancooten', but afterwards he loiters in front of us, lapping up the otherwise universal love. Still don't know what his best position is. Still miss him.

Another loanee arrived this week, Eli King from Cardiff City. He's the defensive midfielder I'd assumed Dan Phillips was going to be. Phillips plays further forwards again today and King stays benched for a game that ends as goalless as it began. I've been to morgues with a livelier atmosphere. Boro number 6 Dan Sweeney grapples with Burton number 6 Ryan Sweeney as ferociously as they surely did when they were kids. It's the first time they've faced each other since their father died in April. Dan – older by three years and a week; the identical distance young Oscar lags behind his sister – is staying in Burton overnight. Hopefully they'll have the best of times.

Having made just the 21 summer signings, Burton are disjointed, but their mascot, Billy Brewer, chides Kane Smith for pinching ground when taking a throw-in, and their goalkeeper Max Crocombe spends a game-delaying eternity in the dugout, seemingly struggling to tie his laces. We shout 'wanker, wanker' at him as he returns. He gives us a cheery wave, so he wins, but when a ballboy dithers late on, he shouts 'quick, quick, quick' at him, so they do want to win. In the end neither goalkeeper makes a meaningful save, although, surreally, one source has Crocombe as man of the match. Tyreece Simpson bumbles around ineffectively, but he gets little service, and a brief yet vicious shower further drenches this already damp squib. Not creating chances is becoming a bigger problem with each passing game, even before the problem of not taking them. Afterwards, Revs rightly points out there were many encouraging aspects, but he claims Boro should have won and doubles down on the notion that they were worth a point at Huddersfield. Does he really believe this? I'm inclined to think not.

The game's talking points – and there were some, for it was fairly beguiling as 0-0s go – all happen at our end. And Oscar and I are overly visible on that night's *English Football League Highlights* on ITV4. When Murphy Cooper (I like him, but I reckon he's too small;

Oscar vehemently disagrees) watches a stray cross hit the post, we're in deep conversation. When Danilo Orsi screws Burton's only real chance wide I, disappointingly theatrically, have my head in the hands, while Oscar slaps the barriers. When Dan Kemp has a cross deflected just wide, I clap overly vigorously, as does a very vocal Oscar. When Dan Sweeney crosses low into the danger zone to no avail, my head is in my hands again and Oscar slaps the barrier again. We watch it together later that night, mutually embarrassed.

'I really hope my friends don't see this. There's nothing to say is there, Dad?'

No there isn't.

30 August 2024
Transfer Deadline Day 1

There's only one hero here: Neil Metcalfe, the Fabrizio Romano of Hertfordshire. He's the sports reporter for local newspaper, *The Comet*, and probably the only Boro-centred print writer. He faces the traditional dilemma of local football reporters: they can only survive with extensive exclusive access (Boro making the first Revs press conference open to all didn't seem especially fair to someone trying to do their actual job), combined with discretion when a Boro player is found insensible in Harpenden town centre (n.b. I know of no Boro player who has been found insensible in Harpenden). Yet to gain reader traction, he needs to ask proper questions without alienating the club. And, this season, he gives each player match ratings that are fair and balanced. Unless you're the player reading them.

Neil also has some very modern dilemmas. Local journalism is crumbling so he won't be earning a fortune, but his management will demand clickbait for *The Comet*'s partly paywalled website and a constant stream of copy during the 24-hour news cycle. He's even started an EFL Fantasy League for Boro fans. Without myself and Oscar, there would have been 28 members. Oscar, in a rare moment of mean-spiritedness, refuses to follow Neil on Twitter. He won't say why …

A Stakhanovite with a fully charged laptop, Neil Metcalfe today is blogging at an insane 6.59am, although why he's blogging at 6.59am is less clear, for no football club is open then. Having broken up his day only by speeding to Bragbury End to interview Revs and preview tomorrow's game, he's still there at 11.21pm. I do hope *The Comet* know what they've got with this man. 'Been good craic today,' he suggests unconvincingly, before possibly breaking down, slugging a single malt and weeping himself to sleep. And his 16-hour stint has brought just a handful of stories, one of which – Jordan 'Robbo' Roberts signing an extended contract (for how long though?) – isn't a transfer story at all.

I ask Oscar if he'd prefer Robbo to have signed on or moved on, as I reckon it was a close call. 'Signed on,' insists Oscar. Me too, but I wish he wouldn't disappear so often. Young goalkeeper Rylee Mitchell goes out on whatever a youth loan is to National League North (North? Seriously?) Oxford City, which should give him the extensive game time he obviously needs, albeit for only 28 days.

Ben Thompson is loaned to Bromley for the rest of the season. It hasn't quite worked out for him at Boro. He came with pedigree, but Evans didn't fancy him and neither does Revs. More than anything he's remembered for his awful miss that would have turned a 0-0 with Bolton Wanderers into 1-0 as last season's play-offs slipped away.

There are two incomers. Norwich City loanee Ken Aboh is a very Boro signing: too young for the hurly-burly of League One, but so promising he got ten Championship minutes last year and scored 11 times in 15 Premier Two games. He looks quite slight, but he may be quick when he comes off the bench. He might get a Second-Hand Car Cup start if he trains well.

More intriguing is Jake Young. The rumours have been swirling since the window opened, and at 7.07am Neil Metcalfe was suggesting the Bradford striker who managed to upset both Mark Hughes and Graham Alexander is bound for glamorous Fleetwood. At 3pm the word from Bradford is that a Boro bid has been rejected. 'It won't happen,' says Neil Metcalfe, wisely caveating, 'I'm fairly certain of that.'

By 5.34pm, following what must have been a steer from Boro, not least because Revs had told him Aboh is the only arrival, it's 'I'm saying no go, I'm 99.9 per cent certain of that.'

At 10.07pm, 'I'm starting to get whispers it's done,' and so it proves. At 10.43pm Boro tweet 'the night is still young' and at 10.47pm Young's arrival is announced. At 11.07pm, there's a Neil Metcalfe article online, saying the 'undisclosed' figure is a six-figure one, possibly eclipsing the record £125,000 Boro paid for James Dunne in 2012.

At 23, Young is a tad too young to be a saviour. Like Dan Kemp, he had a most productive loan spell at Swindon, but, like Dan Kemp, Boro have signed a striker who couldn't get into a League Two team ...

31 August 2024
Stevenage 0 Lincoln City 1

My prediction: 3-1
His prediction: 2-0

Oscar's a tad apathetic today, although he's made himself an expert on Jake Young: 'He might be the one, you know.' Part of him wants to stay home and watch Formula 1 qualifying, I suspect, but here we are. In the club shop we're elbowed out of the way by an oaf from Lincoln who's liberating all the team sheets (if Boro did a programme, etc., etc.) and Oscar wants to eat inside the Lamex, so he goes for the same chicken strips (we're no longer going to persist with the goujon fallacy) and chips as last time. Luckily, I don't do the pie chart or my disastrous burger (£5, stale bread, unidentifiable meat, no onions) would be propping it up.

Revs unaccountably drops Harvey White in favour of Listy. Jake Young was signed too late to be in contention. Aboh makes the bench, although Appéré doesn't get that far. Nothing is auguring well here, other than Neil Metcalfe beginning another blog at 2pm, although internet reception is so feeble nobody at the game can follow it.

It gets worse. Sweens hobbles off before the half-hour (Charlie Goode rather than Lewis Freestone replaces him), and if we thought Listy's miss was bad at Huddersfield, Lincoln's Adam Jackson (he's number 5, so it's Jackson 5 on his back, but Oscar doesn't get it) misjudges a header to let Tyreece Simpson in. With the goalkeeper beaten, the open goal beckons. Rather than rolling the ball into the net, Simpson blasts it high and wide. He puts his shirt over his head and, unlike with

Listy at Huddersfield (away crowds are more tolerant and everyone loves Listy), the crowd turns. 'Simpson, you useless cunt,' bellows the hitherto and subsequently silent man next to me. Needless to say, I'm losing the swear war with Oscar. I feel awful for Simpson, but I'm not sure I can see a way back for a striker who never looks like striking.

Listy is denied a penalty when he's felled by Jackson, and Revs persists with Simpson until the 70th minute when Aboh is unveiled. He falls over before he's touched the ball and I'm not wholly sure he subsequently touches it at all. After the change, Dan Butler foolishly scythes through JJ McKiernan, Jack Moylan wallops home the penalty and there's no prospect of a comeback.

The floodlights are needed late on, the 823 travelling fans laugh at us and Lincoln board their unremarkable Skills – based in Nottingham, once used by Aston Villa, although I may be misremembering – team bus with three more points to their name.

'We're pretty bad at football aren't we?' says a disconsolate Oscar. I can see his point. Few chances created (again) and no attacking focus (again), Dan Kemp's set pieces were uniformly awful and robust Lincoln had a plan they stuck to. Later that night Oscar and I watch the EFL highlights. Barnsley, Bristol Rovers and even Shrewsbury are scoring crisp, well-worked goals conceived on the training pitch. 'Why are they so much better than us?' asks Oscar.

No game next week, because of Wigan's international call-ups. That's two weeks of solid, hardcore, season-turning-around training before Barnsley roll into the Lamex. I can't think of two more important weeks.

Pie chart
1. Norwich City
2. Burton Albion
3. Stevenage
4. Huddersfield Town

September – Quinn The Eskimo's Here

14 September 2024
Stevenage 3 Barnsley 0

My prediction: 3-1
His prediction 2-1

With the Wigan trip postponed, on the spare Saturday we played pitch'n'putt. I haven't played for decades, he hasn't played before. I win. You may feel it's a little on the pathetic side that I need to mention this. You may well be right.

Oscar's school year, the first of his two GCSE ones, has started. As his life is slowly taking shape, he's a bundle of dreams and possibilities. He wants to go to university, he wants to travel the world, he wants to live abroad (as I'd mentioned), he wants to start his own business, he wants to be a professional footballer and he wants to have a pet cat. We already have one: the undeniably chubby Penfold, or Tenfold, as his sister's friends have cruelly but wittily rechristened him.

Oscar and Penfold often sleep together until Penfold wakes Oscar, usually around 3am, with noisy demands to visit the garden, where he can empty his tiny feline bladder. Their tableaux never changes. Penfold is sprawled across the duvet, king of the jungle that is Oscar's bed.

Oscar, meanwhile, is scrunched up in a far corner of that single bed, thus ensuring the noble beast's rest is undisturbed. 'I wouldn't want to live in a world without Penfold,' he says. My heart always melts; what else could it possibly do?

His wants, his hopes are all about after he goes. Needless – and rightly – to say there is no mention of seeing Boro with his ageing dad. Before he goes, though, there is this. Sometimes I just want our season to be over, so it's done, completed without sickness, accidents, travel issues (what if the car breaks down on the way to Bristol as well as Shrewsbury?) and without life intervening, as it tends to. Seeing every Boro game in a season is something we can both take into the next stages of our lives; him to become a man, me to the final years.

Like Wigan, Boro had international call-ups. Eli King went to Iceland, where he played 90 minutes as Wales Under-21s won in Reykjavík, while Dan Phillips flew to Honduras to sit unused on the bench as Trinidad & Tobago lost 4-0, but he did get 72 minutes when French Guiana held them to a 0-0 at the Dwight Yorke Stadium in Scarborough. That's Scarborough, Tobago, not the Scarborough where the lovely Ken Dodd once sat me on his knee, but not in a Yewtree-alerting way. We spend much of the pre-Barnsley week speculating where in the world Dan Phillips might be at any given point. Not in the Stevenage area is our consensus. 'He'll be sleeping now,' suggests Oscar on Friday's school run.

Barnsley haven't lost since the opening day. They are managed by the previously mentioned Darrell Clarke and they turn out to be physical giants. Neither of us has any real faith in our predictions, but to Revs's credit, changes have been rung since Lincoln. Sweens and Kane

SEPTEMBER – QUINN THE ESKIMO'S HERE

Smith are injured, so only diminutive goalkeeper Murphy Cooper, Pidge and Robbo Roberts begin a second consecutive game. Jake Young starts, but so does our very own Quinn the Eskimo ('when Quinn the Eskimo gets here, everybody's gonna jump for joy'), Jamie 'Reidy' Reid. It's a relief to see him back from what may have been a blood clot, but the strapping on his calf looks ominous. Too-frequent flyer Dan Phillips is on the bench alongside the demoted Dan Kemp and Tyreece Simpson, while new boys Appéré and Aboh don't make it that far.

For the first time this season, I'm not wearing shorts and I'm stood between Oscar and a youth on his own who will spend the game on his phone, looking up only to berate the referee ('fuck off you bellend') before returning to the important stuff. In fairness, he doesn't miss much during a wretched first half, which passes almost without incident, as 923 gloomy and mute South Yorkshire folk are shoehorned into the away end. We briefly and quietly sing the 'football in a library' chant, as the dopey visitors can't be bothered.

Boro players are wearing black armbands since Louis and Nathan Thompson's father died in the week. Pidge does all the hollering when the players gather for the pre-match huddle right in front of us. We're getting used to this now and we're warming to it. Pidge inspires, they break the huddle, we clap, they clap back.

Let's talk about Pidge, the man his team-mates call Skip. An ageing centre-back, brought in by Evans to replace Scott Cuthbert, chiefly because, said some, Pidge and Evans live in the same village just south of Peterborough close to the A1. He made just one Football League appearance before the age of 27, having bobbled harmlessly through Peterborough United, non-league,

Australia, Salford City, and Oldham Athletic as they carelessly tumbled out of the EFL. Then he was rescued by Stevenage. Oscar was predisposed to be unimpressed with anyone who'd replaced his hero, Cuthbert. I may have muttered 'carthorse' at some point.

Wrong, wrong, wrong. Solid, mobile, ridiculously brave and capable of scoring a goal or two, Pidge evolved into the poster boy for Boro's rise under Evans and that's why he's immortalised in the underpass mural on the way to the Lamex. But he's more than that, he's a leader, the heart and soul of the dressing room, the epitome of brolic. We feared he might follow Evans to Rotherham (of Boro's players only Alex MacDonald made the journey; make of that what you will), but instead he stayed to run Revs's dressing room too. As a leader of men, he's special. As a centre-half he must be horrible to play against and Boro are so lucky to have him. I'd spout that cliché about trenches, but since the chances of my ever being in a trench are minuscule and the prospect of Pidge joining me there is more infinitesimal still, I won't bother. We adore the man, the East Terrace loves him without reservation.

Barnsley have the better of that poor first half and, but for Cooper's lightning reactions, Josh Earl would have scored for the team clad in lurid pink when Boro's defence enjoyed a communal nap. There are rumblings of discontent as the players amble off.

Forty-five exhilarating minutes later, it's 3-0. Boro are electric and Oscar is elbowing me: 'Nobody saw that coming, Dad.' He's right. Jake Young is hooked after just 51 minutes, having barely had a kick. Then substitute Listy exorcises the ghosts of Huddersfield with a handsome finish after Reidy's shot is blocked. Five minutes later, Barnsley fans begin to leave when Pidge heads Harvey White's corner down and over Gabriel Slonina. After Phillips gets himself booked six minutes after coming on ('jet lag', reckons Oscar), Listy pokes home fellow substitute Louis Thompson's terrific cross for a third. Everyone gathers around Louis Thompson to celebrate and commiserate; we all know who that goal was for.

Apart from Young, whose season had previously consisted of 24 Carabao minutes for Bradford, so let's assume rustiness, it's been a revelation. Eli King is the sort of Rolls-Royce player who creates space for himself, Reidy looked almost there and even broad-shouldered utility man Nick Freeman shed his cloak of invisibility to look majestic on the ball.

Afterwards, Barnsley head home on their swish Eavesway coach – they're from Wigan and carry Wigan Athletic – we take a much shorter journey. The second half was the best performance since Derby were walloped last October. And, for the record, Boro looked properly coached. A blip? Or the way ahead? 'We'll finish ninth,' Oscar now declares. We'll see.

Meanwhile, right now, in a galaxy quite near (I'd never seen a *Star Wars* film before Oscar; I've seen them all now, more than once) another football season has commenced. The day after we didn't go to Wigan, Broxbourne Borough Under-15s began their 2024/25 campaign with a 2-0 defeat at Royston, who could only field ten men. Goalkeeper Oscar reckoned he wasn't at fault for either goal. The journey up the A10 with a couple of team-mates was a loud joy as they speculated upon their chances with the optimism of the untested. The journey home was mute.

Tomorrow, Broxbourne Borough Under-15s will be without substitutes as they lose 6-0 at home. 'You were awesome,' his coach Lee will say to the overworked Oscar as we leave. He glows. The sixth goal was his error but, before and after that, shot followed shot and save followed save. If Boro can turn things around, so can Broxbourne Borough Under-15s. We'll see. Again.

21 September 2024
Exeter City 2 Stevenage 0

My prediction: 0-1
His prediction 1-2

After the final whistle, some of the 123 Boro travellers shuffle disconsolately to the front of Exeter City's St James Road End to clap the players. An older guy claps more lustily than Oscar and I can be bothered to do, but he's also shouting 'not good enough' as he pummels his palms.

It wasn't good enough at all. The Barnsley momentum has been tossed away in 90 minutes of low-intensity ineptitude. How good is Exeter's cherub-faced goalkeeper Joe Whitworth? I can't tell you, since he didn't have a shot to save, unless Luther James-Wildin's late trickle towards him counts. It doesn't.

The day began so well. In Propaganda's 'P: Machinery' there's a moment – several moments in fact – when it grinds to a halt and then starts up again with an almighty motif. It's so rousing we're listening to it at 6.45am on the M25 to get us in the mood for another 12.30pm kick-off, another chapter of Sky's Pretending to Care About the EFL campaign. Again, the viewing figures will bring their own reward.

Oscar switches to Will Smith's 'Miami' and Kanye West's 'Touch the Sky'. I respond with The Whispers' 'And the Beat Goes On' and Curtis Mayfield's 'Move On Up', because I'm a snob. No matter, they all do the trick. We then dissect Bruno Mars's rather one-paced 'Silk Sonic' collaboration with the intriguingly punctuated Anderson .Paak. Oscar loves it. We're so happy.

We both like the look of Exeter too, although we're deep in a student heartland where the graffiti invites us to EAT DISHWASHER TABLETS. It's a stately city built on wool, flattened by the Luftwaffe, blighted by disproportioned homelessness and it's the birthplace of Chris Martin, accountant's son and Coldplay singer.

There's a programme. Hurrah. A cheery steward wishes us a 'good day, but not too good', as if we're moonlighting in *Gavin & Stacey*. As in last season's Carabao, we're given a laminated voucher for a hot drink when we enter and if they make their money back on the hot food – £5 for a steak-and-ale pie, which again has no trace of steak or ale but does include some rogue unpleasantness; £3 for Oscar's 'mediocre' sausage roll – we spurn the pasties after the conspiratorial server reveals 'they're shit here'. In the queue, as The Police's 'Roxanne' blares over the PA, there's talk (not from me and Oscar) of nine points from the next three games and fourth place. Everyone's buzzing. What can possibly go wrong?

The game. That's what can go wrong. For a moment we're happier than Neil Metcalfe. Yesterday was his day off. Neil spent it travelling to Exeter. 'I despise Sky,' he tweets. And this morning when Stevenage tweet the Sky details, he's just as cheery ... 'Or just see everything I'll have on *Comet Sport*. I'll be grafting long after the TV company have packed up and gone home.'

That moment doesn't last long. For reasons the club has taken a vow of Omerta over, there's no sign of Jake Young (you don't drop your record signing after one poor hour, do you?), although he travelled. At a ground where they haven't won in 6,767 days, Boro are one down after nine minutes when Ed Francis swivels on a corner. The handful of Sky viewers could see us behind the goal, as motionless as the Boro defence. The new tactical approach – Neil Banfield's innovation apparently – never looks like working. Since Listy and Reidy are far from best friends, Revs tries to avoid playing them as a joint spearhead. On this grisly showing it's clear why, and they're both hauled off, while there's no midfield tackler to break up Exeter's foraging. To channel my inner Geoffrey Howe, the bat was broken before the batsmen stepped on to the crease.

Then Charlie Goode goes down following a seemingly innocuous challenge. Immediately it's clear he's in considerable pain. Rather than call for a stretcher, the physio takes him to the side of the pitch. When Sweens was injured the other week, he could still hobble off. We're in a different league of agony here.

To get to the dressing room, Goode has to limp around the pitch, past the whole away end and around the corner flag. Each injury-exacerbating step is torture and, after each, he clutches on to the railing, panting and wheezing like a 30-a-day pensioner. Nobody from the dugout comes to help him and the physio, not hunky goalkeeper coach Marlon Beresford, not substitute goalkeeper Bouzanis – neither of whom can possibly have anything better to do – not even Scott Cuthbert. Nobody.

I'm really not one for shouting directly at players, other than the occasional Noël Coward-esque quip they are free to recycle at next day's luncheon. Not here. 'Charlie,' I bellow, 'get a fucking stretcher. Or get someone to help you.' I'm not sure he hears me, but he hears something and responds with a disconsolate thumbs-up. Nothing happens. 'About not swearing dad ...' chuckles Oscar, mid-eyebrow raise. Goode's journey takes nearly ten excruciating minutes, during which another Boro player gets injured, so he's left alone in extreme distress. It's awful to watch.

Exeter are capable. Pierce Sweeney (no relation) has radioactive bright yellow boots, Johnly Yfeko has fabulous hair and Kamari Doyle looks the real deal. They wrap it up five minutes into the second half when Harvey White and Lewis Freestone – love is no longer blooming here; we're going through the bad patch all unsuccessful and some successful relationships most suffer, but Oscar didn't fall as hard as me – allow Doyle the time and space to fire past Murphy Cooper, whose head gets closer to the ball than his arms.

Nobody has a decent game, except – possibly – Luther. Nick Freeman re-donned his cloak of anonymity and somehow manages fewer touches than any outfield player. Hence the lack of service to Reidy – and the pigeons were not running to him here at his former club – Robbo Roberts and Listy, a shadow of last week. By the end of a chant-free lunchtime, a couple of Boro fans are foolishly engaging with a gaggle of Devonian adolescents who are laughing at them. It's that sort of dismal day. 'This is all down to one man,' says Oscar of Revs, who, as Neil Metcalfe toils on his laptop post-match, talks of a lack of desire and says 'this was not us'. I'm not sure who 'us' is right now.

We'd taken motorways in the early morning. Coming back, with Oscar not keeping goal tomorrow (the opponents have folded), we take the scenic A303 route. Oscar films the countryside ('great to look at but no more') and we pass Stonehenge. He doesn't want to go in, but he does film it as we go past, very slowly, waylaid by one queue we don't mind. 'Hmmm, more than just stones,' he admits, before checking out the F1 qualifying times.

Long past bedtime, as if I work for the Dial a Cliché Foundation, I fall asleep in front of *Match of the Day*. When I haul myself upstairs, Oscar is still awake. Go to sleep, Oscar. 'I can't, I'm too worried about Boro.'

24 September 2024
Wigan Athletic 0 Stevenage 0

My prediction: 1-1
His prediction: 1-2

Oscar has a headache. It's so severe he has to leave school early. Luckily it clears up during the walk between school and car. So we're off to Wigan.

Funny old place, Wigan. It's full of fish'n'chip shops, but they're all closed by the time we leave. I haven't been here since Wigan Athletic were in the Premier League, but nothing's changed. It's a trim town, a proud town. Rick Astley hailed from Newton-le-Willows just around the corner and while his determinedly downbeat autobiography, *Never*, mentions that he bonds with co-producer Matt Aitken (the missing link between Stock and Waterman) over Wigan-ish upbringings, Rick Astley's autobiography doesn't mention that Rick Astley's co-producer was raised in the village of Astley. George Formby hailed from Wigan, but his wife Beryl, from

Haslingden, just around a different corner, was always the interesting one.

Saturday's journey was all misplaced optimism. Today's isn't. It's a slog to get up there on time. We don't talk much, but it's a mellow silence. I like it like this and we share vanilla latte Oreos (don't bother; too much filling, too sweet) and we sing along to Alicia Keys & Jay-Z's 'Empire State of Mind' at some volume. He's already packed tomorrow's school bag. I'm impressed, but not as impressed as we both are by Wigan Athletic's club shop.

From the sign ordering PLEASE DO NOT KICK THE FOOTBALLS AROUND THE SHOP, it's a club shop as stocked by Willie Wonka. Everything is branded and beyond the usual tat, almost everything is bonkers. There's a retractable dog lead, a dog bowl, plastic shot glasses, a £10 tape measure, Top Trumps, party invitations, Sekonda watches, £18 ties, whatever a 'divot tool' might be, golf balls, golf tees, dartboards and, of course, a chopping board. Everything, in fact, but a programme (bastards). 'I wish I was a Wigan fan,' declares Oscar, for the first and last time in his life.

I'd liked to have visited the Heinz baked beans factory just north of the town centre, but you can't have everything ('Where would you put it?' asked that great American comedian Steven Wright) and we wander round the giant DW Stadium with visions of divot tools in our heads. They've rechristened it the Brick Community Stadium for some reason, but there's still a statue of the visionary Dave Whelan outside. After chatting with Wigan's then-owner, I mentioned to one of his minions that I quite liked him. 'Nobody's ever said that before,' she replied. The, er, Brick is not deserted, but it's hardly vibrant. We're given vouchers for a free hot drink and our pies – my steak (£4.50, i.e. cheaper than Exeter) and Oscar's cheese and onion – that almost behove a club for whom Crusty the Pie is the circular mascot. Almost.

The official away attendance is 93, but my admittedly flawed headcount stops at 63. The PA plays Joy Division's 'Love Will Tear Us Apart' and 'Laid' by James ('and the Grammy for Best Use of the Word "Skewers" goes to …'), to which I do a vigorous but rubbish drum roll in approximate time. 'Why do you always do this sort of thing?' asks Oscar. 'This is why I don't like being with you.' He moves to some of the hundreds of empty seats nearby. The hood on his Stevenage hoodie remains down. 'My hair looks too good to put it up.'

Charlie Goode has broken his fibula, so he won't be facing the club he fled in such mysterious circumstances. We'll never know how long the shenanigans at Exeter have delayed his recovery, but the word on Neil Metcalfe's street is Christmas. Eli King, Listy, Lewis Freestone and Nick Freeman are benched. The brothers Thompson and Dans Kemp, Butler and Phillips come in, which should mean more midfield bite.

Taye's back. Hurrah. Not in the team though. There's no Marlon Beresford, so Taye warms up Cooper and Dean Bouzanis. Taye must be close to match fitness now but, since Cooper has mostly excelled, Taye probably won't start. How Taye must curse his fingers.

It's another morgue. Half a dozen shouty Boro fans make more noise than the Wigan faithful and the 'you're supposed to be at home' chant makes everyone laugh. The Wigan fans are not especially bright: the keener ones, huddled together for warmth like penguins, have positioned themselves in the one tiny area of the empty ground where they can't see the big screen or the clock. The game's not much cop and, disappointingly, Boro kick towards us in the first half, but they're better defensively than against Exeter.

Midfield bite or not, there's no link between that toothy midfield and attack. Harvey White's range is off and a second game in four days passes without Boro pressure. Let me cut and paste from Saturday: how good is Wigan's firm-jawed goalkeeper Sam Tickle, or 'Super Sam Tickle' as the announcer has it? I can't tell you, since he didn't have a shot to save unless Dan Kemp's late trickle towards him counts. It doesn't.

There's restlessness here. 'Revs, give us a sub,' chorus the singing six. After 72 minutes, on comes Tyreece Simpson and, well, nobody else at all after that. This means record signing Jake Young, marooned on the bench wondering what on earth he's doing here, doesn't even get ten minutes. Murphy Cooper makes a terrific late save and Boro leave with the point they undoubtedly deserve, but there have still been no league away goals from open play.

Revs talks about things being on the right track and, while Nathan Thompson brought defensive stability (except for that moment where he miskicked a Wigan cross and the ball hit his standing leg) on his first start of the season, the attacking issues aren't going to disappear.

The Brick is already almost deserted when we exit after clapping the players into the changing room. There'll be four motorway closures on the way home, which gives us more than enough time to play Kraftwerk's soul-stirring, life-affirming and impossibly beautiful 'Autobahn' in full. It's heaven driving down the empty M6 to this soundtrack. For one of us. 'This is awful, Dad,' pronounces the young heathen. 'Music for people who don't like music. Like you.'

There's even more good news, although Oscar just grunts. Greys of Ely have a coach tracker on their website, so we plot the team's journey as they suffer every closure too. As someone once said, we're in this together.

28 September 2024
Stevenage 1 Charlton Athletic 0

My prediction: 2-0
His prediction: 1-0

The goal, oh the goal. Murphy Cooper catches a corner in front of 1,363 restless Charlton fans. Like peak-period Jonah Lomu, he clutches the ball to his chest, ducks and swerves past some startled yellow shirts and rolls it underarm to Jordan Roberts, 20 yards out on the left. Robbo, who's had a game where everything has almost come off, hurtles down the wing to the other penalty area and crosses for Jamie Reid, who returns the favour. Robbo smashes it first time past Will Mannion. It's a wonderful goal. We go wild, albeit wild mixed with disbelief. 'Did you see that?' asks Oscar, his face a composite of joy and wonder. Where on earth did that come from?

Worry was beginning to take hold. A jerk chicken stall had appeared outside the '76 Lounge. Oscar's keen, so we share a £5 portion. The spice kicks and the rice is manly, but the chicken's gristly. Much as I fear a boneless bucket, chicken really is better without bones. 'You're so old-fashioned, Dad,' he decides, over-securely.

Wigan had filled us with both trepidation and intrigue. Charlton were flying high-ish. Reidy (rightly) and Dan Phillips (wrongly) were back on the bench, where they were joined by Taye, who surely didn't expect to march straight back into goal. Tyreece Simpson starts and Oscar and I plan to be nicer about him. Effort? No issue. Holding the ball up? Not bad. The other stuff? Might get better. Scoring? We're not that nice.

Another 45 minutes stumbles by without a Boro shot. Charlton aren't any better, although Matty Godden was once here (there's a very brief but kind chant before kick-off) and Lloyd Jones is bigger than a truck. At times we can hear their manager, the stratospherically intense Nathan Jones, shouting from the other side of the pitch. I saw his meltdown at Brentford – the club I used to manage – during his cataclysmic spell at Southampton. He has much more to melt down about here. Boro are making them look impotent.

The watershed is Reidy's introduction in place of Simpson long before the hour. He's sensational, the Jamie Reid of the first half of last season, the one the club still call BGR (Big Goal Reidy) and the pigeons really are running to him now. Suddenly things begin to click. Louis Thompson is having his best game for the club by a country mile, Jake Young arrived with Reidy and he forces Mannion into a fine save.

Charlton rally and suddenly the clock starts to turn very slowly indeed. 'I've never been so tense,' mumbles Oscar, at least not since the last time he was this tense. When Charlton finally create a golden opportunity, Pidge comes from nowhere to head clear from under the bar, while heading Dan Butler at the same time.

The whistle finally goes and Boro have three points, plus the most clean sheets and fewest goals conceded after eight games since joining the league. Heavens.

Afterwards, Revs comes over and leads us in a massed chant. We still have our issues with him, but Boro looked tactically astute today and the guy looks so happy. We just want the best for him and the team. There's much here to build on, but we said the same thing after Barnsley.

Charlton have swapped their traditional apostrophe-unfriendly Kings Ferry coach for a Bayliss. 'The windows are very tinted aren't they?' notes Oscar, proof of a burgeoning interest in team buses at last. He'll be wondering what happened to Hallmark coaches next, and he's so excited that he's forgotten his prediction was correct. 1-0 to Oscar, in every way.

Tomorrow, Broxbourne Borough Under-15s will score their first goals of the season and take their first point. Oscar's last-second save cannons off a striker's knee and over him for the equaliser, but there's something here to build on too.

Pie Chart

1. Norwich City
2. Burton Albion
3. Wigan Athletic
4. Stevenage
5. Exeter City
6. Huddersfield Town

October – Kwame Poku, We'll Never Forget You

1 October 2024
Stevenage 1 Wrexham 0

My prediction: 2-0
His prediction: 3-2

It's 5.30pm. We're raring to go. 'I've got such a good feeling about this,' declares Oscar. Me too. Season tickets? Check. Money? Check. Phones? Check. Let's go!

Let's not go. It's been raining heavily round these parts and there's a pitch inspection. 'Tinpot club' is the general reaction on Twitter, as if Phil Wallace controls the weather. He may do, of course. Half an hour later, not a peep from the Lamex. We're still at home, joining in with the tinpot clamour.

A minute after six, the club decides the game is on ('keep the ball in the air lads' advises a Twitter wit), but we're late. It's all very frenetic. In our programme-free world, we have to get a team sheet and Oscar is resisting.

'It's just a piece of paper.'

Yes, but this is our record of what we've done together.

'And what when you're gone? They'll just be pieces of paper on the floor.'

Just do it. We do it.

This delay means we're late and hungry. It's time for our maiden Boro Burger. It's £7 and includes two patties, cheese, onion and bacon. Oscar tips his to the ground. A river of grease/oil/whatever pours out. Mine's better, but, but, but ...

There's some kind of medical emergency towards the end of the first half. A bunch of fans run to the front of the East Terrace asking the linesman to stop the game. I can't see what's going on, but the stewards – one of whom is the size of a child – look terrified. The linesman ignores the hullabaloo (cue instant 'lino you're a cunt' chant) and someone leaps on to the side of the pitch to press the point. Eventually order is restored, but the bitterness lingers and the guy who was on the side of the pitch (he didn't actually encroach upon the playing surface) is escorted out of the Lamex by a smirking police officer, which doesn't seem wholly fair. That said, last season when Oscar needed a doctor before the Derby game (he couldn't move his neck following a gymnastics incident), the stewards were supremely helpful and efficient.

Anyway, Drackers is on fine form during the half-time entertainment, where hardy souls attempt to kick a football into giant buckets. Harder than it seems, trust me ... and Oscar asks a question I've been waiting for him to ask for two years: 'Do you think Wrexham's team coach will be an Ellisons?' Truly, the boy is my son.

Wrexham are supposed to bring Hollywood glamour, but they are small-town Wrexham and they will always be small-town Wrexham, despite the recently granted city status. Oscar assumed the Netflix cameras will be here, that Wrexham will be promoted and that they're building a 60,000-seater stadium. I dispute all three things. Wrexham's 855 make more noise than others with greater numbers and while their team look composed in possession, they'll create two chances all evening: Jack Marriott skims the bar, and Pidge, for all that he's having a slight form dip, makes another brilliant headed clearance. Murphy Cooper, the fan-voted player of the month (Oscar voted for him; I went for Robbo Roberts), has little to do.

It's a terrific performance. We're both falling deeper in love with Dan Phillips: 'He must be horrible to play against,' notes Oscar. Nathan Thompson is making it difficult for Freestone, Goode and Sweens to displace him. Brother Louis has another blinder and he scores the winner as early as the tenth minute with a speculative long-ranger, to which jittery goalkeeper Arthur Okonkwo reacts too late. Reidy isn't the player he was on Saturday and Jake Young finally gets a start. I can't make Young out yet and he's replaced by Simpson who has his finest half-hour in a Boro shirt. Love? Not yet, but I'm shaving my legs and getting hopeful.

Dan Kemp arrives off the bench. He's still so short of confidence we can almost smell it. Of late, he's taken up diving. I have no moral qualms here and neither does Oscar, but Kemp tumbles too often when he's in a promising position, and even the most dullard League One referee hasn't fallen for it. Eli King – not one of life's goalscorers – misses a straightforward late chance, but Boro aren't hanging on like they were on Saturday. It's a 1-0 again, but a different kind of 1-0. On the whistle, Revs comes over and gives what's becoming his trademark gesture: three rapid-fire elbow pumps. The East Terrace grunts ecstatically at each one and Revs pounds his heart, repaying the love. We couldn't be happier.

As Wrexham head north on their apostrophe-unfriendly Pats coach – a magnificent beast and local, so hats off to Hollywood and they used Eavesway in the 80s – we pick our way through the estate up the road from the Lamex to find our car. At one point a woman in a van is being hooted because she's stationary. She gets out to chastise the hooter: 'There's no point pipping me, I can't get through,' although you could get Arnold Schwarzenegger's Hummer through the gaping gap.

The street is deserted, but we're laughing, and a familiar voice behind us laughs with us at the absurdity of it all. Yikes! It's Drackers! In the unlikely event of him recognising us from Phil Wallace's meet'n'greet, he doesn't let on and he trundles past us, smiling and shaking his head. For the record, Freestone can't get in the starting line-up, Kemp hasn't scored and Appéré has vanished.

Then Drackers turns into what we assume is his house. It's bathed in light. Grinning from ear to ear, Drackers issues a cheery 'olé olé' to his family as he walks through the door, into the – in every way – warmth. It's a beautiful sight: they must have been a happy household that night.

That's what football does to people, I explain to Oscar. That's why people who sneer at it are wrong. They can't or won't understand what it can do; how it can bring colour to black-and-white worlds, how it can uplift and enhance us, how it's important.

'Please shut up, Dad. I know all that.'

We're giddy on the way home. Boro are now ninth in the table. Oscar yawns. 'You know we couldn't have picked a better team to support, Dad.' We really couldn't.

5 October 2024
Peterborough United 2 Stevenage 1

My prediction: 0-2
His prediction: 0-1

Who's your favourite wife of Henry VIII? I'm quite the fan of number one, Katharine of Aragon. She was a most competent regent while he was off fighting in France, she was fluent in English and she was extremely fertile, although of her many children, only the future Queen Mary survived longer than a few weeks. Oh, and she got a raw deal off Henry.

Oscar and I are stood at her grave inside Peterborough Cathedral (*Encyclopaedia Britannica* calls her Catherine, but I'm going with the grave). Of course it's not her original grave; that was ransacked during the Civil War. This one was paid for by a *Daily Mail*-instigated campaign to encourage the nation's Catherines/Katharines to contribute a penny each. Even so, her remains are apparently directly under our feet.

Peterborough Cathedral is wonderful, beyond beautiful. Nobody's spirits could fail to be lifted. Except mine and Oscar's. We are in mourning.

'How did it happen, Dad? How?'

I really don't know.

It started so well. To shake things up a little, we took the train.

I know train travel should cost a mortgage, but if we change in Stevenage and take the stopping train it's £12.65 for me and £2 for Oscar. We're buoyed by Tuesday's triumph, it's sunny, the trains are on time and there are seats to spare. It may be a Sky-ordained morning kick-off (hence the 'we hate fucking Sky' chants later) as part of their Pretending to Care About the EFL campaign, but our morale is stratospheric.

We take a lunchtime stroll through Peterborough. There's the distant noise of Stevenage fans putting on a show a few blocks away. We're familiar with Peterborough's ground, with its uncomfortable seats built for dwarfs (not that we'll be sitting), with its blocked sightlines and silent home support, but their pie – a Pukka – goes to the top of Oscar's pie chart. The programme is bulky and if you walk past the club shop at the right moment – as we do – you can pick up a team sheet too. Again, it's all going well and I've managed to accidentally smuggle an apple through the frisk. Revs, for once, hasn't changed his starting XI. This is going to be a great day. We can feel it in our bones.

As we know, there's no better mascot than Boro Bear, so in a frankly feeble attempt to compete, Peterborough have four. Although the numbers don't tally, I have a 'Village People Have Let Themselves Go' gag to hand. Oscar hasn't heard of Village People. There's a rabbit called Peter Burrow with a giant carrot ('you can stuff your fucking carrot up your arse', chant the Boro fans when he comes to say a provocative hello), which he twirls as he runs alongside the pitch. There are two more dressed as builders and finally the splendid, top-hatted and suited Mr Posh, who first led the team out just after the Second World War. Even Oscar is impressed, although he can't fathom why one end of the ground is closed and spaces abound elsewhere. Nor can I.

After 45 minutes, Boro are somehow losing. A disastrous opening saw sloppy defending and lugubrious goalkeeping allow Donay O'Brien-Brady to put Peterborough ahead with a daisy-cutter, before

Nathan Thompson hobbled off. Murphy Cooper looks traumatised by his error and he's uncharacteristically unsafe. More uncharacteristically still, Dan Phillips can't hit a pass to a team-mate or time a tackle. Yet Boro still miss a hatful of clear-cut chances: Jake Young, Reidy and Robbo Roberts should all have scored, but look back to Burton, Exeter and Wigan, where chances didn't even exist. It's a different team and Louis Thompson is again a steamroller, a classy steamroller.

The Boro fans are wonderfully loud and I'm hoarse after 45 minutes of tuneless bellowing. 'I'm not worried,' says Oscar at half-time, as a skip is placed on the pitch. People will attempt to chip balls into it from 40 yards without them bouncing out. Nobody succeeds. Boro are so lambent that, like Oscar, I'm not worried either, and nor is anyone else in the away section. We've got this.

It's more of the same in the second half when the true Dan Phillips emerges. Substitute Tyreece Simpson is stripped and ready after 49 minutes. He takes his hi-vis vest off. Then he puts it back on again. Repeat for ten baffling minutes. Young dithers when put through alone, before he's finally replaced by Simpson. Just after the hour, nature finally takes its course when Harvey White's cute ball finds Louis Thompson, who wallops home with the glee of a Lottery winner. Someone in the Boro section lets off a flare. Big time.

On and on Boro press, but the second still doesn't come. On the touchline, Peterborough boss Darren Ferguson is so incandescent with his team that when they come over for a drinks break, he refuses to speak to them, like a cuckolded husband. But Peterborough look dangerous when they break clear and I begin to feel uneasy. In the 87th minute, I ask Oscar if he'd stop the game and take a point.

'Absolutely not.'

I would.

Then it happens. Of course it happens. In the fourth of four added minutes, Dan Butler gives away a needless corner, although he seems to have expected a call. Jack Sparkes floats it over. Lewis Freestone doesn't clear it properly and – I can see the angle and gap perfectly – Kwame Poku impressively sweeps in the winner. For the first time all afternoon, I use my seat. All the colour has drained from Oscar's face and a shocked, stunned silence has replaced the incessant away din. Fuck. Fuck. And furthermore, fuck.

Then, as we try to come to terms with what's just happened, there's a figure in blue hurtling towards us. Why, it's Kwame Poku. He scored at his fans' end, but rather than celebrating with them or his team-mates, he's sprinted the length of the pitch to make shushing gestures towards the 775 of us.

Nobody knows how to react. It's like being distracted by a clown during a funeral. Then of course we shower Poku and the similarly engaged James Dornelly with abuse and, as he joins in, the colour returns to Oscar's cheeks. Even so, there's only one winner here and it's not us, but Poku does have to run down the Lamex wing in February.

Why he did it, I cannot say. Later, there's some sort of apology from him on the Peterborough website, but it's so half-hearted and the club are so embarrassed by it, that they will only let Peterborough account holders see it, as opposed to, say, the ones he's theoretically saying sorry to. We shall remember him.

OCTOBER – KWAME POKU, WE'LL NEVER FORGET YOU

Boro kick off. The final whistle blows. The players come over and we clap until our hands are even more sore. Outside it's a little tense. On what has become the Boro fans' side of the bridge leading into town, there's a guy carrying a traffic penalty notice and a Boro fan in the middle of the road calls a driver a twat for trying to drive down said road.

On the opposite side of the road there's a gang of Peterborough fans aged around 15. One of them is topless and swinging his shirt around. As Boro had in the ground, they have a drummer. Twat Guy has charged ahead and suddenly there's a commotion that Oscar is rather too keen to investigate, although he has taken my advice and zipped up his coat over his Boro shirt. The Lilliputian Peterborough fans have surrounded Twat Guy Gulliver and are chanting 'There's only one fucking Boro' at him with a fair amount of venom. He naturally chooses to take them all on and is immediately arrested. Someone is having a worse day than us. Sorry, Twat Guy.

We head for the cathedral in search of spiritual succour. Oscar's so upset (about the game, not the arrest) that he refuses to go in until I guarantee we'll be there for no longer than five minutes.

He's never had an undeserved last-seconds crusher before. 'How long am I going to feel like this for?' he sighs. Well, you know the Exeter game where Boro were awful from first to last? The one where we knew Boro weren't getting anything from the first minutes, so there was no tension?

'Yes.'

It's not like that. In the decades to come, lower league football has more unpleasant surprises in store for you, but at least you'll be able to say, 'This wasn't as bad as Peterborough 2024.'

After we've stood over Katharine, we have a Subway sandwich (I know, I know, but, look, we've nothing to celebrate) and a free golf putt at an exhibition on the main square, where we both win a tiny packet of Haribos. Just before Peterborough station we see the Boro team coach (not on the Greys tracker today, although Cambridge United's journey to and from Exeter is) coming towards us around a roundabout, having set off in the wrong direction, but about to glide south. Oscar unzips his coat to reveal his Boro shirt and we wave and clap in their direction, but the windows are too tinted to see if there's a response. 'I'm sure someone saw us and waved back,' says Oscar. I really hope they did …

On Sunday, Broxbourne Borough Under-15s will also lose 2-1. The boys fought hard, but after Oscar's save hit a striker's knee and looped in – for the second game in a row – it obviously wasn't going to be their day either. It has not been a great weekend.

8 October 2024
Peterborough United 2 Stevenage 0 –
Bristol Street Motors, EFL Trophy

My prediction: 1-3
His prediction: 2-3

Who's your favourite wife of Henry VIII? I'm quite the fan of number one, Katharine of Aragon … That's not going to work is it?

Three days later, we're back at Jake Jarman's home town, the one place in Henry Tudor's kingdom we don't want to be. It's the same feeling for all the away support. Boro lose tonight, it's more misery. Boro win, it won't compensate for Saturday.

Peterborough are holders of the Second-Hand Car Cup, so while they close two ends tonight, they do rustle up a couple of thousand diehards, or 'suckers' as some might call them. Boro's own rustling totals 103 – mostly 12/13-year-old boys for some reason – and there's a police presence. Still, there are compensations. It's an early kick-off. We can park outside the ground. It's £1 for Oscar to get in. And although they're not doing a programme (poor planning bastards; they could have doubled up on Saturday, but what do I know? Nothing, that's what) we pick up a team sheet again.

Ever the adventurous gourmet, Oscar goes for a Rollover hot dog. Because I fear change, I stick with the Pukka. We're both happy.

Ding dong, Revs rings the changes. Eli King and Reidy are on international duty, but oddly Dan Phillips isn't, so he's on the bench rather than a beach in Cuba, the island where Trinidad & Tobago play on Thursday and where I was once robbed. Luther turned down Antigua & Barbuda, so he has to be excluded. Of Saturday's heroes/losers, Pidge starts so he can work on that awkward partnership with Lewis Freestone. Former Peterborough defender Dan Butler and Jake Young – just to get a bloody goal at last – begin too.

Elsewhere, Taye's in goal and Kane Smith is fit again, Ken Aboh gets his first start and there are two 16-year-olds on the bench. Kwame Poku is amongst the Peterborough subs and an emboldened Peter Burrow wanders amongst us with his carrot. I fist-pump him. Oscar fist-pumps him. This makes us both more happy than you might imagine. Let's not hold grudges. The seats – unused in Saturday's adrenaline factory – are fiendishly uncomfortable, but I knew that already.

Boro are soon one down. Kane Smith gives away a needless free kick on the edge of the area. Jack Sparkes whips it across. Smith accidentally heads on and Malik Mothersille heads in. Oh dear. The scorer celebrates like he's Kylian Mbappé. 'Really,' sneers Oscar. He'll be saying 'really' like that when he's 70.

Young and Nick Freeman spurn chances, while Simpson manages to miss a sitter and then gets in the way when Aboh looks like following up. Simpson puts his head in his hands. He's obviously going through trauma, but our feelings of potential love are waning. Peterborough score again when, with Pidge and Freestone both running back and out of position, Sparkes beats Smith again and shoots across Taye and in. Same old story.

After half-time the deluge begins and the, ahem, 'ball retrievers' look like they've entered a monsoon. It's the heaviest rain I've seen since that morning I bumped into Nick Cave on a São Paulo street. Soon, the players are splashing and squelching like schoolkids who might get themselves injured. Nicholas Bilokapic's penalty area is a puddle, and 67 minutes in referee Stephen Parkinson takes the players off for what the PA promises is a five-minute break.

Forty minutes later, men have jumped on forks to reduce the surface water. In the centre circle, there's a man without a fork but with a blue jacket. He does a lot of pointing, as if the forkmen don't know what grass is. We even manage a chant: 'Groundsman give us a wave.' He does too. Bless. In the centre circle, the referee rather theatrically bounces a ball on all areas of the pitch and we're ready to go again. It's a farce, of course, but Ryan

Doherty (16 years, 43 days) becomes Boro's youngest outfield player (the Watford friendly doesn't count, but this does) and Lenny Brown (16 years, 97 days) becomes the second-youngest.

After the restart, there are 23 minutes to go and another eight will be added. For the players it's about avoiding injury and Poku not coming on. For us it's simply surreal, not least since Boro will almost certainly still be in the trophy nobody cares about, certainly if Gillingham are dispatched next month, possibly if it's a draw. Oh good. I do hope this is all tax deductible for Bristol Street Motors.

We chat with a Peterborough fan outside. 'You were unlucky Saturday,' he admits. 'Tonight was nothing. Not everyone did, but I liked Dan Butler when he was here. Not as much as Nathan Thompson though.'

Afterwards, Revs is on the website, bemoaning missed chances and sloppy goal concessions, but not his lack of tactical astuteness. There are A1 closures on the way home, but they're all northbound. To complete our Peterborough circle, we pass Kimbolton, where Katharine of Aragon died, and we're home soon enough. 'I've never felt like this before about a Boro game,' argues Oscar. 'But we've wasted our time tonight.'

19 October 2024
Mansfield Town 0 Stevenage 1

My prediction: 1-2
His prediction: 1-2

It's 12 days before we're scheduled to be off to Mansfield and I'm perched on the end of Oscar's bed. He's just been invited to his best friend's birthday party. It involves go-karting and it's on Mansfield Saturday. I knew this moment would come, but I'm unusually inarticulate.

My plan is to assess the lie of the land like a far-sighted parent, back down and let him go. I can't make him suffer for a book. The party, Oscar?

'What about it?'

How do you feel? (n.b. Never, ever ask a teenage boy how he feels, unless it's about Tyreece Simpson or Formula 1.)

'It's done. I told him I'm not going to his party. It's not that deep. Get out of my room.'

He's angry. I get out of his room. The shame is on my side. We'll come back to this, but not until after the game.

It's been a decent international break. Jamie Reid started for Northern Ireland against Belarus in Hungary (events, dear boy, events), missed four chances and was taken off after 76 minutes as the teams drew 0-0. Unsurprisingly, he didn't start the epic 5-0 crushing of Bulgaria, but he did manage a 16-minute cameo. He didn't score then either. He's a confidence player. This doesn't bode well.

Eli King played 90 minutes for Wales Under-21s as they lost to the Czech Republic and thus failed to qualify for the Under-21s Euros. He was dropped for the subsequent friendly against Slovakia (hey, imagine how good the Czech Republic and Slovakia would be if they joined forces) but he was given his own 16-minute cameo. They were both in Friday training, unscathed.

In the meantime, some figures have appeared. Boro have the second-lowest average attendance in League One, ahead only of Burton (TVC's move there still baffles us), but it's distorted since Boro have entertained

Charlton, Barnsley and Wrexham. And Boro are 14th in League One's percentage of ground filled: 67. That won't get better either. It's not a carp – some teams have more fans than others – but it is another reminder of what Boro are up against.

We're not up against much today. It's sunny. The traffic is light and even the worker-free roadworks passive-aggressive 'you may not see us, we're working at night' sign doesn't rile me. We've actually been through them at night, although they'd forgotten to put up the 'you may not see us, we're working during the day' signs. Okay, it did rile me.

The road from the M1 takes us through the nicer parts of Mansfield and even Oscar approves. It's the town of Rebecca Adlington and Ed Davey, although he was raised in Eakring out Newark way. But although it's had a market since 1227, it was also the head of the in-no-way-government-funded/organised UDM during the miners' strike and it's still known as Scabsfield in former mining regions outside Nottinghamshire. Like a Frenchman in the 50s wondering if every stranger he passed collaborated with Vichy, I look at everyone over 60 and wonder if they worked through the strike.

The answer is probably 'yes' and the collective shame still lingers, which of course makes things morally blurred when everyone we meet, from the guy at the ground's pie counter to the man afterwards who stops us to declare 'you were the better team today', is kind and generous of spirit. Such is life. And if Scargill had called a ballot, etc. As if to remind us how beautiful life can be, even in Mansfield, there's a swan in the lake we walk past opposite the ground.

There's a surprise on the Boro bench: Aaron Pressley. Crikey, that was quick. I know people who've taken longer to recover from a night out. Tyreece Simpson doesn't even make that bench, where we find Dan Butler (weakened after a bout of glandular fever) and Dan Kemp. Intriguingly, Revs is so mistrustful of the Pidge/Freestone partnership at centre-back that he deploys Luther alongside Pidge and Freestone at left-back.

Before the game we talk to the lovely Mrs Chatty. She's oldish in years but young at heart, and when Luther, her favourite, became a father she left a heap of goodies for him at the club ('everyone else leaves clothes, I left nappies and stuff: things he'll need every day'). Luther was delighted and as his Fiat-driving mother told Mrs Chatty, 'He was born with a smile on his face that one.' She told Oscar off for swearing a couple of years ago at Port Vale. 'Why didn't you back me up, Dad?' Because I was on her side, not yours Oscar. 'I love Mrs Chatty,' says a mildly repentant Oscar. So do I, and she – as well as Drackers going 'olé olé' to his family, Revs fist-pumping and silly songs about the Thompson brothers – is why we love this club. Among other things. So many other things.

We're especially fond of Luther too. He plays the trumpet and piano. Oscar follows his TikTok, which concerns his property portfolio and Wildin Ventures, the company he runs it through, alongside his older brother Courtney, a former footballer and model, to whom Luther gave blood when Courtney was diagnosed with leukaemia. Blood brothers, you see. Today, after an early wobble, Luther will be a central-defensive hero, especially when he throws himself into the path of Lee Gregory's goalbound drive late on.

The pie doesn't quite work. The friendly pie man admitted he preferred the sausage rolls. We should have listened. I have steak, Oscar has peppered steak. 'They're meaty though,' pie man had promised. So they are, but they're lukewarm and claggy too. Oh well.

Mansfield had won their five previous league games and theoretically could have gone top if they'd hammered Boro. There's no programme (bastards) and the disused fourth side of the ground looks very much like it did when we last visited in 2022, but the atmosphere is exuberant. Mansfield are pretty, but Murphy Cooper isn't tested and Boro began to look distinctly threatening. Not as in the first Peterborough trip threatening, but they break quickly and former Boro loanee Christy Pym makes actual saves. He'll be named man of the match later on.

Then George Williams hacks down Reidy. The free kick is a metre or so outside the corner of the penalty area. Jake Young – already having showcased his customary mix of wonderful approach play and less than wonderful finishing – steps up and curls it past Pym for his first Boro goal.

It's a wonder goal by any yardstick, one that even the unlikely lovechild of Lionel Messi and Cristiano Ronaldo would struggle to emulate. It's at the opposite end to where the 216 of us are sat and there's a moment of shocked silence when it sails in. Then, pandemonium at our end, silence everywhere else. Oscar jumps up and down, not wholly sure what to do. 'WHAT A GOAL,' he bellows. What a goal it was.

The second half is something of a siege but, apart from Luther's block, Boro have the two best chances and it never feels inevitable Mansfield will score. There's a giant clock to our left. 'Why does it go so slowly?' asks

Oscar, adding his customary refrain of 'I've never been so tense.' Pressley comes on to hold the ball up, Dan Butler emerges in the last of the five added minutes and I don't think I've ever seen anyone under 90 move so slowly as he shuffles from dugout to pitch. Incensed, the Mansfield fans seem to think he's wasting time rather than recovering from glandular fever. I'm sure I saw him wink, at least I hope I did. I don't think he managed a touch, but he did his bit.

It's been a glorious performance, a season's first away win (a first home defeat for Mansfield while we're at it) and a seventh clean sheet, even if Revs over-eggs it slightly afterwards by saying Boro were wholly dominant in the first half. Boro had a better gameplan than Mansfield, better spirit and they almost always looked in control.

The plyers come to us on the final whistle, but nobody's grinning more than Revs. He does his three right-arm horizontal fist-pumps, and there's even a chant: 'Revell again, Revell again, olé olé.' 'This is fucking great, Dad,' hollers Oscar between chants. Stop swearing Oscar. But he's right and we're falling in love with Revs all over again.

On the way home, we talk about the game, berate FotMob (why isn't it FootMob?) and their typically random player ratings. I ease the conversation back to the party he missed. 'Yeah, I turned down the Nando's after the go-karting too …' he shrugs, sadly, but he's nowhere near as angry as he was a few days ago. I know Boro won and it's been a day to remember, but for all we knew it could have been Exeter again rather than Revell again. There are no guarantees. 'I know that, Dad. But it wouldn't have made any difference. I wanted to go to the party, but I had to be here. I told the truth about the book to my friend. I'm fine with it. He's fine with it. It's not that deep.' I guess he's right: it's not that deep.

That said, I like his friend's mother, so I engineer a school gates meeting with her the following week. I'm aiming to apologise, to get Oscar off the hook and to confirm that what she knows about the book is true and that his non-appearance is all my fault. She doesn't know anything about the book. Oh Oscar.

On Sunday, Storm Ashley breaks in Hertfordshire so the wind blows and the rain drives as a depleted Broxbourne Borough Under-15s (two boys have fractured kneecaps) lose 4-6. Oscar argues that two of the goals were deflected and the rest weren't his fault. They were a little unlucky, all things considered, but they're bottom of the league now. Stevenage will not be finishing bottom of League One.

22 October 2024
Stevenage 0 Cambridge United 2

My prediction: 2-0
His prediction: 3-0.

It's the second half. The ball comes to Dan Phillips, the one new arrival we're now unreservedly in love with. He's on his own, close to the centre circle near us. He has two options, both of whom are waiting for him to play a simple rolled pass towards the touchline. Instead, Dan smashes it into the advertising hoardings, between the two options. That's tonight in one wretched pass.

It was so peachy before a ball was kicked. We were in good time, in buoyant spirits after Saturday and Boro were entertaining bottom-of-the-table Cambridge United in a local derby. Drackers sported a hitherto unseen, Piet Mondrian-style red-and-white jacket (think Joseph's coat of many colours, but with just two colours). The night was mild and, as if to taunt the away fans in the wake of last year's hilarious power-cut-enforced abandonment moments before kick-off, the floodlights don't come on until less than an hour before the match begins. How we chuckled.

It started to go wrong when we saw the team sheet. Revs had lost Luther with an unspecified (it's always unspecified) injury. That was force majeure. He dropped Eli King and replaced him with Dan Kemp rather than Harvey White, so there was nobody to rule midfield with arbitrary sway. I'm not sure voluntarily changing the starting XI after a season's-best performance is the way ahead. I never did it when I was Brentford manager.

Cambridge don't look like bottom dwellers, but much more disappointingly there's an announcement ordering the homophobic chanting to stop coming from the East Terrace, where we are. We hadn't heard anything, but soon the players are briefly taken off and Boro's comically inept stewards – don't they train stewards these days? – stand at the bottom of the terrace, too scared to go up. 'He's behind you!' someone shouts. The quivering stewards don't laugh. We do. Eventually two men are gently ushered outside. Good ... if they were guilty.

Everything's disrupted and Cambridge score. It's an awful goal with awful implications. Dan Kemp's abominable header falls to Korey Smith, who pokes a shot towards goal. Freestone sticks a leg out. The ball hits it, loops over Cooper and in. Pidge is behind Freestone and he's livid, impersonating Freestone's wafting limb. He wouldn't have done that to Sweens. Call me a blushing old romantic, but I'd like my centre-back pairings to be besties. A left-footer playing on the right side of central defence in this formation, Pidge has never looked comfortable alongside Freestone. One of Cambridge's travelling 926 lets off a flare and we both see the immediate future, especially Oscar's tomorrow morning when he meets his Cambridge-supporting schoolfriend Frankie.

Boro are dreadful to a man – even Murphy Cooper gets bawled out by Dan Butler for poor distribution – and a Pidge booking means he's suspended for, oh no, Rotherham.

Revs attempts to correct his mistake by bringing on both White and King for the second half, which instead compounds it. Until King drops back to become a third centre-half, he and White get in each other's way. I'm not seeing much evidence of Neil Banfield's in-game tactical nous now. Unlike his predecessor Paul Raynor, he's never a touchline presence either. I'm not sure what he is, what he does or whether he tells Revs what he wants to hear, as opposed to what Revs needs to hear.

Boro have almost all the possession, but they're soporific, uncommunicative and empty of ideas, so they go back, back and back, usually to Pidge, rather than distribution maestro King, and while Pidge is many things, he's not a ball-playing centre-half. For the first time this season, Boro look like they don't care; at one grisly point, Harvey White chickens out of a challenge. 'You've got to get that Harvey,' bellows the non-teetotal guy behind us whom we shall christen Mr Loud – he's right of course – and when Cambridge break out in added time for the first time in the second half, Sullay Kaikai scores their second after Freestone puts in a feeble challenge and King doesn't seem to know how to put one in at all. Cambridge goalkeeper Vicente Reyes ('any good?' you ask; how could I possibly know?) runs the length of the field to celebrate a first away victory since March and they can leave on their Greys coach (the actual one Boro use? Sometimes, and it was on the Greys tracker before the game) fulfilled. It's lovely to see. Or it would be in other circumstances.

'I hate this team,' snarls Oscar. 'I hate these players.'

But you loved them on Saturday.

'Yes, but that was before tonight.'

Oscar is so furious that we agree we don't want to hear Revs tonight. Instead, we listen to him on the following morning's school run. Revs wasn't asked to address his team selection, but he was incandescent. Unlike Steve Evans, he didn't throw individuals under the bus, just – rightly – the team: 'Unacceptable ... fell way short everywhere ... just not good enough.'

After the game, *The Comet*'s Neil Metcalfe goes on strike, refusing to submit his player ratings until the morning. 'Quite frankly,' he tweets, 'if the players can't be bothered, I don't see why I should stay up till 2am grafting.'

Neil is as good as his word. Next morning, Dan Kemp is awarded a 2/10, Kane Smith a 3 and there are four 4s. 'I expect better in South Yorkshire,' he thunders. 'I *DEMAND* better.' Hero ... again.

26 October 2024
Rotherham United 2 Stevenage 0

My prediction: 0-2
His prediction: 0-1

OCTOBER – KWAME POKU, WE'LL NEVER FORGET YOU

We're 30 seconds out of the car. It's sunny and Rotherham's mighty minster is standing guard over the town like a Mr Byrite version of Christ the Redeemer. There's a woman at a bus stop in a tracksuit, with two similarly attired males. She's talking loudly to a second woman, who's sat on a wall across the main road. We walk past the first woman. She's covered in facial scabs and she's jonesing. Oscar looks at me and before he can compute what he's seeing, there's a commotion. Those who have been waiting for the man need wait no longer. Here he is, shambling across some waste ground. Rather more quickly than you might imagine, all things considered, the quartet run to him. I regret blowing my Quinn the Eskimo line on Reidy.

Before Oscar and I have walked another 20 metres, two of them are squatting on the wet waste ground shooting up. We walk another 50 metres and we're in front of the police station, the one where the miners who were charged with (and fully acquitted of) rioting at Orgreave during the strike were taken. If any police folk were looking out of the window between eating doughnuts, they'd have seen everything. 'What exactly have I just seen, Dad?' Well, Oscar ...

Rotherham United, that's the team I should support. I once asked Justin Hawkins of The Darkness how many mistakes he'd made. 'So many, so, so many,' he sighed. An hour later he was still cataloguing them. I am Justin Hawkins. My life hasn't been one long mistake, it's been a succession of them, be it career, finance, women (for some reason I still wonder where two of them, the one whose surname I never knew and the one whose surname I can never forget, are now; hope they've had the good lives they deserve) and the catch-all of general decision-making. And I should have been a Rotherham United fan.

I spent the first 18 years of my life in Rotherham, mostly (it seemed at the time) standing on a bridge over the M1 dreaming of escape. When I did escape, I returned only to visit my late father, but I haven't been to the town centre where I perfected the art of underage drinking for, let's say (because I can't remember), 20 years. Ever hypocritical, I now want Oscar to embrace his Yorkshire roots. 'Why do you keep saying I'm northern, Dad? I'm not.' Today is not entwining us as I'd hoped.

I want to tell him about Harpers (I can't remember where they stood, apostrophe-wise), the bookshop I'd loiter in; about The Sound of Music and Circles, the record shops I'd loiter in (there was a lot of loitering); and about the ODEON (Oscar Deutsch Entertains Our Nation, but I digress), where I was a member of The Saturday Club. There, for 5p, we'd watch a morning's worth of films, mostly made under the aegis of the Children's Film Foundation (it's still going as the Children's Media Foundation, something that fills me with joy) before my father picked me up in his milk float.

Oscar doesn't get this at all, any of it. Maybe this whole enterprise is for me, not him. Betrayed by those who sacrificed the town on the alters of the Parkgate and Meadowhall shopping centres, Rotherham is dead. Harpers has been demolished, The Sound of Music is now Johnny D Schoolwear, and the Odeon – where top pop group Sailor once played – is derelict. The replacers have been replaced and even Costa has closed down. In fact, bar a couple of pubs and, surreally, my childhood dentist, it's all changed and it's all changed for the worse. Apart from a Christian woman with a microphone underneath

OCTOBER – KWAME POKU, WE'LL NEVER FORGET YOU

the minster, where a big bride with big tattoos and a big vape is getting wed, it's silent.

I take Oscar into the covered market, where I'd buy *Superman* comics when I was tiny. It's almost deserted, a Potemkin Village of stalls with no customers. A spavined Rotherham fan straight out of a *Scooby Doo* cartoon comes up to us: 'Go back to Stevenage; there's nothing here.'

'It could do with an air-freshener,' says Oscar. Since he's never seen one before, he's awestruck by a weighing machine; Bronze Age man confronted by iron for the first time.

Me? I'm heartbroken by all this, as I had been when the Far-Right Riots came to town in the summer, chiefly to the Holiday Inn at Manvers, a rare sign of local regeneration on the site where the Manvers Main pit once towered over a tightly knit community. A couple of years ago, without going into the centre, I'd taken Oscar, his sister and my cousin John around my Rotherham. All my old houses – the bungalow in the mining village, the tiny terraced house near the centre, the nice semi where we lived next to big blond Rotherham United centre-half Trevor Swift (he did like a loud party; I'm still traumatised), the nicer detached residence before financial collapse, the shop my mother shouldn't have tried to make work, the high-rise flat overlooking the town my dad lived in, always with his budgerigar and with me for a few months after my mother kicked me out. All my schools: my still-thriving primary school, my once thriving secondary school, my intermittently thriving sixth form college. John and I loved that day. Oscar and Jessica were bemused.

This morning, though, we stop for a drink at the apostrophe-unfriendly Noshys Coffee Lounge on the central All Saints Square. It's warm enough to drink outside. There's greenery, it's quite pretty, but it's eerie. Noshys is empty inside and out and the server is poleaxed by Oscar doing the most southern thing imaginable and asking for the chai tea latte that's on the laminated menu, surely by mistake. He settles for ordinary tea and, for a gratifying second, turns northern: 'Best tea I've ever had.' We sit in the sun watching the smattering of passers-by until a vaping 50-something man in a Rotherham United sweatshirt spots Oscar's Boro shirt.

'Mind if I sit here?' He doesn't wait for an answer. We are now three. 'Do you want any advice?' Well, yes I do, where do you want to start? Sadly, he's only talking about getting to the ground. He's great. Travels everywhere with Rotherham, went to see a Guiseley vs Huddersfield pre-season friendly because that's the sort of man he is. He's no fan of Rotherham manager Steve Evans. 'His style of football is abhorrent to me,' he sneers loquaciously. He reminisces about Revs's late, late 35-yard winner for Rotherham at Wembley in the 2014 League One Play-Off Final when Evans was manager, but he worries about his club right now, although he says nice things about the Lamex. When he visits in April, he'll get the bus from the station. 'Oh, it's not far to walk,' trills Oscar. He pats his ample stomach and bids us a cheery farewell. 'Do I look like a walker?'

Rotherham United's old ground, Millmoor, is still there, floodlights and all, opposite Needle Park. They play youth football there now, but a sporting use covenant I don't understand means the land can't be expanded by scrap metal giants CF Booth into their core business. Ken Booth, the late family patriarch, was a United chairman, although far from beloved. Attempts to attract speedway and rugby haven't worked since United fled in 2008 and Millmoor remains a monument to clichéd Yorkshire stubbornness.

We amble to the ground, me in reverie, him impatient for a pie. On the way in, we almost bump into Sweens (Pidge turns up too; that's a good sign, spirit-wise). Sweens speaks first. 'Alright lads,' he says. I don't know whether I'm more delighted by Sweens's friendliness or being called 'lad' by him. When you back, Sweens? I ask. He's had two operations since he last kicked a ball, the second one keyhole. 'Soon,' he says, believably.

Our Noshys friend loves the New York Stadium (so called because the land it's stood on is also called New York, although that's not what I remember) and he's right. It's a bowl with ample legroom, even for those with longer legs than my stubby pair. There's the best programme in League One so far, but for Oscar it goes horribly wrong on the pie front. He wants to try a Big Yorkie, which is some kind of Yorkshire pudding with pulled chicken and/or unspecified sausage. It's out of stock. My pie is delicious but his breaks at the bottom, scalds his hands and leaves brown marks on his trousers. 'It's bottom of the pie chart and it's not coming off the bottom,' he snaps, petulant and embarrassed. It splatters when he throws it on the floor. It will not be the last thrown pie of the afternoon.

The game, the game. It's our first reunion since Evans dumped us, a reunion we dumpees can't avoid. For all that, though, there's a faux delirious atmosphere in the away section, as if the 437 of us are having the same awkward meeting with the ex-girlfriend/boyfriend who found someone better-looking and wealthier.

As we know, Pidge is suspended, while Louis Thompson is injured, but Luther has made a miraculous recovery to fill in at centre-half. Kemp has been dropped, but Taye replaces Murphy Cooper, which hardly seems fair.

Evans and Revs embrace, as they must. A brass band plays 'Another One Bites the Dust' before the remembrance commemoration and Oscar giggles when the 'Last Post' trumpeter messes up the minute's silence. The first half is scrappy and almost chanceless. Dead-ball specialist Harvey White (Revs is still playing White and King) messes up six dead-ball opportunities. Boro have no shots or attacks, but they're good value for the 0-0 and the natives are beginning to get restless.

It goes wrong in three disastrous minutes. Firstly, for the second time in a week, Lewis Freestone deflects past his own goalkeeper when Jordan Hugill's shot loops off him in freakish fashion, over Taye and into the bottom corner. Then Mallik Wilks squeezes a drive past rusty Taye at his near post.

The atmosphere turns toxic in the away end. Some moron at the back throws a pie and it hits a Stevenage-supporting woman at the front. It's all too much for one fan. Like a livid mountain goat, he bounds upwards over row after row of seats and starts pointing his finger and shouting at those he believes to be the culprits: 'You're a fucking embarrassment. If you want to support our club like that, fuck off.' He's accusing a couple of lads who look like and snigger like naughty schoolboys while pleading their innocence. The stewards come in and, presumably with the aid of CCTV, find and eject the culprit. He's not (I think) one of the accused.

There's more. An anti-Revs but pro-drink group start slurrily singing of Boro's uselessness: 'How shit must you be, we lose every week.' The leader of a smaller pro-Revs but equally pro-drink faction replies: 'Stop fucking lying, we've won over half our games,' which isn't true, but hey.

The game finishes. Our former lover, Steve Evans, comes over, pounds his heart and claps us. I feel like crying over what's been lost, and not just on this dispiriting afternoon. Even Oscar, who's turning more against Evans with every week that passes, is moved.

Here's the thing. If we count Jordan Roberts and Elliott List as midfielders, here are the strikers: Aaron Pressley, Jamie Reid, Tyreece Simpson, Dan Kemp, Louis Appéré, Ken Aboh, Jake Young. Here's the number of league goals they've scored this season between them: one.

And there's no midfield to provide service. Ben Thompson's at Bromley, ex-Boro striker (15 games, 0 goals) James Daly has been gently propositioned, but ye gods, he's happy at Harrogate. It's looking bleak again.

The bleakness continues after one Boro fan has stood like Christ the Redeemer (again) at the bottom of the terrace, staring as players and fans exchange half-hearted applause. As we exit, one bunch of worse-for-wear Boro fans take it upon themselves to taunt the home support. Another Boro fan in similarly altered state, tries to drag them away by draping himself around them. It's sad and tawdry, and why has everyone had too much to drink? And yes, I drink my body weight in wine and cry myself to sleep in quiet desperation each night, but that's not the point.

Oscar is spooked and shocked by this trip. A goalless draw would have been fine, but it's been a rotten few days and he's unnerved by Rotherham. In another attempt to nourish his roots with those who share his blood, we visit my cousin John after the match. Here, we do find what I'm looking for.

John lives in the same street he was born. It's the same street where his mother (my aunt) and my father (his uncle) were born, as were mine and John's grandparents and their parents. If I'd spent more time with John, my life would have turned out better. He and his lovely wife Ange, who can roll her eyes and raise her eyebrows like no woman on earth, are kind and generous and they make a fuss of Oscar, even when he explains the intricacies of Revs's tactics to them at some length. He loves them, loves being around them.

We eat pizza, we sip tea, we catch up and, more than anything, we laugh. John and Ange's son calls from Folkestone and he's put on speaker phone. Their daughter Gemma drops by with her impossibly beautiful daughter Amelie, so there are three generations of our family under one roof and, since I'm getting sentimental now, a fourth generation – my father and John's mother – is here in spirit.

When my father died, John inherited my father's treasured bowls set. John has kept them for nearly 20 years without playing. This year he's joined a bowls club and he's using those bowls. I feel like crying again, but in a good way now. It's exactly what my dear old dad would have wanted. There hasn't been a lot of love today, but it's overflowing in this kitchen in a village just outside Rotherham. Oscar gets it now; he even gets the bowls thing. We're a happier, more content pair as we drive home, him with slightly stained trousers, me with slightly damp cheeks.

The following day, Broxbourne Borough Under-15s win their first game of the season. With no substitutes, they overturn a 1-0 deficit. They look the part, Oscar makes a decent save or two and their opponents are denied what even Oscar admits was a clear penalty. Everything went their way, just as it's not going Boro's way. It doesn't deserve to right now.

29 October 2024
Stevenage 1 Bolton Wanderers 4

My prediction: 1-0
His prediction: 2-1

Oscar's sister Jessica wants to talk. 'I love what you're doing with Oskie. Can I come to a game too?'

Of course. That would be brilliant. I'll give you a fixture list. Choose whatever game or games you fancy and come with us.

'Thanks Dad. My rate is £15 an hour.'

She won't be joining us. And, yes, I love her more than life itself. And she'll take a surprisingly evocative picture of her father and brother for the book cover.

Just the two of us then, but we're unsettled now. Our naïve early season optimism dissipated with the Cambridge and Rotherham defeats. Bolton are on a roll, and vicious roadworks on the A602 make us snippy too.

Oscar's mood isn't helped by one of his friends being here. Sam is somewhere in the away end with his mum, although Bolton only bring 590 fans, which, for such a relatively big club, seems oddly apathetic, roll or not. Bolton Sam is a lovely, serious young man, not the teasing type, but since Oscar is a 14-year-old boy, he fears being teased should Boro lose, even more than Boro actually losing. He has little faith in his own prediction.

'Must I predict only Boro wins?'

Not at all. He thinks for a second.

'No, I can't do it, but I'm not confident.'

Nevertheless, we wander around the Lamex like angsty meerkats, necks long and swivelling, desperately trying to catch sight of Sam and his mum, if only to warn them about the chicken 'goujons' and chips. We don't see them. Oscar is simultaneously disappointed and relieved.

Revs shakes things up a little. Pidge and Louis Thompson are back, and Eli King, Harvey White, Lewis Freestone and Jake Young are defenestrated. Tyreece Simpson warms up in his kit, but he's not even on the bench, Boro Bear wears some kind of sexy negligée to celebrate Hallowe'en and I rediscover the uneaten pack of Haribos we won in Peterborough.

Sixteen minutes in, Boro are hit by two goals in three minutes for the second time in four days and it's all over. Both Bolton goals are from set pieces. Sloppy defending from Jordan Roberts and (I think) Reidy following a corner allows Ricardo Santos to head in his first league strike since February 2023. Then a poor Pidge header out from a Bolton free kick falls to the outstanding John McAtee, who volleys into the ground and over Taye.

There's no realistic expectation of a comeback. We weren't the only tetchy, edgy ones, and as the Boro bench sits sullen and silent, the mood on the bitter, miserable East Terrace turns gallows-humour dark. 'A Sunday League manager for a League One team,' shouts somebody into the ether, and when a chant strikes up, it's the old faithful 'we're fucking shit'. Boro are booed off at half-time.

'It's not just one player,' sighs Oscar. 'It's collective. I can take losing, but not losing this pathetically.'

It's better in the second half. Boro began to move the ball forwards as quickly as Bolton and there's even a shot on goal but, when Bolton break, the hungry Hungarian Szabolcs Schön crosses low. Luther completely miskicks and Victor Adeboyejo slots in number three.

Doughty Boro pull one back when – praise the Lord – Dan Kemp expertly tucks in after goalkeeper Luke Southwood spills Reidy's shot. In no way confirming that football fans are inherently fickle, the 'we're gonna win 4-3' chant starts up, and such is Bolton's propensity to panic that Southwood is booked for time-wasting. For a heady moment it looks like the impossible is possible, but of course it's not. It wouldn't be impossible if it were.

Bolton notch number four when Taye lets Dion Charles's gentle poke slide under him. Six minutes are added and there's more booing from the home support, or what's left of it. Being lunatic optimists, Oscar and I don't boo or leave, but he's waxing poetic. 'Put the dog out of its misery,' he demands.

Before the game, we'd sort of hoped to bump into Bolton Sam. After it, Oscar is desperate there should be no contact whatsoever. 'If I see him, I'll walk right past him and not say anything. He knows how I feel. He'd do the same if Bolton had lost and I'd totally respect that.'

We turn our collars to the cold and damp and look at the floor, hoping not to be spotted. In truth, I wouldn't mind, I like Bolton Sam and his mum, but Oscar's tension is infectious and party lines are there to be toed. We don't see them. Phew. Oscar exhales long and loudly and Bolton scuttle back home on their rather fantastic Van Hool coach, which is packed with televisions, as if they'd ram-raided the Currys just off the M1 near Milton Keynes on the way down.

It's been a grisly evening but, as Revs points out, the performance was better than against Cambridge and Rotherham, although that's hardly setting the bar high. Is his job safe? Right now, yes, although he's lost a fair portion of the crowd. Oscar wants to give him another month. I want Revs to prove me wrong. Defeat on Saturday will open and widen the discussion. Where do we go from here? Oscar and I bumble home in contemplative silence. Boro? We just don't know.

Pie Chart

1. Peterborough United
2. Norwich City
3. Burton Albion
4. Mansfield Town
5. Wigan Athletic
6. Stevenage
7. Exeter City
8. Huddersfield Town
9. Rotherham United

November – Our Unhappy Home Life

2 November 2024
Stevenage 1 Guiseley 1 (aet) – FA
Cup, Stevenage win 5-4 on penalties

My prediction: 4-1
His prediction: 3-1

A few weeks ago, we watched the FA Cup first-round draw on BBC2, ruined as ever by the BBC telling us which teams were which numbers beforehand. We both wanted to avoid Barrow away. We were keen for a pulsating local derby with Barnet or Boreham Wood and I wanted a new ground to visit. Failing that, an easy draw at home to a non-league club would suffice. Guiseley at the Lamex – 80-something places and four tiers beneath Boro – more than sufficed.

Poor Guiseley. All that effort, all the joy of the 84th-minute winner at Kidderminster Harriers, which took them to round one for the first time since 2019, all that expectation of a televised draw, all wasted on a trip to an atmosphere-free Lamex. No wonder only 329 of their fans made the journey.

We're not anxious. 'I don't want just a win, because we all know that will happen,' notes Oscar. 'I want to crush them, I want our strikers to score and I want our season to start again today.' I don't contradict him. In fact, I even splash out on a Nando's to boost his spirits. We listen to a Formula 1 sprint in the car, we spot Mrs Chatty and say hello and, although we're 2.45pm arrivals, there's space to spare and a barrier to hang off on the East Terrace. I've asked his question before and I'll surely ask it again: what can possibly go wrong? Since this is Boro, quite a lot.

Pidge and Dan Phillips managed to injure themselves against Bolton, so they're out. Luther does something to himself in the warm-up, so little full-back Kane Smith has to play centre-back without notice, as Revs refuses to chance untried kiddie centre-half substitute Alfie Thornett or even Eli King. Aaron Pressley starts for the first time this season and Murphy Cooper is back after Taye's unfortunate display against Bolton. Revs has few cards to play, but he's playing them all, taking no chances. Good. Let's fill our boots.

Here's something else you can see coming a mile off, although we didn't, despite Oscar wearing contact lenses for the first time: no boots are going to be filled today. He's trialling those lenses and he's so desperate to succeed that the membrane of his irises could be peeling off and he wouldn't speak up. It's another step to him leaving, of course, so I'm vehemently against it. My opposition couldn't be more wrong on every level. And what was I doing at his age? Exactly the same thing and with evil hard lenses.

Sod the romance of the FA Cup, Guiseley aren't great and, since I hadn't known the draw when we met the Rotherham fan who'd been there pre-season, I hadn't asked him about them. Their low status is reflected by their name-free shirts being numbers 1–11 and their J&B coach, which has just a couple of tables. 'Like what we use on school trips,' reckons Oscar. Ominously, they score early on when Will Longbottom heads in. Mercifully, the referee had spotted his almighty shove on makeshift full-back Nick Freeman. We sing the 'football in a library' chant before Guiseley do.

Boro sneak ahead when Jamie Reid scores at last, bundling in Dan Kemp's cross. 'Wemberlee, Wemberlee, we're the famous Stevenage Borough and we're going to Wemberlee,' we sing, if only to make ourselves laugh. I explain to Oscar that Boro's superior fitness will triumph over these butchers, bakers and candlestick-makers and, yes, the traffic does indeed turn one-way. Alas, said traffic is driven by Guiseley. Smith heads against Lewis Freestone and the loose ball drops to Longbottom, only for Cooper to rush out and block. Then Cooper judges his angles again to brilliantly block both Gabriel Johnson's drive and Longbottom's follow-up. Finally, Smith and Cooper mess up: this time Longbottom rolls the loose ball in.

The English language has many words – c.600,000 according to the *Oxford English Dictionary* – but there are not enough to explain just how awful this Boro showing is. That Murphy Cooper is the only player to emerge from the rubble with credit (although Dan Kemp is improving) speaks some of those words, but everything is wrong and Joe Cracknell is yet another goalkeeper whose gifts remain elusive, owing to their lack of use. 'We're really not very good are we?' mumbles Oscar, sadder than a 14-year-old boy deserves to be.

Having been booed off at half-time, Boro are booed off at full time, but with much more gusto. The atmosphere is poisonous, but it's muted by disbelief. Fans stream out rather than watch an added half-hour. The covenant between players and fans has been unbreakable since Paul Tisdale left, but Reidy – who's been shown nothing but love during his struggles since Christmas – breaks it by showing his exasperation with the reaction, as if the performance hasn't been diabolical. What does he expect? I'm disheartened by his attitude, but I was disheartened when Marmite peanut butter was phased out, so I might not be the best judge of disheart. Boro have the best of added time, but Guiseley have the actual best chance when Joe Ackroyd is put through alone and, as Cooper charges out, pokes his shot wide.

It's penalties. After Jordan Roberts has hit one out of the ground via the bar and Harvey White's feeble effort could have been saved by my grandmother (and she's been dead for almost 60 years), by penalty number five Boro are going out. All Guiseley captain Lebrun Mbeka has to do is score. Cooper dives to his left and sticks out a paw to foil Mbeka's not-that-bad-actually kick. We go cautiously wild.

In sudden death, Kemp has already scored when Jameel Ible steps up, Cooper dives to his right and pushes it aside. There's been no love today, none at all, but it now comes in floods. Murphy Cooper has saved the penalty, saved Boro's cup run, possibly saved Revs's job and perhaps saved Boro's season. 'We did not deserve that,' says Oscar.

At the final whistle, Scott Cuthbert charges across the pitch to confront some Guiseley players. Doubtless they laughed at him on the bench, but it's not really the moment, Scotty. Accompanied by a midget security guard – why does he need a security guard, even a small one? –

Revs comes over and applauds apologetically. There are no fist-pumps, so at least he's read that room. Even the steadily growing Revs Out faction doesn't actively dislike him and nobody could possibly think he's not putting his heart and soul into every working day. Afterwards, he's surprisingly chipper: 'Say what you like but we're in the next round.' He's right, and if Boro win in round two and if some magic happens in round three, we'll forget today.

'Doesn't feel like we won, does it, Dad?' asks Oscar. No it doesn't.

The following day, Broxbourne Borough Under-15s win again. It's a doughty performance, and they overturn a deficit, although they have no substitutes. Oscar makes a few handsome saves and things are properly looking up. It can be done, Boro.

9 November 2024
Stevenage 1 Reading 1

My prediction: 1-1
His prediction: 2-1

A survey appeared this week and found its way to Twitter, so it must be true. Apparently 4.82 per cent of Stevenage residents attend Boro games. Obviously it's heavily flawed as they're counting away support such as the 1,363 who noisily follow Reading at the Lamex today, but if not, that's almost one in 20, which is incredible (i.e. not true) since it includes those who don't like football and who favour Arsenal or Spurs. Boro are 12th in that League One survey. Huddersfield are top (12.89 per cent), while Bristol Rovers are bottom (1.6 per cent), a place behind Birmingham City (2.34 per cent). Perhaps Boro are bonding with the community more than it appears sometimes. Perhaps.

We're not in great form ourselves today. Because he's a teenager he can sometimes be sulky, so Oscar is in sulky teenager mode. He finally starts talking as we pootle down the A602. There's a new food truck outside the 76 Lounge. It sells curry for £5, heated on a flaming stove inside the van. 'Can you put in the book that we didn't get any because you don't like curry, Dad?' I will.

Even though we're stiltedly talking, we're despondent and without hope after last week's farrago, but Pidge and Nathan Thompson are back from injury. Pidge doesn't look fit at all, though, and his distribution is awry, while the hero Nathan Thompson will finish the match with a bandage around his head. Although Tyreece Simpson wasn't considered good enough to kick a ball against Guiseley, he starts. It's said there's a guaranteed gametime clause in his contract, but I don't believe it. Luther's still injured and Robbo Roberts doesn't make the bench.

The first half is fantastic. Reading – especially slinky Wolverhampton Wanderers loanee Chem Campbell – are easy on the eye and they move the ball quickly, but Boro sweep ahead when Dan Kemp, who's finally hitting form, guides Nick Freeman's cross under Reading's dodgy keeper, Joel Pereira. There's even a Kemp chant now: 'Dan Kemp's on fire,' to Bruce Springsteen's 'Dancing in the Dark'.

Oscar jumps about, I jump about too but more warily, Dan Phillips puts himself about and Boro go in ahead. Even Neil Banfield stands up at one point, looking for all the world like Penfold (the cartoon character, not our pet cat named after it), although he might have been simply stretching his legs. 'This was the half I wanted,' says

NOVEMBER – OUR UNHAPPY HOME LIFE

Oscar with a massive grin. Then he says something else: 'I don't think we should get season tickets next season, Dad.'

This isn't something I'd got around to thinking about. I'd kind of assumed we would. I know this is all getting a little Michael Bluth and George Michael Bluth, but I don't let him see how I feel.

Why's that? Are you not enjoying our season? 'Oh I am, apart from having to spend so much time with you. It's not that, Dad. But it's my GCSEs. Even you must accept they come before a Stevenage game.' He may have detected some of my anguish, because he never calls them Stevenage. Of course I accept that, Oscar, but let's talk about this in March.

The second half is another thriller, but Boro's game management is wobbly. I'd always enjoyed chatting with Rubén Sellés when he was at Southampton, already doomed after the Nathan Jones madness. His Reading look strong, Revs makes the wrong substitutions again, changes the shape, and front foot becomes back foot. Murphy Cooper, last week's hero, repeats his performance but even he can't stop Harvey Knibbs's close-range equaliser after Campbell had wriggled past Dan Butler in the area. 'Sing when you're drawing,' our weary chant goes, 'you only sing when you're drawing.'

It's all Oscar's fault. At least it is according to Mrs Chatty, who we've been stood next to. When Dan Kemp scored, he looked up where Boro might be in the table at 5pm. 'DON'T DO THAT! You'll jinx it by looking at the table!' she shouted. Oscar blushed. At the final whistle, she reminds him of her warning. I'm not sure she's joking. Neither is Oscar.

A draw is a fair result – my first correct prediction, you'll note; not that it brings any pleasure – and for all the flawed second half, it was the best overall performance since Mansfield.

Reading glide west on their superior coach. It may or may not be an apostrophe-unfriendly Stewarts – both parties may have moved on – as unlike Watford's Stewarts, there are no identifying marks. Most peculiar.

We don't chat much on the way home. There's not too much to say, but we're relieved and we're as one again.

Tomorrow, Broxbourne Borough Under-15s will lose 7-0 to a far superior team. Unlike Murphy Cooper, Oscar dives over a couple, misjudges a couple more and has 'my worst-ever game'. Oh dear.

12 November 2024
Stevenage 1 Gillingham 1 – Bristol Street Motors EFL Trophy,
(Gillingham win 5-4 on penalties)

My prediction: 2-0
His prediction: 1-0

I do love a clunking great metaphor. We already know that Boro players who can walk but aren't selected must attend home games. Tonight, this includes Jordan 'Robbo' Roberts. As Marcus Wyllie's penalty sails past Taye to give Gillingham a victory almost as Pyrrhic as my correct Reading prediction, Robbo is out of his seat and presumably off home, moving rather quicker some might say – but not me or Oscar, since we love him – than he has during his recent games.

Soon after, Robbo is in the car park, he's in his car, he's raring to go. He's not going anywhere. He's blocked in. And people are knocking on his car window asking for selfies. To his immense credit, Robbo lugubriously gets out of his car each time, wearily puts his arms around some urchins and smiles a grin most rictus. I stare at him, trying to convey empathy via telepathy. As James said in the oddly bracketed 'Sometimes' (Lester Piggott)' – Tim Booth cooked me salmon in his Hove flat once; very possibly the worst meal I've ever had – 'When I look deep in your eyes I can see your soul.' I look deep into Robbo's eyes and I can see his soul is crushed.

After Guiseley, we were wary of assuming progress in any competition, even though tonight's maths are simple enough and heavily loaded in Boro's favour. Since Peterborough United and Crystal Palace Under-5s have completed their Second-Hand Car Cup group games, all Boro must do to qualify for an away tie in the knockout stage of the tournament nobody wants (but I'm warming to actually) is to do better than losing by two goals against an out of sorts League Two team.

We're not going to Birmingham on Saturday because of international call-ups (mostly Birmingham's, plus Reidy), so Revs picks a strongish team and he's so committed that he'll be yellow carded. Taye's in goal – his kid brother Luca is in Gillingham's goal; they have equally lovely hair – the boy Ryan Doherty gets a start, Kane Smith goes to right-back, Harvey White and Eli King have slightly different midfield roles and Pressley and Jake Young try to build a partnership up front, rather less passionately than Klaus Kinski building that opera house in *Fitzcarraldo*.

The East Terrace and North Stand are closed and, although under-12s and those who look under 12 are admitted free, the crowd will number just 832, officially including 147 (which to my flawed headcount looks a wild overestimate) who must return to the Medway towns this evening. The away fans will manage a couple of chants. We Boro fans prefer to talk quietly amongst ourselves.

We're in the seats right above the tunnel on the halfway line. I tell Oscar that Boro will win this trophy. He laughs at me. We can hear Scott Cuthbert bellowing in Scottish throughout the game – we can't decipher him, so surely the players can't either – and getting all Glasgow overspill with the fourth official. We both think we hear the referee swearing at the Gillingham bench and we see Revs put his head in his hands and turn away distraught when the far-from-Stakhanovite Listy messes up again.

There's so much to take in that we have a fine old time, which is fortunate since the first half is so poor. Not Guiseley wretched, just poor. Managed by Mark Bonner, who I still hold a tiny flickering torch for, and pulling out of the sort of run that cost him his job at Cambridge, Gillingham deservedly suck their half-time oranges ahead after Kane Smith falls over and Josh Andrews sweeps in. Oscar can't quite fathom how Jonny Williams was in the Wales squad at the last World Cup, but is now revenge-tackling a 16-year-old in front of a three-figure crowd. I can. I admire Jonny Williams. Oscar is less sure.

Boro Bear isn't here, but Drackers is and even he chirps up with a pointed, 'Ah! A shot on target!' during the half-time entertainment, where grown men still have to chip a ball into a rubbish bin. Trust me, it's great fun.

This game may mark the end of Aaron Pressley, although he's contracted for another season. He loses his heading duels, he still poses no threat, and when he gets a shot in, it goes straight at Ashby-Hammond Minor. 'You're shit Pressley,' shouts someone – the loudest shout of the evening – as he's substituted. Pressley looks like he's about to cry. Oscar could cry for him too, but this relationship isn't going to right itself.

The impish Dan Kemp comes on and scores the equaliser that will take Boro through with a little to spare. He jiggles past a few half-challenges, refuses to pass to better-placed fellow substitute Tyreece Simpson and fires past Gillingham's Ashby-Hammond. Oscar jumps up and fist-pumps. At the end, to Drackers's obvious disdain, we're treated to what he calls the Ashby-Hammond Cup (i.e. the compulsory penalty shoot-out that must conclude all Second-Hand Car Cup drawn games). Strangely, Oscar relishes the idea that both Ashby-Hammond boys are goalkeepers but not first-teamers. 'A battle between the mediocres,' he declares, unkindly. It's a first for crowd and players: a penalty shoot-out without tension. The players don't even bother to put their arms around each other.

Even here though, Boro can make drama out of mundanity. Bravely, Tyreece Simpson looks to redeem his season with the first penalty. Less admirably, he slugs it wide. Deary me. He's broken. Boro score their next four, but Gillingham score all five. They win the drawn game, yet losers Boro are through. Bully for Boro. I suspect there will be no champagne on Gillingham's sturdy Bayliss coach as they cross the Thames at Dartford. Like Charlton, they've defected there from Kings Ferry. There's something going on in the world of Kent luxury coaches. Probably.

Afterwards, Revs says he wants a home draw in the knockout stage, but since Boro are group runners-up they will automatically be away to a southern area group winner. Odd he didn't know that.

Before the game, we'd visited the deserted club shop and, unveiling my inner Jocelyn Wildenstein (the spending, not the surgery, although if I did have plastic surgery I'd emerge looking like an apricot), I'd splashed out on a Boro polo shirt. I'm no merchandise maven, but it was cheap (just £12 in the sale) and Oscar gave the purchase his seal of approval, something I keep searching for. Predictably, I left it under my seat after the Ashby-Hammond Cup. Before we discover Jordan Roberts in the car park, I charge back into the ground, shimmying past the stewards, who really don't like returning fans for some reason. Oscar heads them off with some boyish charm and assurances that I'm a buffoon rather than a more volatile member of the Revs Out faction. It's still there. 'I have to do everything for you, don't I?' he mutters.

On the way home, we talk about the forthcoming draw. Oscar says he doesn't care, but he cares enough to want the conversation. We can't meet Peterborough in this cup again at this stage, so it's one of seven, all (Walsall, Cheltenham, Charlton, Burton, Wycombe, Colchester) just about doable on a December school night, plus Exeter. I wanted a new ground. When pushed, Oscar fancies Wycombe, with the optimism of one who's never been there, but he isn't keen on going back to Burton. 'It's going to be Exeter isn't it, though, Dad? Can I get some time off school?'

23 November 2024
Stevenage 0 Leyton Orient 0

My prediction: 3-0
His prediction: 2-0

NOVEMBER – OUR UNHAPPY HOME LIFE

Oh my. It's the first really cold day of the season – a wind whistling in from the north carrying freezing pellets of water – but Oscar pays homage to his northern roots by wearing neither hat, nor hood, nor gloves. That's my boy.

Even so, we're glum. This weird run of home games is sapping the team's momentum, the book's momentum and our momentum. Just the two to go.

Anyway, Leyton Orient is geographically the closest Boro come to a local derby. Last March when Orient won at the Lamex, their facile manager Richie Wellens taunted the East Terrace until Sweens intervened (Sweens is always intervening), grappling with him on our behalf. Wellens talked about the 'cream rising to the top', but whatever the cream was, it wasn't Orient, since they left the Lamex in 10th and finished the season in 11th. And they have Sean Clare, who I secretly love, but I can't share that love yet, since he isn't in the squad.

Speaking of love, as we must, we bump into Boro Bear outside. Oscar and I high-five him. Would you like a photograph with Boro Bear, Oscar?

'What do you think?'

Actually, I think he should, but I don't pursue it ...

Orient arrive in their striking Anderson coach (mostly white, but with a deep, deep shade of the richest red), their 969 fans make a little noise, since, because of the Sky's Pretending to Care About the EFL campaign, it's a lunchtime kick-off so a handful of viewers can watch it. As is the way with lunchtime kick-offs, those viewers will be rewarded with a low-tempo game played in near-silence. 'Why, Dad, why?' I don't know, Oscar.

It's been a funny old week. Trinidad & Tobago didn't play in the break, but Dan Phillips seems to be injured, and since Wales Under-21s were knocked out of their

Euros, Eli King wasn't going anywhere. Jamie Reid managed 14 minutes in Belfast against Belarus and the identical time in Luxembourg against Luxembourg. I like Luxembourg. At a time of some emotional trauma, I visited Luxembourg on my own. It's the right sort of place for healing. It didn't heal Reidy, for he didn't score for Northern Ireland in Luxembourg (or Belfast) and he won't score his first league goal of the season today.

'I'm not turning against Reidy,' confides Oscar. 'But I don't think he should start any more. He's only getting starts because of how he played in the first half of last season.'

There is real darkness too. Matt Lawton in *The Times* breaks a story about Thomas Malins, lead coach of Boro's Elite Development Programme between November 2021 and April 2023. Stevenage's DBS check didn't cover abroad (i.e. Norway) where he was, to quote the headline 'deemed guilty of child sex offences'. Boro's response? Unless I missed it, silence. I'm not sure that's the way ahead here.

Boro have opened a bar at the back of the East Terrace, but for reasons beyond human comprehension, they have decided it won't actually open until half-time. Phil Wallace's Meet the Fans forum suggested demand and Boro have responded, so fair enough, but it's too cold for beer today, it's illegal to drink alcohol in view of the pitch, the drinking space to mill around is tiny and there's one steward. Old question: what can possibly go wrong? We'll see, but not today.

Jake Young and Aaron Pressley don't even make the bench. Ken Aboh, who looked purposeful against Gillingham, does, but he won't get a kick. Mrs Chatty stands next to us. 'How are you, young man?' she asks

Oscar, who does manage a 'very well' and doesn't swear all lunchtime. Oscar is hungry, still banging on about his Rotherham pie and he's now claiming he didn't have enough footroom at the New York. And since he's in a stats mood, he points out that Boro's scoring ratio, 0.7 goals per game, is the worst in League One, just beneath Wigan.

Today, Boro will have one shot of note, spurn one chance after Orient's nervy goalkeeper Josh Keeley failed to hold that shot and Louis Thompson will hit the bar with a cross the wind evolved into a shot. That's all, and when Tyreece Simpson – gloved, the big jessie – comes on with five minutes remaining, the chant is 'we're on the pitch when Simpson scores'. Never has grass been less likely to be trod.

Murphy Cooper will have even less to do against thuggish Orient, who take advantage of referee Ben Speedie's gullibility. At one point, Jack Currie shoves Listy over and gets a foul for his trouble. He jogs back smiling broadly at us. We shout 'wanker, wanker' and football's circle turns again, as it always will.

'The first half was funny,' sighs Oscar, immune to my suggestion that Orient are there for the taking. 'The second was just awful. Can we talk about Formula 1?'

Last week, there was no international break for Broxbourne Borough Under-15s. They lost 8-0, although it was a superior performance to the previous week. As he was keen to point out, Oscar played better when conceding more.

Tomorrow, the wind will howl and they'll cruise through their cup tie (there's a lot of cups; I struggle to keep track of which is which) 4-1. Like Murphy Cooper against Orient, Oscar won't have much to do, but he performs his tiny workload just fine. And just as Richie Wellens was booked, an opposition parent will become so worked up that he has to be restrained by the other grown-ups and was last seen stomping off to the car park on his own, as Oscar giggled like the schoolboy he is. So did I.

30 November 2024
Stevenage 0 Mansfield Town 1 – FA Cup

My prediction: 2-1
His prediction: 1-0

My Stevenage polo shirt has emerged from the wash. Oscar insists I wear it to the game. It's washed well, although the club crest, being considerably thicker than the rest of the material, has sort of creased in on itself. I'm still not a club merchandise sort, but it might bring a change of fortune, although luck has nothing to do with this rotten spell.

We're wary. Of course we're wary. The first round of the FA Cup was the lowest of the many lows this season is gifting us, but when Mansfield-raised Alvin Stardust posited that he felt like Buddy Holly, he probably meant that when you squeeze through in the cup, it doesn't matter any more.

We jointly refuse to discuss the possibility of Manchester City in round three, but Boro haven't won since our life-enhancing trip to Mansfield seven stuttering games ago. We've purchased seats very close to where we sat against Gillingham. We invest in a hot dog (organised crime in the West End type of sausage; indeterminable meat, rather than a frankfurter) for Oscar.

NOVEMBER – OUR UNHAPPY HOME LIFE

For me, it's a Pukka pie that doesn't burn the skin off the roof of my mouth. We're literally above the tunnel, so we can see Mansfield manager Nigel Clough chatting with punters, cheerily posing for selfies and generally being a good egg. There's a noisy, 742-strong travelling support, showing they could have done the flying pickets thing during the strike if they'd wanted, but the East Terrace is quiet, morose and sparsely populated.

With Dan Phillips still injured and the midfield thus out of shape, Revs has finally dropped Reidy (I wish it hadn't come to this, but it's the right thing to do) and gone for attacking broke. Jesus, the first half is good, banishing the ghosts that too often overwhelm Boro. When Boro break, there are a swarm of players hurtling forwards. For the first time in a while, Listy is cutting in behind full-backs as he did in League Two and everyone is playing well, apart from Jake Young, stranded on the left.

There are chances galore. As we know from his loan stint at Boro, Christy Pym can't hold shots, but when he spills one and Dan Kemp fires the loose ball past him, Baily Cargill hacks off the line. This is the Boro we fell in love with.

I move to discuss Manchester City's upcoming third-round visit to the Lamex. After two chances in the first two minutes of the second period, I'm ready for that conversation again, but Oscar shushes me.

Then – once again, you've seen this coming haven't you? Once again, I hadn't – the hitherto unemployed Murphy Cooper saves well from Cargill, Boro struggle to clear the corner, Jordan Roberts's clearing header is floppy, Jordan Bowery helps it on and Stephen McLaughlin expertly wallops home from the edge of the area.

These things happen and there are 42 minutes left. It shouldn't be a problem, but the way Boro attempt to solve that problem makes it massive. Boro's fragile morale collapses, so they revert to the lumpen long ball and speculative crosses of recent weeks.

Mansfield's Ben Quinn flops to the floor with no one near him. There's a rare moment of noise when the Boro fans – we included – jeer. Exasperated at our ignorance, Clough turns around and announces to the crowd that 'his shoulder's popped out'. So it has. Off goes Quinn. We've been silenced by a better man.

On the bench, Revs does nothing, and for endless swathes of time during which empires rise and fall, nobody stands up in the technical area, leaving the players to fend for themselves. As late as the 74th minute, Revs makes a quadruple substitution in a bid to buy 30 minutes of extra time. Even with seven added minutes and Neil Banfield deigning to stand – in the name of all that is holy to dignity, he's finally replaced his baseball cap with a stylish woolly hat – Pym isn't really tested again and Mansfield return north in their apostrophe-unfriendly Nottingham-based Sharpes coach (with rather fetching MTFC livery and bordello lighting), eagerly anticipating a third-round draw against a club Boro would have equally relished facing.

Oscar is incandescent. He refuses to clap the players off. 'I've never seen such contrasting halves. This is a turning point for me. Revs has got to go. Now.'

He's not as down as after Peterborough (league), but it's close. Even though the first half was excellent, I haven't felt so bleak, so bleak in fact that I don't sleep properly. I have 99 problems and Boro are unquestionably one now. In truth, I'm more disconsolate than Peterborough. That defeat was agonising, but there was so much hope, so much promise of more and better to come. Now, I have no hope. Partly that's self-indulgence; I really wanted a third-round tie and I really wanted to take Oscar to our first Premier League ground since Villa Park. Selfishly, it would have given the book another dimension – obviously it could have been Harrogate Town away, but that would have been winnable – and it would have given us a Christmas with something to look forwards to.

There's something else: what now? Boro are 17th, four points above the relegation slots and the only way isn't up. It's going to be a slog from here. I need to keep Oscar on side for the book, but his dreams are getting crushed and he thinks it's because of one man. It's not all bad news though: for a change that man isn't me.

On the final whistle, Revs shakes hands with his conqueror Clough and scurries down the tunnel, head down. No apologies, no communication. The Revs Out faction is gathering pace and personnel. His position is in a little peril now, as is Boro's in the League One we must return to. Afterwards, Revs says much the same as we'd been saying, but we didn't have the option of changing things.

Next morning, relegation-threatened like Stevenage, Broxbourne Borough Under-15s stroll into a three-goal lead; think a Boro who take their chances. The rain pours and another opposition parent has a hissy fit, this time about a throw-in on the halfway line. He's chanting, 'Cheat, cheat, cheat,' at the linesman. I'm usually above such nonsense, but even I speak up: 'Mate, it's a throw-in on the halfway line in a children's football match.' I feel better for it, honestly. Alas it finishes 3-3, but Oscar doesn't finish the game, having dived (genuinely bravely it must be said) at a striker's feet. Both players are forced off. A qualified medical professional, Oscar theatrically limps to the car and diagnoses that sushi followed by a chocolate croissant are the officially recognised cures for his ailments. Strangely enough, he's right.

*Phil Wallace:
boss of bosses.*

Alex 'Revs' Revell: he's the manager. Again.

Neil Banfield: he's the assistant manager, footballistically speaking.

Scott Cuthbert: he's Scottish and he's the number three.

The Stevenage FC mural.

Boro Bear: he makes everything better.

A view from the East Terrace.

Murphy Cooper: 'never fall in love with a loan player'.

Luther James-Wildin: 'always has a smile on his face', but not here.

Nathan Thompson (l) and Dan Butler after exiting the Carabao Cup at Norwich.

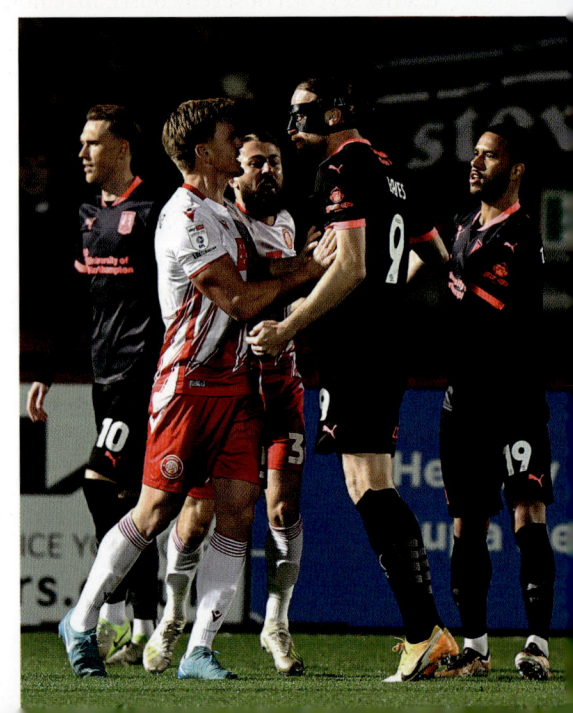

Carl 'Pidge' Piergianni introducing himself to Northampton Town's Tom Eaves at the Lamex. One of these men wouldn't make half-time.

December – The Most Footballistic Month

3 December 2024
Stevenage 2 Northampton Town 0

My prediction: 2-0
His prediction: 4-1

'We go again' is one of those sanctimonious phrases managers trot out to mask defeats. But it feels right here. It's the seventh of seven consecutive home matches – the whole of November! – which have turned Boro's season around, but not in a good way. Before tonight, those games have yielded four Boro goals, a cup exit and two points. As Amy Winehouse – I very awkwardly had to reassure her she wasn't ugly when we sat in the deserted Jazz Café shortly before *Back to Black* one weekday lunchtime – might have said, 'What kind of fuckery is this?'

I'm still not properly over Saturday – rather than Manchester City, Mansfield drew Wigan at home in the third round, so it feels like progression to the fourth for them – but Oscar is, even though his Boro top is in the wash. I ask him who Boro's manager is going to be for Saturday's game at Crawley. 'If we win, Revs. If we draw, it depends on the performance. If we lose, I'm not sure.'

I thought I might have to bribe him with a Nando's again. Instead, he's so upbeat and so positive that we have one anyway. Because of him, I begin to feel optimistic once more.

That said, Boro are 17th, Northampton Town are 18th, so in theory it's the first relegation struggle of the season. Hurrah! Northampton are in poor form too. Even worse than Boro against Guiseley, they actually lost at home to non-league opposition in the FA Cup first round: Nile Ranger's Kettering Town. To add mild spice, Northampton field a couple of ex-Boro loanees, Sam Hoskins and Nesta Guinness-Walker, but the chants of 'Boro reject' are half-hearted from the season's first sub-3,000 league crowd.

Jordan 'Robbo' Roberts is suspended, but otherwise Revs keeps faith with the Mansfield defeatees. Reidy's starting again and we haven't, in fact, seen the last of Aaron Pressley, since he ousts Ken Aboh from the bench.

It's my favourite opening to a game in yonks. Barely 30 seconds have passed when, right in front of us, Pidge starts grappling with giant, mask-wearing centre-forward Tom Eaves. Let's just say that for a man who never goes down, Pidge tumbles to the ground with surprising ease. Then joy of joys (if this were on television we'd be told 'this is not what anyone wants to see', but of course it's exactly what everyone wants to see) almost every player from both sides piles in as we chant 'off, off, off'. At Eaves rather than Pidge of course.

The referee yellow cards both players. Now we have a problem. Pidge has to play the remaining 89 minutes, 30 seconds with a yellow card to his name. One bad tackle and it's goodbye to him, to three points and perhaps to Revs too.

Both teams are fired up; the 491 Northampton fans are so fired up that they start a 'shit referee' chant, which the whole ground joins in with, although Scott Jackson is fine and he gets the big decisions right. Maturely and craftily, Pidge leaves the bulk of Eaves-policing duties to Nathan Thompson, but Eaves himself is a man in thrall to his demons. Referee Jackson warns him again for a foul by the dugouts (i.e. near the halfway line in a zone of no danger). In the 28th minute, Elliott List sprints away from Eaves, who, as if winning a keenly fought contest for the Nation's Stupidest Footballer, crudely fouls him from behind. Off he pops. We celebrate as if a goal had been scored.

What those shenanigans were about, I cannot possibly say. Afterwards, Jon Brady, managing Northampton for the 200th time and under more pressure than Revs now, admitted Eaves was 'naïve', but no more. Brady will not manage Northampton for a 201st time. Eaves is a lump but he's genuinely not that sort of player. He hadn't been booked all season, hadn't been sent off since 2022, and history tells us that over a career that began in 2010, the very physical centre-forward tends to pick up just three or four yellow cards a season. Oh well.

This means another problem beyond Pidge's yellow. If Boro don't win after over an hour against ten men … Revs is certainly feeling the pressure after a first half where only a Nathan Thompson long-ranger troubles lanky stand-in goalkeeper Nik Tzanev. When the teams re-emerge for the second half, Stevenage's Twitter tells us that 'Alex Revell was shown a red card at half-time', but no more.

It's Luther's 27th birthday. 'A birthday pass forwards,' trills Oscar. 'A birthday throw-in …' and so forth until he misses a tackle. 'Go to the birthday bench, Luther.' Never change, Oscar, although he's changing almost every single day.

By the 80th minute, it's not going well. Expertly marshalled by Jon Guthrie, Northampton have defended deeply and well. Jake Young has shown us his six-pack after failing to throw a bottle of water off the pitch. Ironically, he himself is soon off, subbed once again. I still can't make him out. One volleyed cross that whips across goal just waiting for a touch is a moment of Premier League quality. Then he's alone in the penalty area with time and space for a shot. In a moment of park-level quality, he skews it high, wide and almost on to the A602.

Camped in Northampton's half, for all Boro's hegemony of possession, they are ponderous until, from somewhere at the back of the West Stand, the banished Revs makes his substitutions. Unlike Saturday, he plays his cards brilliantly. With 90 minutes ahoy, Eli King guides over a low cross from the left. The impish Dan Kemp nips in ahead of the dozing Akin Odimayo and the one man whose reputation has waxed during these home games sweeps in.

Oscar leaps high – at that moment I can't help but note we're not hugging after goals any more – bellows a 'YEEEESSSS' and the feeling of relief is almost palpable, both on the pitch and around us. That's that. Boro press for more. Kemp has one cleared off the line, and when Luther enjoys a birthday one-two with another substitute, Nick Freeman, the latter crosses from the right and Reidy guides in his first league goal of the season. At last, at last, at last. Welcome back Reidy.

Until his surrender speech of 15 August 1945 – 'the war situation has developed not necessarily to Japan's advantage', etc. – the good people of Japan had not been allowed to hear the voice of their Emperor, Hirohito. It's said those Japanese people were disappointed that he sounded so unassertive, although they probably had to deal with more pressing disappointments in 1945 than a father of seven's weedy voice. Similarly, until his post-match briefing of 3 December 2024, Boro supporters had not been allowed to hear the voice of assistant manager Neil Banfield.

Bizarrely, Neil Banfield claims he doesn't know why Revs was red carded, but he has a lovely voice and he's taken off his woolly hat to deliver his wisdom. It's Cockney but not overbearingly so. It's sing-song, a little like a post-lozenge Glenn Hoddle. Better than that, infinitely better than that, he introduces us to a new word: 'footballistically', as in 'footballistically, we've been outstanding'. 'Did you hear that, Dad?' laughs Oscar, linguistic horizons expanding by the second. I did, I did. We play the recording over and over again, savouring it as we drive home.

We would like to formally apologise to Neil Banfield for mercilessly mocking his baseball cap and for suggesting he slightly resembles Penfold (the cartoon character, rather than our cat). We also forgive him for his tactics at Exeter. We've fallen in love with him in a footballistic instant. We hadn't bargained for that.

10 December 2024
Burton Albion 0 Stevenage 4 – Vertu EFL Trophy

My prediction: 1-2
His prediction: 0-3

The duo who run the Stevenage club shop are great. She's really helpful, super-efficient and has an appealing take-no-prisoners undercurrent. He's super-patient, calls me 'sir' and wishes everyone have a great afternoon/evening as they leave, even when the shop is at its busiest. I'd hope his parents are proud of him. And when I purchased my polo shirt the other week, they both insisted I used their storeroom to try it on first.

This tiny club shop isn't spectacular. It was refurbished in the summer but nobody noticed. Should you so wish, you can acquire a Boro rubber duck in exchange for £10.

Even the salesman's eyebrows raised, though, when we bought our Burton tickets last Saturday.

'How many tickets have we sold?' asks Oscar, who had noted the eyebrow-raising.

'Er, one,' he replies.

Oscar finds this hilarious and, just a little too loudly, announces to all and sundry that 'me and Dad have just trebled our away support!' Shop Guy's grin is fixed, but he still wishes us a great afternoon.

This of course raises the notion that the person who has bought his (and it will be a he) ticket is going on his own. To Burton. On a really cold December evening. Doesn't he have anything better to do? No, he does not. Of course he doesn't. Neither do we.

That said, Oscar is not wholly happy. The 7pm kick-off means we can make it without him skipping school, although it's tight.

He's not a fan of this trophy at all. 'We could win 30-0 and it would still be a waste of my time,' he mutters from the back of the car, as he changes from his school uniform into his Boro top and jogging bottoms. 'Have you brought snacks?'

I have. That settles him. He's right about this shambles of a competition though. A few weeks ago, when Gillingham simultaneously won, drew and lost at the Lamex, the Second-Hand Car Cup was officially the Bristol Street Motors Trophy. Now, apropos of absolutely nothing, the name has been changed mid-season to the Vertu Trophy. This hasn't happened to a cup before, has it? There must have been a Führer Cup in Germany at one point, but I'd wager it ran until the end of the 1944/45 season before changing its name. I don't know who or what a Vertu is and I don't care. Nor do any of the, wait for it, 329 people who turn up at Burton's Pirelli.

Before the game, we wander around the near deserted car park. The Boro kit van, as driven by Keith Bell, aka Kitman Keith, who, magnificently, got himself booked at Exeter last year, is next to Boro's Greys coach. Oscar is delighted to note a six-pack of Red Bull, some Walkers Max and a bag of Candy Kittens left on the seat, ready for hungry Kitman Keith's return. Like Oscar, never change, Kitman Keith, never change.

Almost understandably, Burton don't do a programme (still bastards though). At the poky club shop, they promise free team sheets for all, but that isn't true. Three and a half sides of the ground are closed, so entire the 329 of us are crammed into half of the main Carling Stand.

Both sets of fans must therefore mingle and share the food outlet. Think *Abigail's Party* without the belly laughs. The menu isn't quite as extensive as it had been at the league game, so Oscar has another London-mafia style hot dog ('not good, not good at all') and I have a burger, ruined only by the soggy box it was served in. We buy water, but manage to lose the bottle. Or it was stolen.

We have padded seats ('I bet Phil Wallace has sat here,' speculates Oscar) and there are several available, since Boro – away area infiltrated by elderly Burton fans, presumably players' families – have brought just 13 supporters, over a seventh of whom have travelled in my car.

It's fantastically, wonderfully surreal. I don't think I'll be part of a more exclusive, good-natured club than we 12 white men and one white schoolboy. Since the whole squad were eventually awarded medals, there are more England World Cup winners than Boro fans at Burton tonight. I'm at my happiest here and, for a moment of unprecedented serenity, truly content. I try to tell Oscar; he doesn't wholly get it, but he will, because he's partly me. Whatever happens in the game, this will be amongst the greatest nights of my life.

I do realise how sad this is. I realise it suggests I have a warped outlook. I realise why Oscar and his sister think I'm autistic. I realise that it only confirms a life lived without triumphs (I did sing backing vocals for Iron Maiden at a Brazilian football stadium though; that was good) and I realise that it means I deserve to have no relationships. I realise all that, but, right here, right now, in the Staffordshire cold on a December evening, I don't care. It's only so impossibly good because I'm sharing the experience with someone I love though.

In fact, I could die here and now and it would be okay. Naturally, they'd have to abandon the game. This would cause Boro more fixture chaos, but although only one of them knows my name, the remaining 12 would revisit the Pirelli in my honour, wouldn't they? Wouldn't they? Someone would have to take Oscar home and he'd forget where the car is parked, but I'd pass on in a beatific state, oblivious to the mess I've left behind. Oscar liked the padded seats.

There's no Revs Out faction (except wavering, plain-clothes Oscar), so the feeling is warm, especially when the Boro team trots off after the warm-up and Pidge looks up. Instead of clapping us, he just shakes his head and laughs with us at the wonder of this Last Supper-sized gaggle supporting him this evening. We love him; he gets it. Everyone chats to everyone. We meet the guy who'd bought a ticket before us. He's lovely and he's wearing shorts, so hats off. Nobody's drunk and nobody can be bothered to start a chant. We all want: a) starter Simpson and b) substitute Pressley to score.

Burton somehow won at Peterborough last week, but they're enduring an awful season. They sacked their manager shortly after Boro's draw here, they lost here in the FA Cup to local rivals Tamworth, who drew Tottenham at home in round three, and they already look doomed. There's no Terence Vancooten tonight either.

We should have gone to Crawley on Saturday, but Storm Darragh and Crawley's jerry-built ground intervened. The moral of the story: don't buy train tickets in advance. This also means Revs – in the naughty seat, on our row, for the first of his two-game touchline ban after his sending-off against Northampton – can field a strongish team, albeit one with eight changes from Northampton. Taye gets a run-out in goal, Dan Phillips is finally back, Pidge, Nathan Thompson and Dan Kemp are on a kids-free bench, and there is no sign of Louis Thompson, Listy or Reidy.

It goes right from the sixth minute when Eli King slings a corner over. Goalkeeper Harry Isted makes the first of many hashes. Showing unusual keenness, Jake

Young has a shot and then a slice which falls to Lewis Freestone, whose header loops in at the far corner. We applaud gleefully. In fact, Young tries so hard, he's injured and off before ten minutes are up. Scott Cuthbert is barking at Robbo in Scottish and even Neil Banfield rises to make some footballistic points. Oscar is regretting not putting his Stevenage hoodie over his Stevenage top, but the more Boro press against hopeless opposition, the more excited he gets.

Boro are rampant in the second half. Robbo's through ball is deflected into Simpson's path by Jason Sraha's deflection, Alex Bannon's misjudgement and Jack Armer's non-tackle. He thunders forwards and thwacks home like a natural-born scorer. Hell's bells! Leading Second-Hand Car Cup scorer! We go quite wild. Goal machine Tyreece! It's happened!

Number three stems from Pidge heading a corner down, Pressley shooting aimlessly and Ken Aboh (the more I see, the more I like; his pace saw two Burton players booked) thrashing in his first Boro goal. Harvey White tapped in the fourth after Pressley had hit the post following yet more fine work from Aboh. 'We're counting that as a Pressley assist,' explains Oscar. We certainly are.

The few Burton fans sing 'you're not fit to wear the shirt' to their team. Oscar points out that it's only a Burton shirt and they're only kids who've given everything. On the way to the car he's so happy he'll skip and shout 'yabba dabba doo' at the top of his voice to no one in particular. There's a rotten journey home with M1 closures and the M25 exit blocked, but we hear Simpson talk of his goal ('He sounds like someone who'd be really intelligent if he hadn't taken up football,' suggests Oscar) and those roadworks can't hurt us.

I know Boro didn't win 30-0, but was it a waste of your time, Oscar?

'Absolutely not. Not a second.'

14 December 2024
Stevenage 2 Stockport County 1

My prediction: 3-1
His prediction: 2-2

Do you prefer F1 or football Oscar?

'Football's number one, but do you remember Pidge's block on Tuesday night? Did you put it in the book?'

I do remember Pidge flinging himself in the path of a goalbound drive like the hero he is. I remember us going 'phwoar' like 70s builders confronted with a moderately attractive woman after a session on the Double Diamond, and I remember Oscar saying, 'That's why we love him.' But, no, it didn't make the book.

'Because we follow a small club with no media coverage, I can't talk about it with anyone at school. They don't know who Pidge is. With F1, all my friends know all the drivers. I love everything about our little club and I love our little stadium, but I wish I could share it with someone who's not you.'

He breaks my heart sometimes. We watched the Vertu Cup draw on television this morning (Orient away, so no school issues, but it's a tricky one, footballistically speaking) and saunter to the Lamex in cheery fashion, although Stockport have won four of their last five league games. We're pressed for time, chiefly because Oscar has become addicted to *Suits* (a crush on Meghan Markle? I do hope so), so we don't get a great spot on the East

Terrace. They're playing Orchestral Manoeuvres in the Dark's 'Electricity' (there's sappy Christmas music at half-time rather than, say, The Waitresses: 'you forgot cranberries too!'). I'm stood next to an older, heroically sweary, Cockney gentleman with a magnificent thatch of Kirk Douglas-style hair. We're fast friends by the end of the game. 'Facking hell, get closer,' may well be the inscription on his tombstone.

Boro Bear, English football's finest mascot, is wearing a Christmas jumper, but he's off form today and perhaps his identity has changed. Instead of running out ahead of the teams, pumping his fists and thumping his big old beary heart, he saunters like we'd just sauntered. 'That's ruined the afternoon for me,' laments Oscar, without irony.

Phil Wallace is here, and Revs – again on the naughty seat for the second and final game of his suspension – makes eight changes from Burton, meaning a fortunate Reidy and Listy start.

It's 1-1 after a first half where Stockport are the better side, although their 667 travellers aren't especially vociferous. Pidge pings the ball forwards, Reidy plays the flick of the season, which sets Dan Kemp free to waltz through some dozy defenders (I'm thinking of you, Ethan Pye) and score in what's becoming Kempino fashion. Moments later, Harvey White gives the ball to Callum Camps. Nathan Thompson is too slow to notice the peril and Camps's scuffed shot bobbles past Murphy Cooper, at fault for the first time since Peterborough. Damn.

The second half is all Boro, and Stockport manager Dave Challinor will refer to his team's performance as 'a complete shambles'. As against Northampton, Boro win via an act of jaw-dropping opposition stupidity. This time, there's little danger for Stockport as Robbo runs into the area but away from goal towards the corner flag. In a moment of madness, Ibou Touray trips him up. Reidy hammers the penalty past Ben Hinchliffe. It's not an enjoyable game. I'm as tense as ever, but there's an unease to my tension. We both think Stockport will equalise, but they don't – in fairness, Cooper isn't overworked – and there are positives aplenty.

I was wrong about Reidy, he has his best game of the season, so when Harvey White – stagnating by the game – is announced as man of the match, the East Terrace giggles as one. Robbo runs his heart out, the defence is immense and goal machine substitute Tyreece Simpson ensures the Stockport defence never settles. Three wins out of three and Stockport glide north in their splendid (and tall) Beeline coach with much to ruminate over. Boro are back and Oscar is ecstatic. 'On afternoons like this you don't feel the cold,' he muses. He's right there too, and the 'Revell again, olé olé' chant is resurrected.

Afterwards, Oscar formally rescinds his membership of the Revs Out faction and shouts 'yeassss' a lot, although he will point out that since Revs was sent off at half-time against Northampton, Boro have won everything. 'Neil Banfield's stepped up hasn't he?' Oscar speculates, before trying out Scotty Cuthbert's Runrig accent. Humbly, Revs doesn't come to share the love, so Cuthbert comes over to briefly applaud us clappers, alongside the players.

They leave with us still applauding, leaving only Drackers, who has mooched in our general direction, not quite sure what to do. We know exactly what to do. The East Terrace makes the thumping tom-tom sounds backed by the low growl that's always the invitation for Revs to delight us with his fist-pumps. Drackers steps in, flashes the broadest of grins, does the Revs first-pumps and does them very well indeed. It looks like it's one of the great moments, a bucket list moment, of his life, although he seems slightly sheepish afterwards. We couldn't love him more and he couldn't love the club more. We're so happy, every one of us.

Like Boro, Broxbourne Borough Under-15s had their game postponed last week. Tomorrow, their last outing until mid-January, will see them triumph 2-1 in a closely fought contest with no parental aggro. Oscar is powerless to stop the goal past him but, in truth, like Murphy Cooper, he doesn't have much to do, other than shout and, for the first time, punch away a corner. He's delighted afterwards.

21 December 2024
Blackpool 0 Stevenage 0

My prediction: 0-2
His prediction: 7-0

I'm holding on to my hoodie hood, bent double. Oscar's carefully sculpted hair has gone all Don King. We're giggling hysterically at the absurdity of it all, but we're crying too because it physically hurts and we're drenched. We're trying to walk back to the car that's somewhere in Blackpool town centre. The winds are officially 40mph, the freezing rain is horizontal and we've just seen a 0-0 draw. 'Nobody will believe us, Dad,' he splutters, grinning his broadest. I'm not sure life could possibly get any better. What a day we've had.

It's the Saturday before Christmas and the fixture-list gods have dispatched Boro on the longest trip of the season. This is another of the many reasons otherwise reasonable folk despise football and how weak people such as myself and Oscar allow it to control us. It dominates time and resources, it reduces choice, it wrecks family life, it destroys relationships, it's expensive, it's inherently pointless and we should grow up. But what do they know?

Today there are yellow weather wind warnings and circa 22 million cars are on the roads. Boro travelled early yesterday and stayed at the Boston Manor & Spa just off the M6 ('a stylish contemporary setting, extensive gardens, over 100 parking spaces, a grand piano and Starbucks to boot'), but we're off at 8am, fuelled by a McDonald's – only those who have attempted to rouse a grumpy 14-year-old boy from their bed at 7.30 on a Saturday morning may judge – and Master Miserable Oscar has decided 'we don't have anything to play for, for the rest of the season and we're going to lose 7-0'.

I have a plan. If we're not bogged down by traffic, we'll have fish'n'chips before the game. Wisely, I task Oscar with choosing the finest such emporium in Blackpool and he discovers the incongruously named Yorkshire Fisheries, the oldest chippery in Blackpool, Lancashire. The traffic's fine, we do have time and the world is finally turning as it should.

Oscar has chosen expertly and at half-time we're both in such postprandial food comas that we can only share a pie which would have disappointed, even were we not too full. Inside Yorkshire Fisheries, it's warm enough for Oscar to display his Boro shirt. 'Everyone's looking at me,' he grins.

I once loved Blackpool. In 1922, Paul Robeson made his British debut at the Opera House, which is still inside the Winter Gardens, but for me there was a family holiday when I was a kid, there were night trips to the Illuminations and there was a guest-house Christmas with my mother. Here's another reason why football matters: I can't remember a thing about that maternal Christmas, other than the match I sneaked off to see – and I've checked, although I didn't need to – finishing Blackpool 3 Chester 0.

Later, there was another holiday, solo but in the bosom of another family, which was marvellous, although I'd eventually behave shamefully to the guy who'd persuaded his parents to take me. A little later still, there was a violent, drunken post-football evening that ended with knives (not on me and certainly not by me, not ever by me; but if you put yourself in those situations …). So Blackpool and I have history. I even tried and failed to get Oscar and his sister to come on a Blackpool holiday with me this year. For some reason, they preferred Croatia.

Today, Blackpool is like bumping into a once-glamorous old flame who's sunk into addiction. It's the most deprived area in the UK. One in 45 children are in care, they attacked JD Sports during the Far-Right Riots and it has the lowest life expectancy in the land (73 for men against a national average of 79), but it's top of the tables for alcohol-related deaths and mental health issues.

After the fish and chips and mushy peas and bread and tea, we park nearer to the ground in a derelict alley. Oscar swears he sees a guy on a bicycle cycle up and look through our car windows seconds after we leave, and we amble around town and along the seafront, shuddering in the wind. It's more dystopian than I remember. The smell of what Oscar calls 'weed' is overpowering, one of the piers is closed and the few shops that are open on the promenade are doing no business. On the doorstep of one of the closed shops a broken couple huddle in a wet sleeping bag. 'How does anyone get like this?' asks Oscar. I don't have an answer for him.

It's our only trip to the coast this season and I'd wanted us to touch the North Sea as a kind of anointing, but the beach is chained off, the waves are towering, the signs say NO ACCESS and I don't fancy tempting our fates.

Oscar is cowed by the whole experience, especially after he's researched the house prices. 'I will never live here,' he declares. I still love Blackpool, but ...

We walk over waste ground to Bloomfield Road in silence, me haunted, him shocked. I've always liked the ground (turns out I've always liked every ground we go to), even when they placed the press box as a buffer zone between opposing sets of supporters in Blackpool's Premier League season – it's still there, but now there are no home fans in the other half of the East Stand. The ground's shabby – they do a programme so lots to be forgiven – but weirdly there are precisely six padded seats in our section. We bag one each; two away games, two padded seats. Oh yes. We are princes.

The wind makes things tricky on the pitch and, while the deluge that soaks me and Oscar is hours away, there has already been rain. Yet Blackpool still water the pitch. Encouragingly, Revs has picked the same starters and substitutes as the Stockport game and Oscar wants to change his prediction to 0-2.

Blackpool start well and Murphy Cooper saves smartly from the excellent Albie Morgan, but they're more Bernard than Stanley Matthews. Accidentally assisted by Blackpool's shaky custodian, Everton loanee Harry Tyrer, whose meal of choice is ham and cheese omelette with beans, Boro look fairly sharp up front and solid at the back. Pidge is magnificent and Luther's not far behind. The Boro fans are cheery – there are even two Father Christmases amongst us – and we're next to a couple of older guys whose confusing sweary anger is leavened by their flashing woolly hats. I have a chat with one of them about Harvey White's insistence on passing backwards rather than forwards.

As he always is, Oscar is absorbed by the game and is convulsed with laughter when Morgan blasts well wide, slumps to his knees, puts his head in his hands and thumps the ground. 'If I die before you, that's how I want you to behave at my funeral,' he chuckles. I probably would too, but without the irony he's taken as a given.

In the second half, Cooper makes a truly marvellous flying save from substitute Jordan Rhodes's fierce header, and in the last seconds of the seven added minutes the excellent Jordan Roberts is trampled on by Odeluga Offiah (Martin's nephew), which afterwards Revs will say was an 'absolute stonewall penalty'. He's right, although anyone who puts the word 'stonewall' before the word 'penalty' should be subject to Iran-level sanctions. Oscar jumps up and down in frustration and screams 'wanker' at referee Martin Woods. I would stop him, but I'm doing the same thing. As I chant, I pause: this is the moment I must accept defeat in the swearing war with Oscar. Fuck.

That said, it's a hugely enjoyable 0-0, although Louis Thompson and Dan Kemp (who trained just once in the week) are forced off. Boro just about deserved three points – or even their first-ever goal in this particular stadium – but a draw at Blackpool is just fine and it's now five undefeated in League One. There's much to be optimistic about right now. Most of the 183 travellers rush to the front and the team come over to clap us, Revs joins them and the love and mutual appreciation is strong. 'Revs is growing on me,' admits Oscar.

We don't talk much after our subsequent soaking but, after we find the unscathed car, even Oscar is impressed by the Illuminations, I have a reverie, the roads south are clear and we've had yet another ball.

Glad you came Oscar?

'Absolutely. One hundred per cent. And it was a penalty, wasn't it?'

26 December 2024
Stevenage 0 Wycombe Wanderers 3

My prediction: 2-1
His prediction: 3-1

'Season-defining.' That's my phrase before today's game and I couldn't express it more pompously if I tried. Oscar shrugs. He's had a fine Christmas, thanks for asking. He received the present he wanted: 'A robe, or as you probably call it, a dressing gown.' He's disappointed to discover his thin white calves poke out from underneath the hem. Turns out Little Lord Fauntleroy did actually want a robe after all.

We're in super-high post-Christmas moods. Boro's five undefeated could become six and a springboard for the play-offs. Toppled from the top of League One by Birmingham's midweek victory at Crawley, Wycombe are tough, though; they haven't lost a league game since August and they won 11 on the trot in October and November. That said, they're only a slightly bigger club than Boro.

Pre-match is brilliant and our spirits soar even further. Boro Bear is his old self in the wake of the Stockport imposter and it's peak Drackers. First, he and Boro Bear go over to some of the 875 Wycombe fans and get a kid to read their team out. Rather than just holler the names, the kid sings the individual player chants. Even Oscar smiles in benevolence.

Then, Drackers and Boro Bear bound into the East Terrace and pressgang individual Boro fans to read out individual player names. They don't come close enough to us alas: 'I'd have said "Tyreece Simpson goal machine",' chuckles Oscar, but it's the most life-enhancing pre-match atmosphere in a while.

Mildly ominously (Stephen King tells writers to avoid adverbs, but Stephen King has never swaggeringly anticipated a Boro game), Murphy Cooper isn't in the squad. He's 'ill', apparently, so Taye starts. Louis Thompson hasn't recovered from his Blackpool injury, so he's out and Elliott List is demoted to the bench. Before a ball is kicked, there's a 'Revell again' chant. 'I've got a really good feeling about this one,' smiles Oscar. Me too. Olé olé. Game on!

We're idiots. We're morons. We're fools. Revs had let the players off Christmas Day training – I don't know, but I'd wager Matt Bloomfield had his Wycombe team in – and after seven troubling minutes, Pidge of all people messes up a Dan Phillips pass. Ipswich loanee Cameron Humphreys nips in and finds Richard Kone, who slots past out-of-position Taye.

The atmosphere deflates there and then. Before half-time, it's two when Taye taps a pass out to Kone, who lobs it over him and into goal. Oscar's head is in his hands. His Boro top is in the wash again.

Pidge will have his worst game for some time – these things happen and now's the moment to show him love, so nobody even thinks of jeering – but he's annihilated by Kone, who's stronger, quicker, smarter, craftier and more skilful. If Pidge wins a duel, I don't see it.

Kone's quite something. He came to the UK as part of the Ivory Coast Homeless World Cup team, ostracised by his family 'because I am homosexual'. Sexuality being a broad church, he seems to have a girlfriend and daughter now. I'd love to see an openly gay Boro player; they'd surely be cherished. And that player could have been Richard Kone. Last January, while Boro were recruiting Kane Hemmings and Vadaine Oliver, Wycombe picked up Kone from Athletic Newham in the Essex (i.e. closer to Stevenage than Wycombe) Senior League for a packet of felt tips and a salted caramel Cornetto. Kone won't be at Wycombe long.

For a fleeting moment, it seems there may be a post-Christmas miracle when one substitute Simpson hits the bar and another, Listy, accidentally clears Dan Kemp's shot off the line. But Boro are outclassed in every department and Franco Ravizzoli is yet another goalkeeper I can't evaluate because he had nothing to do.

Unlike the driver of their far-from-swish Motts coach (they've used the Aylesbury firm for over 25 years, but the double-decker they used to navigate the M40 seems to be no more), Wycombe barely need to exit second gear. For Boro, worse becomes worser when Taye fails to come for a cross. Big Beryly Lubala leaps above little Dan Phillips and heads in. There's a victory most Pyrrhic at the end when Pidge – who else today? – clumsily fells Luke Leahy in the box. Wycombe allow Kone to take the hat-trick-securing penalty. It's hard and low, but Taye saves brilliantly. The East Terrace barely raises a cheer.

At the whistle, Wycombe full-back Daniel Harvie faces us, grins and thrusts his arms into the air – nobody has the will to get too upset and I'm always impressed by people who love their jobs – as Revs dashes away on the whistle, although later he will cite 'catastrophic errors' and being 'outplayed and outfought' against a better team as mitigation. Led by the admirable Dan Butler, the players slope over and, do you know what, the few of us who remain don't have the heart to abuse them. All Boro players have had stinkers and other than a familiar weary chant of 'we're fucking shit', we've mutely accepted it. We clap back dispiritedly and stumble off into the mist.

Season-defining? Wish I hadn't thought it before the game, but I hope I'm wrong again. As we head to the car for a journey home in crushed silence ('Nothing to say is there?' laments Oscar again; correctly again) we mingle with the Wycombe fans. In front of us there's a little boy, six or seven maybe, in a Wanderers bobble hat. He's grinning from ear to ear, so happy he can't contain himself or hold his dad's outstretched hand. Instead, he's skipping – literally skipping – with delight, so full of energy and joy that he runs up and down the grass slopes on the way to the car park.

'I used to be like that after Boro games,' sighs Oscar. 'I wish I was him.'

29 December 2024
Stevenage 3 Bristol Rovers 0

My prediction: 2-0
His prediction: 1-0

We're subdued. We're late again, which makes me stressed, if not Oscar, for whom time remains an abstract concept. His Boro shirt is out of the wash, and if that sounds like barrel-scraping for something positive to say, yes it is. On the speed-limit-challenging way to the Lamex, we mull over who Revs might drop after the Boxing Day debacle. We're in broad agreement: nobody would sacrifice Pidge after one nightmare (astonishingly Wycombe drop Richard Kone for their trip to Charlton; he comes on and scores, but they're already two down and will lose), but Taye must go, alas, assuming whatever Murphy Cooper's 'illness' is has cleared up. Weather vane record signing Jake Young, Harvey White and Reidy too. And we'd both like to see Ken Aboh start to inject pace and oomph.

We're not far off. Taye is dropped, as are White and Young, but Jamie Reid stays. There's not even a place on the bench for Aboh – oh – but, hallelujah, there is one for Dan 'Sweens' Sweeney for the first time since Lincoln in August.

If Boxing Day pre-match was full of life-affirming joy, today the Lamex is desolate. The crowd is sparse, the PA somehow more muffled than usual and even Drackers sounds tired. There's no Afghan hound-style bounding into the East Terrace from him and Boro Bear (who does lighten the mood by trying and failing to prise someone's phone out of their hands) today. Tellingly, though, there is a brief Murphy Cooper chant.

Bristol Rovers are ideal opponents: in freefall with just one win since October and a crackpot, brand-new managerial appointment in Iñigo Calderón, plucked from helming Brighton's under-18s. Whether he has seen a League One game since playing in one for Brighton in

2011 is a matter of speculation, but he has certainly never managed anyone anywhere before.

It's a different Boro today. They're patient and firm. As Wycombe were on Boxing Day, Boro are assisted by extremely poor opposition, but the failures of Thursday are the successes of Sunday. Pidge is imperious again, Luther is turbo-charged, Robbo Roberts fights for everything and Reidy Reid always has the beating of Clinton Mola, who clearly isn't related to the Spanish general Emilio Mola, whose, ahem, accidental death in 1937 was so handy for Francisco Franco.

Dan Butler is accidentally taken out by Murphy Cooper – lesson: never get in Murphy Cooper's way – and he staggers to the changing room and then to hospital in a daze, but Boro are well on top. The first goal is a joy. Dan Phillips finds the returning Louis Thompson, who in turn picks out the overlapping Luther. Luther takes one touch to steady himself and another to cross deep, where Listy – more alert than his marker Joel Senior – sends a fabulous diving header flying past nervy Josh Griffiths.

The goal also teaches us another lesson. Hard but fair, Pidge had got the better of Promise Omochere, who elected to stay down and who would prove to be far from injured. The referee and Boro rightly played on, but Rovers were so distracted that they give Boro free rein to make ground and score. Play to the whistle: the most basic football lesson of all.

Just as the East Terrace was silent on Boxing Day, it's now in full voice. The two drummers – too soon to cite The Glitter Band at this point? – drum their drummiest and there's even a delightfully self-deprecating '1-0 in the library' chant. Fickleness? No, things have changed.

'There is,' states Oscar between chants, 'no chance we're going to lose.'

He's right. Just after the restart, as if desperate to emulate Northampton's Tom Eaves, Jamie Lindsay self-immolates with a spectacular triple whammy of idiocy. 1: already booked, he foolishly hacks down Louis Thompson. Cheerio Jamie. 2: the free kick he concedes is in a dangerous position. 3: Dan Kemp dinks it in. James Wilson lazily heads it on. Butler's replacement Lewis Freestone nods it back and the unchaperoned Robbo guides in his first goal since – gulp – September.

Some of the 541 travellers head west out of the ground and west again for 140 grim miles, soon to be followed by the team in their rather cramped KB of Stonehouse coach. As in so many other aspects of Bristol football, City always had the best bus, through 38 years with the now defunct Peter Carol (as in married couple Peter and Carol Collis, who cannily advertised in the Bristol Rovers programme while they drove Bristol City) and lately Turners, complete with missile-attracting Bristol City livery.

That's it for the game really, but the team who can't score goals (it's Boro's second-ever lowest at this stage of the season) score another when Louis Thompson sets man of the match Robbo free to drive forwards down the right and unselfishly cross low for Reidy to slot home his 50th Boro goal. The final game of 2024 has produced the same scoreline and the same scorers as the final game of 2023.

There's one last pot of joy. With the game long secure, Sweens replaces Nathan Thompson. The Sweens chant (it's an appositely violent one) gets a lusty airing and when he shakes hands with Pidge it's a beautiful moment.

Afterwards, there's love to spare. Unlike Boxing Day, there's nothing to be embarrassed about. The players look buoyant and when Revs comes to do his fist-pumping we all join in and holler the 'Revell again' chant. Everything is different to Boxing Day and maybe, just maybe, this was the season-defining game after all.

He's not a tot any more, so Oscar doesn't dance like the little Wycombe fella on Boxing Day but, nevertheless, his heart is dancing as we bounce to the car park. And, as all football fans do, he's getting forgetful. 'It's a long time since we went home in complete happiness, isn't it, Dad?' I know what he means, though, I really do.

Pie Chart

1. Northampton Town
2. Peterborough United
3. Norwich City
4. Burton Albion
5. Mansfield Town
6. Wigan Athletic
7. Stevenage
8. Exeter City
9. Blackpool
10. Huddersfield Town
11. Rotherham United

January – Includes the Best Night of Our Lives

1 January 2025
Northampton Town 0 Stevenage 0

My prediction: 1-2
His prediction: 0-2

I spent New Year's Eve bingeing *Veep* with Oscar's sister and mother, so it was perfect and nostalgic. Oscar and his chum went to a friend's house. The friend's father brought him back at 2am. Another end-of-our-days sign. The friend was a girl, but Oscar is not going to elaborate. He's tired and not really up for Northampton, but who could be?

The rain – nasty, heavy stuff – stops as we exit the M1 and for the first time at Sixfields, I find a free parking spot, an oasis of triumph in a desert of defeats. Last season opened with a trip here. The electric atmosphere, the scrumptious pie and a Pidge winner aligned to provide a memorable afternoon.

Things are different today. We wander around their cramped club shop (a 'Snuggle Hoodie' for just £30 anyone? Thought not), but the stewards on the gates are unpleasant and feral. They are cowardly too, and when we enter they take out whatever is making them angry on the schoolboy rather than the adult. Until now, League One club stewards have invariably been sweet and smiley. Hats off to Northampton for going against the grain.

Unprompted, Oscar bids a non-sarcastic 'afternoon' to the pig-ignorant first steward, who just glares at him. Though most clubs, including Boro, don't frisk children, Oscar is prodded around like it's a Five Families summit and he yelps in pain. When he's through the unnecessary cordon, he's yanked back by his hood so these louts can rifle through that hood. I did ponder this before, but doesn't anyone train stewards any more? Probably not. Budgets, I guess.

The kiosk where we bought last year's pies is closed. At the one that is open, we both plump for a humble Pukka. According to Oscar, it's the best Pukka of the season. We go to the back row so nobody's behind us, but even my stumpy legs are too long, while Oscar is forced to go side-saddle like Queen Maxima of the Netherlands. Sixfields is only 31 years old, but it's looking tired, old, unloved and the PA is broadcast through a duvet. Oscar was right, it's a nice Pukka though, and they do the best programme of the division. It asks squad player Ali Koiki what's the first thing he would do after winning the Lottery: 'Leave the country.' Love you, Ali.

Northampton are a bigger club than Boro, but they're an example of how things can go awry without a steady Phil Wallace-style hand on the financial tiller. They're over £7m in debt and on our right the renovated East Stand is nearly ready. It's been a painfully slow construction since planning permission was granted in 2012 and what was initially projected as a community hub with shops, offices and a hotel, partly funded by a £10m council loan, will now be just a few corporate boxes, against a backdrop of court cases, bankruptcies, home seizures and six-figure fines, but not much actual building.

Dispiritingly, Boro haven't come close to selling out their allocation for this near-derby. Last season there were 961 of us and we had to go on the side as urchins had purloined our seats, but Boro's self-policing away policy is 'sit anywhere', so we didn't mind. On this Bank Holiday, there are just 585. New regime apathy? Dank weather? I don't know, but there's hardly any chanting until the (ignored) demands for a second substitution, perhaps involving the introduction of former Northampton striker, Tyreece Simpson. It's as if a plug has been pulled.

For Northampton, it's the first home game of the Kevin Nolan regime, but their fans are somnambulant too, and when Nolan picks up an early yellow card, it's as if he's trying to rouse fans and team from their collective slumber

Worryingly, Dan Butler is still in hospital, so centre-half Lewis Freestone – rather than full-back Kane Smith – steps up at left-back. None of this matters. It's a horrible game, free of chances, free of interest and free of creativity. Boro's sole strategy is to pass backwards to Pidge, who hits forwards diagonal after forwards diagonal, invariably finding touch, like the world's most attritional rugby player.

We do say hello to Northampton's Tom Eaves, who gifted us the game at the Lamex. He's scored just once since that day's dismissal and, like everyone else, never looks like adding to his total here. He's still a grappler, so the Boro fans abuse him, but mildly. Nothing is getting anyone going and Oscar loses his bottle of Diet Coke.

'It's the longest half ever,' sighs a deflated Oscar of the first period, even before seven minutes are added after

Northampton's Jon Guthrie is stretchered off. Murphy Cooper makes a fine stop from Mitch Pinnock and the contest is encapsulated by a Freestone free kick on the halfway line, which he launches square to the other side of the pitch, where no player lurks. The laughter is quite loud. I spend the second half gazing longingly at the Wagamama on the hill. I don't even like Wagamama.

Afterwards, there's some guilty applause from the players, but love's in short supply here. Revs makes little sense when Boro put up his post-match comments on Facebook, half-heartedly defending his refusal to inject new blood ('sometimes it's very difficult to come on') and repeating yet again that 'we have to do better going forwards'. We know this, Revs.

5 January 2025
Lincoln City 0 Stevenage 0

My prediction: 1-2
His prediction: 0-2

We have a new chant. To the tune of 'Revell again, olé olé', it's '0-0 again, olé olé'. How we laugh at ourselves. What wags we are. For the record, today will be the second blank in four days, the sixth of the season and now no League One club has scored fewer goals. But, swings and roundabouts, everyone bar Huddersfield, Birmingham and Wrexham have conceded more.

There's snow a-comin', but not on the A1, although Oscar's mother insists we pack a duvet. We oblige. We're still too numbed by New Year's Day, the most soporific match of the season, to argue. Lincoln will be better. We know this.

I like Lincoln a lot. We amble down the High Street. It's almost franchise free. There is Couling, a sewing machine shop (a machine could be yours for a reduced £149), Brickz Kingdom, which seems to sell only Lego, and a cute tearoom amongst the vape shops and fast food shacks. Like Lincoln itself, it's endearing and a little bit eccentric.

On the way to Sincil Bank (I've never worked out what a Sincil is and suspect I never will, although it's been rechristened the LNER Stadium for money), we pass tiny narrow houses in tiny narrow streets ('How do they turn their cars around?' asks practical Oscar), a police notice explaining there's been a recent arson attack and a tiny narrow river. Sixfields it ain't.

There are two club shops, one a narrow (what is it about Lincoln and narrow?) Portakabin, the other a much more salubrious space where a Lincoln City golf towel has been 'reduced' from £11.99 to, um, £17. They don't do a programme (bastards) but, in an idea Boro won't countenance, they've printed an 'enhanced' team sheet, which features a news update and an explanation of the team picked by head coach Michael Skubala ('we need to be ready for a crash, bang, wallop kind of match') for 50p.

And there are food outlets, albeit just outside the turnstiles. We are warned off the in-ground pies and we ponder a Yorkshire pudding wrap, but since Oscar has now pledged to go local, we both alight upon a Lincolnshire sausage in a roll with a bed of mashed onion sold by a pretty woman from Harpenden. The roll falls apart under the weight of it all, but it's £7 of joy. 'Not as unique as I thought it would be,' decides Oscar, whose baggy blue Christmas jeans are making their public debut.

The ground befits its city. It's not narrow, but it is eccentric. Oscar notes there are five stands and there are wooden, hotel-style doors to the toilets where the only graffiti is by New Year's Day visitors and victors Rotherham. You can see the cathedral on the hill, where the future Edward II was invested as the first English Prince of Wales in 1301, although not from the half of an end we've been allocated.

There are only 312 of us, but with the Lincoln fans above us to our right in full voice, we're back to making noise, after the silence of Sixfields.

Revs has revised the team. Lewis Freestone is apparently injured (precisely the mystery a Boro-enhanced team sheet could explain) so full-back Kane Smith gets to play at full-back. Yay. Reidy, Listy and the Dans Kemp and Phillips are benched in favour of Harvey White, goal machine Simpson, Jake Young and Nick Freeman, who will benefit from playing a more advanced role than of late. Louis Appéré is on the bench and Charlie Goode travelled, although the actual squad headcount hasn't been boosted, since Norwich have recalled Ken Aboh, presumably because Revs didn't fancy him, although Oscar and I certainly did. More surprisingly, young Ryan Doherty and Louie Henry have been loaned to Potters Bar, managed by Boro's all-time record appearance holder Ronnie Henry, grandson of Spurs double-winner Ron Henry. I'm with Revs's changes today, though, he'll be delighted to know. Let's shake things up. And shake things up Boro do.

Moments before kick-off, right in front of us, Lincoln goalkeeper George Wickens has fist-pumped the ballboys behind the goal, before engaging them in conversation, explaining exactly what he wants them to do. Very impressive, George Wickens.

JANUARY – INCLUDES THE BEST NIGHT OF OUR LIVES

Revs will later suggest that Boro did everything but score and he's only slightly delusional. The result matches New Year's Day, but it's a different game entirely. Boro are terrific, making in-game changes, playing through the middle to Simpson, who doesn't look like scoring, but does give the defence a torrid physical time. 'When Simpson scores we're on the pitch' is sung with affection and irony these days.

Wickens has other qualities too, athletically tipping over a Pidge header, but he's beaten by Louis Thompson's drive, so close to us that we hear it cannon off the post. Oscar's barking like a dog: 'We've got this, Dad, we've got this.' We haven't though. Lincoln are poor, but ominously, in first-half added time, Murphy Cooper is finally called upon, flinging himself across goal to foil Conor McGrandles's howitzer.

Alliances bloom. Jake Young and right-footed Kane Smith down the left, Robbo and Nick Freeman down the right. From a footballistic point of view, Neil Banfield, in the stand rather than the dugout, must have been delighted.

The second half is more balanced. Boro are still on top, but late on Lincoln have the best chance of the game when the unmarked Jovon Makama blasts over from inside the six-yard box. To Oscar's delight, Makama is hooked before play restarts. 'Cheerio, cheerio, cheerio,' he sings.

On the whistle, the players and Revs come over. No inappropriate fist-pumps from Revs but, after the bleak hollowness of Sixfields, love blooms once more. Snow is coming, apparently, so we hurry back. We don't see a flake.

At 1am, I'm still up, watching *Match of the Day* (I know, I know ...) when Oscar appears fully dressed.

'Come outside, Dad, come outside.' I come outside. Our road is deserted, but it's covered in a thick coat of snow. The streetlights and the silence make everything more wondrous still. He does what 14-year-old boys the world over do and throws a snowball at me. With Murphy Cooper-style reactions, I dodge it. 'That was very Aaron Pressley of me,' he winces, as I hit his turned back with one of my own. 'I'm Tyreece Simpson now. He's not allowed to miss.' I stand still. The ball hits me in the chest. 'And Simpson scores! Just as he will on Saturday because nobody can go against what the snowball predicts.' We shuffle back indoors, the snow crisp under our feet. Like a Poundland Bon Jovi, we're halfway there. Oh oh.

0-0. Again. O-bloody-lé. O-bloody-lé.

18 January 2025
Stevenage 1 Wigan Athletic 2

My prediction: 4-1
His prediction: 1-0

Two games should have taken place since Lincoln, but the freeze postponed both Boro's hosting of Burton and Leyton Orient's FA Cup tie with Derby Couty. The latter's rearrangement meant Boro's Vertu Cup (unless it's changed its name again) trip to East London was deferred. Sorry, I'm boring myself here.

In other news, Ben Thompson's loan to Bromley has been made permanent and Aaron Pressley has been offloaded, albeit temporarily. Barrow are the lucky recipients, although their manager, Stephen Clemence, will be sacked after Pressley's non-scoring debut at

Swindon. Press will miss a penalty and be dropped without scoring before January has passed.

My instinct had firmly told me Boro would reach the third round and be drawn with Brentford, the club I used to manage, in the FA Cup third round. As a rule of thumb, my instinct is wrong about everything – how does instinct work for normal people? Do you just picture things and they happen? Or is there a voice in your head saying 'do that'? – so obviously it was wrong here.

I had planned to explain how I was recruited as Brentford manager in 2005. After a less than productive training session at their Jersey Road training ground, my predecessor (and, as it turns out, successor) Martin Allen flung a training bib at me and said, 'I resign. You're the manager. Talk to them.' Now, from a legal point of view – and I'm sure I'm right here – that constitutes a formal job offer, not least because football managers are legally obliged to appoint their successors. I know I should have discussed terms, made plans to renovate my office and acceded to the photoshoot with a scarf, but such was my eagerness and with a trip to Port Vale looming, I leapt in and gave my first team talk in Churchillian terms. That's Churchill the insurance-flogging dog, rather than the Churchill who would have had Michael Turner and Sam Sodje fighting them on the beaches of Ealing. Isaiah Rankin may have sniggered, the rest looked as baffled and as contemptuous as Hibs (or was it Hearts?) players did when Roman Roy addressed them in *Succession*: 'Go hard, go fast, go ya lovely bastards.'

'See you in Burslem, guys,' I may have trilled, as my rallying parting shot. Bafflingly, they ushered me out of Jersey Road there and then. They never did call with the bus's departure place and time. Martin Allen still seemed to think he was manager, as, in fact, did the rest of the football world. I didn't sue; I'm a bigger man than that, but what really rankles isn't merely the absence of my framed photograph at the Gtech, the subsequent absence of opportunities to do match punditry alongside Billy Reeves or the absence of invitations to ex-staff reunions, which would offer the opportunity to discuss Paul Priddy and Gordon Sweetzer with Phil Holder and Eddie May, but that according to every football history book, it never happened. And because Boro didn't make the third round, I can't even tell that tale here.

'You're lying aren't you, Dad?' shrugs Oscar as we speed to the Lamex, late again because he's been faffing with his contact lenses. For the record, which doesn't include me, without my hand upon the tiller, Brentford lost at Port Vale.

It's cold, but it's still. We're both really up for this one, both confident, both wondering if the push for the play-offs begins this afternoon against a team who looked pretty feeble at their place. I'm buoyed by Secret Affair's 'Time for Action' on the still-too-quiet PA, but Oscar had already been more buoyed still by the never-to-be-explained arrival of a Red Bull Mini Cooper on the grass outside the Lamex, which he somehow knows is one of just 500 in the world. The student marketeers are too lazy to actually hand out their product. Instead, they leave some Red Bull cans next to the Mini. We both take one, I drop and dent mine instantly, but Oscar smuggles both cans past turnstile security. I go reckless with my prediction and we're stood next to Mrs Chatty, who's as excited as we are. Dan Butler is still injured – hope he's okay, it's been a while now – and Tyreece Simpson doesn't feature at all. He's injured himself, apparently, although I wouldn't be surprised if that means he's being loaned out.

It certainly doesn't go wrong in the first half. Wigan goalkeeper 'Super' Sam Tickle doesn't look very super at all, but he saves well at Reidy's feet after a lackadaisical back pass, and he bats aside Kane Smith's piledriver. Boro, being Boro, don't create many chances, but they're infinitely superior to an overly physical yet lacklustre Wigan, whose clumsy new loanee Will Goodwin had been linked with Boro. Bullet dodged there, I reckon.

Inevitably, it does go wrong after the restart. Louis Thompson gives a cheap free kick away and is booked. Jensen Weir whips it in low and hard. Half-time substitute Dale Taylor loses his man and guides it in. Pidge is furious and for the first time this season there are real post-goal arguments. Pidge seems to think Dan Kemp lost Taylor. I couldn't see clearly enough, but caring is a good sign, I reckon. Tough love is still love.

Hitherto supportive, the East Terrace turns a little. Mrs Chatty gets angry at the swearing and the negative chants. 'I've got a right to an opinion,' mutters the guy behind us. I agree with everyone. Oscar looks sick, but I'm not too concerned. 'We'll get this back,' I tell him, a true believer today.

It does get better. Louis Appéré appears for the first time since Burton away, chosen ahead of Jake Young. Better still, Wigan are down to ten men when Weir is given a straight red for brainlessly chopping down Louis Thompson. The 83rd-minute equaliser is lovely. Robbo Roberts zips down the right and crosses deep for substitute Dan Sweeney to cushion a header into the path of Dan Kemp, who gives 'Super' Sam Tickle no chance. Sneaky 'Super' Sam Tickle immediately tumbles to the ground and is treated for some time, coincidentally allowing Wigan's outfield players to receive instructions. 'That's a lot of added time,' notes a delighted Oscar. 'We've got this, Dad, we've got this.'

He's right on one count. 'Super' Sam Tickle's antics mean there are eight added minutes, to the lustily expressed delight of the East Terrace. We have, indeed, got this. Except we haven't. After three of those eight minutes, Wigan break and Taylor finds himself through on goal. Louis Thompson takes one for the team and commits the foul on the edge of the area. His second yellow card means he's the first Boro player to be dismissed this season.

'They're not going to score are they, Dad?' asks Oscar. They are. Thelo Aasgaard curls it – wonderfully curls it, it has to be said – around the wall and beyond Murphy Cooper. Wigan have finagled the points and the 446 travelling supporters go as bonkers as we'd have done. The team escape on their long and plush Eavesway coach – local and used for decades following the even more local Hursts, whose Mr Malcolm Hurst personally designed the Wigan Athletic vehicle – having triumphed over Boro for the first time. Bastards, bastards, bastards.

Oscar is devastated. 'Worst since Peterborough,' he mutters. 'How could that happen? Again.'

This time, we don't journey home in defeated silence. Revs will say it was a game Boro should never have drawn, let alone lost. He's right, but he also says something he's hinted at before: that what Boro do in training isn't carried through in games. 'And whose fault is that?' Oscar asks, almost tearful. 'I love Revs, I always have,' he says. 'And our club is better with him around. But while I accept there's no reason to sack him at the moment, I just don't think he's the right man for this job.' Love moves in bet-hedging ways.

The following day, after an extended Christmas break and a slew of postponements, Broxbourne Borough Under-15s return to action in a cup game. Like Boro, the boys face physically demanding opponents. Oscar lets one in when – unlike the referee – he believes the ball has gone out and doesn't play to the whistle. Then he stumbles to concede a second. Yet with doughty Broxbourne leading in added time, he makes what may be his save of the season. Victory is theirs. No late heartache here, and it all goes off in the car park afterwards when a disgruntled opponent – who'd been caught crying on the pitch – has to be restrained from continuing the physical side of the conflict with Bolton Sam, who Oscar calls 'my centre-half'. 'That was fun,' he chuckles, when we're safe in the car. 'Unlike yesterday.'

21 January 2025
Leyton Orient 0 Stevenage 1 –
Vertu Trophy

My prediction: 1-1
His prediction: 1-2

I've always thought Neil Diamond's Robbie Robertson-produced 'Beautiful Noise' was a subjective thesis. I should have asked him when we met beneath a badly drawn mural of, er, Neil Diamond. We enjoyed high-quality cigars and hand-crafted chocolates. Actually, that last part isn't true. He enjoyed high-quality cigars and hand-crafted chocolates, but chose not to share them. Even so, I now know what he meant, since I have now heard the most beautiful noise audible to human beings.

It comes in the tenth (tenth!) minute of second-half added time tonight. Leyton Orient are desperately trying to claw their way to fortuitous penalties when, right in front of us, their Sonny Perkins lays the ball into the path of Jordan Brown in the penalty area D. Brown shoots first time. Time stands still in the Vertu Cup silence. Boro goalkeeper Taye Ashby-Hammond doesn't move. The ball sails beyond Taye towards the top corner and hits the bar. The sound of the clang, very much how you'd imagine, but more beautiful, immeasurably more beautiful, echoes around the ground. Already stood, Oscar leaps into the night stillness as if Boro have scored, as do those around us. Me? I can't help but laugh long and loudly. It is – again, I accept the implications and how they're not good – another one of the great moments of my life. When the referee finally blows for time, Oscar is still jumping and I'm still laughing. Love? Too right it is.

This ultimately glorious evening began as omnishambles. The shambles that is the EFL Trophy still doesn't really know what it's called (there will be electronic perimeter advertising, which gives no clues as to what a Vertu might be). The shambles that is Leyton Orient have sold away tickets for a part of the ground they've closed. And we're a shambles because we're on the platform of Woodford underground station before we realise we've left the tickets we will be later forced to exchange in the car. 'Both our faults, Dad,' he insists. It's his fault.

We're in a sort of mourning too. As we suspected, Boro's claims that Tyreece Simpson was injured were spurious. On the day Simpson's FotMob rating finds he's in the bottom one per cent of European strikers at a similar level for shots taken, he's journeyed up the A12 to Colchester United for the rest of the season. He'll play at Harrogate tonight. We send him thoughts-and-prayers-style cuddles. He doesn't score.

Oscar is now up for the Vertu. I remind him I said we'd win it, but I don't confess that I only said this to maintain his interest. In the last round, Burton was an evening of unmitigated glory, but Orient went through seven December games without conceding, haven't lost in ten and, gnash those teeth in jealousy, Manchester City will arrive next month in the FA Cup. Since the quarter-final draw has already been made, whoever triumphs tonight will host Birmingham City some time next month.

Brisbane Road is now the Gaughan Group Stadium, but such is the lure of the Vertu that tonight they're already selling half-and-half Orient/City scarves, the handful of Boro fans – if you happen to have 71 fingers – are huddled in the corner of the main stand. There's no programme (bastards) but, hurrah, no queue at the food outlet. There is, though, food choice in excelsis. Oh my. Oscar's keenness to sample local delicacies leads us both to pie (lovely crispy crust, not quite enough meat) and creamy mash. Later he'll acquire a large tub of popcorn for a very reasonable £2.50. Others devour nachos, the giant hot dogs are proper frankfurters, and my Bovril isn't (too) watered down. It's a local derby, if local derbies had no atmosphere.

Revs rings the changes. Ding, and furthermore, dong, once again. Louis Appéré starts for the first time since Norwich, Sweens for the first time since Lincoln at home, Charlie Goode for the first time since the Exeter horror and Taye has another opportunity for goalkeeping redemption. Still no sign of Dan Butler though; he's been a long time missing for what looked like a minor concussion, although him still being in hospital three days after that injury didn't feel right at all. Turns out it wasn't just concussion; there was some kind of spot (or clot; I don't know, not being medically qualified) on the brain. 'Revs knows this cup is the best way for him to keep his job,' argues Oscar, still stung by Wigan. The Revs Out faction don't travel to Vertu away games, so Revs gets the free pass he needs.

And we finally get to see Sean Clare again. As if to show that love transcends all boundaries (hi Hallmark cards, I'm available for work), we love him. An opposition player. We love him tonight especially, for not only is he Orient's captain, but he has his hair in pigtails, like Snoop Dogg once did. We love him because when he came to the Lamex with Charlton for a 2022 Carabao Cup tie, he scored Charlton's first penalty in the shoot-out and, when Charlton won it, he did a little Pac-Man style jig, grinned like someone who loved winning more than anything and waved at us before celebrating with his team-mates. We chanted abuse back at him but, secretly, Oscar and I fell in love with him. We haven't seen him since. Hi Sean. We both hope you're well.

Even before the bar-hitting thwack, Boro are terrific, aided by an Orient who play like Boro at their worst – ponderous build-up, reluctance to press forwards, fear of shooting – with an added layer of playing out from the back, but badly. A smarter club than Orient would have offered Manchester City ticket guarantees to those who turned up tonight. In that case, they certainly wouldn't have had to close two sides of the ground.

JANUARY – INCLUDES THE BEST NIGHT OF OUR LIVES

Oscar is disappointed there's no cat-calling of Orient head coach Richie 'cream rises to the top' Wellens. 'I bet he votes Reform,' Oscar speculates, with absolutely no evidence to back up this assertion. He mocks Wellens's white trainers, but he's delighted to hear Wellens afterwards blaming his fringe players for not seizing the moment.

Orient goalkeeper Josh Keeley saves brilliantly from Appéré and a slightly revitalised Jake Young, but Boro win it when Harvey White's vicious corner (his set pieces are a malevolent delight sometimes) cannons in off the unlucky Brandon Cooper. Or, as the graceless Orient website had it: 'a corner hit an unfortunate man in red and bounced into the net'.

There was much to savour. Taye made splendid saves of his own and looked like the confident, super-efficient Taye of yore, Nick Freeman always seems better in a more advanced role, Dan Kemp was everywhere, while Sweens and Goode were defensive solidity itself. I hate to say this, Quinn the Eskimo and everything, but right now Boro look better without Jamie Reid. Can I dream for a heady moment? Birmingham, then a semi, then Wembley, then Pidge holding a cup. I love the Vertu Trophy. Even Oscar's falling. 'We can win this can't we, Dad?'

Afterwards, we rush to the touchline to clap the players off as the Orient fans sneak away around us. A kindly looking, elderly man and his wife shuffle towards us, presumably to offer sporting congratulations, as benign old folk so often do. 'You're a bunch of fucking wankers,' he hisses. My evening, already marvellous, is made. Oscar didn't catch it, so I tell him, loudly. He points at the pensioner and laughs at him, as do the other Boro fans who did hear. His wife (or carer perhaps) smiles and rolls her eyes, for this may well have happened before. As she drags him away, he turns to face us: 'But you are fucking wankers.' I have seen my own future.

There are Boro fist-pumps, led his time by erstwhile Orienteer Dan Kemp. I never knew he could smile so broadly and his grin is almost as broad as Oscar's. Hey Phil Wallace, looks like I was wrong about Dan Kemp. I'm sorry and I couldn't be happier in my sorrow.

Such was the evening's cavalcade of joy that we'd forgotten about Sean Clare. There was nothing for him to jiggle about tonight. Sorry again, but we hope your family are well, Sean.

We skip to Leyton underground where there's an Orient fan on his mobile. 'Awful, we played six in midfield and Sonny Perkins was terrible.' We leave him to his publicly expressed private grief. 'What a night,' trills Oscar. 'What a night.' And who'd have thought that the Vertu Trophy, the runt of everyone's litter, could bring two nights of untrammelled joy?

25 January 2025
Barnsley 0 Stevenage 1

My prediction: 0-1
His prediction: 0-1

On Saturday we're still reliving the Vertu. Oscar's on a high all the way to Barnsley. 'That was the best trip ever. It couldn't get any better.'

Prising him out of bed is getting increasingly fractious. He wants to cut everything fine. I don't. To prevent him working out his own timings, I've stopped putting the route in the satnav the day before away games while he's in the car. I've started lying about departure times, so when we leave 15 minutes after the time I've told him, he thinks he's secured a victory.

We're early into Barnsley, but not early enough to wander around the town centre as I'd hoped. The grim mining town from where the maternal side of my family line hails is an odd place, home to both pride and deference. I tell him about his great-grandfather, who – I think; it's all terribly murky – fought in the First World War, but I know none of the details. He died when I was an infant, but there are photographs. He – my maternal grandfather – was, my father believed, a miner, but a lazy one. Then, I try to tell Oscar of the grandmother who I never met; nor did my father, although she wasn't dead when he squired my mother. It's a treasure trove of hard-to-follow family secrets I don't have the key to. Rather than this, Oscar wants to discuss tracks that have over a billion streams to their name, mostly it seems by The Weeknd. By the time he gets properly curious about his family history, I'll be long gone, unable to answer his own questions. There isn't anywhere to show him anyway.

My match ticket had cost a whopping £26, the programme a similarly whopping £4, but it's a feeble affair (despite the gloating vis-à-vis the women's team: 'We took our foot off the gas … and ran out deserved 16-0 winners') and a pattern is born. There's a club shop (a, ahem, Superstore to give it its official name) full of the usual tat. This matchday it's almost empty. Barnsley FC are big in Barnsley and the club represents the community like nothing else, beyond the contrasting claims of Arthur Scargill, Dickie Bird, Michael Parkinson and Danse Society, but demand for £20 Barnsley FC cufflinks may be limited.

They're not keen on outsiders either. Next to the away turnstiles (turnstile to be more precise; home clubs mostly need just the one for Boro), a docile, bovine steward is restricting entry to a grown man with a child's ticket, although Oscar, who seems to have an adult one, sails in. Inside, it's dank. We're hungry. Oscar goes for a hot dog, which somehow costs £6.50. The packaging promises a sensibly sized Rollover. Instead, buried deep in the heatproof bag, is a cocktail-sized mini hot dog. Do they rip off their own fans like this? Obviously, I don't know, but Oakwell will be less than half full this afternoon. Perhaps the biggest thing in the community isn't really bothered about being a part of their community after all; not when that community can be squeezed for every last penny they can't afford. Oscar is still hungry after his morsel. A £4.50 sausage roll is reasonably sized, but by comparison Greggs is Michelin starred. I play safe with a trusty bog-standard Pukka. It's lovely, although for £5.50 I'd expect shares in Leicester-based Pukka Pies Limited tossed in.

Inside, our day dips further still. The stewards are vicious, volatile and not all of them are displaying accreditation details. The winter sun is bright and we're looking straight into it. This being Boro, there are hundreds of empty seats and some of those seats – at the back and side, far from the home fans – are in the shade. We make for them, as do others. The stewards force us to sit where we're blinded. 'I can't see a thing,' laments Oscar. 'This is the worst place ever.' Worse than Barrow and Gateshead, Oscar? 'Oh absolutely. Maybe not Barrow ...'

More day dips? Oh yes. Inside Oakwell we discover that Nathan Thompson has fled Boro for the siren charms of Milton Keynes, and by the time we'd reached Barnsley he'd already started in MK Dons' lunchtime kick-off against their friends from AFC Wimbledon. He's 34, out of contract in the summer and there was no two-year deal – perhaps not even a one-year deal – on anyone's table. That said, he's been a colossus of late and we'll miss him. Now Boro are down to one Thompson and, since Louis is suspended today, no Thompson will appear for Boro for the first time since Guiseley.

We dig in and so do Boro. Barnsley may be in fifth place, but they are so poor and so disorganised (as they were at the Lamex), I wonder why I yearned for Darrell Clarke to succeed Steve Evans. Seems like I was wrong there. Again. They have a new signing, albeit from Shamrock Rovers. He shares his birthday with Joey Ramone and former Northern Ireland international and future prison guard Hugh Dowd. He's a biomedical science graduate, but Neil Farrugia's major contribution is his attempt to flick the ball over Lewis Freestone. He flicks it into his own face instead.

Robbo goes close early on with a deflected drive Ben Killip does well to tip over, Jake Young does his thing where he skips past a clutch of defenders like Messi and then messes it up with a mess of a shot. By half-time, we're beginning to think there's something more than pelf to be had here. For the second half the sun has set and Boro are kicking towards us.

It begins to happen. Boro break fast down both wings and, unusually, create chance after chance. Reidy fails to make contact with Robbo's incisive low cross by the width of his toe, Robbo spurns a chance of his own and, when Dan Kemp adds to the misses, Oscar pummels my jacket in frustration and I have my head in my hands yet again. 'This cannot be happening,' bellows Oscar, and when the '0-0 again, olé olé' chant resurfaces, it's a lament in the style of Nick Cave's 'The Ship Song'. I admit to Oscar that I've lost hope. 'I haven't,' he says, as six added minutes are announced.

After three of them, Eli King spots the outstanding Luther gambolling down the right. Georgie Gent obligingly stumbles. With one touch, Luther controls, with another he crosses. 'Please, please, please,' wails Oscar. For the second moment this week, time stands still. Scoff all you want, but I'm being literal here; it's a moment of stillness to be preserved forever. The ball sails over dopey keeper Killip. Time readjusts itself *Matrix* fashion and Dan Kemp crashes in from nowhere to head home.

We go wild, insane, crazy, all 195 of us. Oscar howls at the non-existent moon with his customary 'yes yes, yes'. I punch the air in a way I incorrectly believe maintains my dignity. 'Told you, Dad, told you!' shouts Oscar. The humiliations of the day evaporate in that instant.

The players charge towards us, grinning like loons and Barnsley offer no threat as the game winds down. They exit to a cascade of boos, and as Clarke later admits, his team were 'miles off'. Better still, Barnsley's Corey O'Keeffe chooses to respond to our taunts; he exits abused by both sets of fans.

Oscar and I punch each other as we hurtle down to the front to clap the players and shout 'yes' a lot. A 1-0 away victory is rare enough. A 1-0 away victory in added time simply doesn't happen to Boro. It's happened.

Revs joins in and he takes over the fist-pumping. He does it more slowly than usual, but after each he unleashes a mighty, mighty roar and after the third he emits a long, loud lengthy cathartic growl of joy. The love, oh the love.

After noting that we've both got our prediction right for the first (and surely last) time this season, we're still giggling – Oscar has caught my affliction from Leyton Orient – when we reach the car. We're still hungry too, so we look up the finest fish and chip shop in Wath-Upon-Dearne, my maternal family's former mining village home. We find Broadway Chippy on an estate smelling of assorted marijuana products (not a smell my miner/soldier/whatever grandfather probably ever sniffed), but we strike gold and £15 secures us both a large cod and chips, plus gravy (him) and mushy peas (me). We eat it in the car with our fingers, wipe our hands on the damp grass and drive home. God, we're happy.

With almost uncanny symmetry, the following day Broxbourne Borough Under-15s will have added-time glory too, in Harlow. (Shall we talk about Harlow's traffic system? Sadly there isn't time.) Oscar throws an early one in ('I went for it with two hands; should have tipped it over with one') and throws his water bottle down so hard it almost bumps up and smashes him in the face, like the Barnsley guy yesterday. All looks doomed at 2-0. But, faced with a superior team, Broxbourne claw it back to 1-2, Oscar makes a series of flying saves behind his resolute defence and the boys equalise with the last kick of the game. They celebrate like Boro celebrated yesterday. The opposition goalkeeper is crying. Oscar puts his arm around the sobber and tells him everything will be alright.

28 January 2025
Wrexham 2 Stevenage 3

My prediction: 0-1
His prediction: 1-2

Oscar has a stomach ache. It's so severe he has to leave school early. Luckily, it clears up during the walk between school and car. So we're off to Wrexham.

It should be joyous. This is the game Oscar has been looking forward to more than any other. It's a night trip and the high of Saturday is still fuelling us. It's not joyous, though, for tomorrow Oscar has a maths test. Not a mock, not an actual exam (it's not a GCSE year, I must defensively stress again, should the Parent Police be on patrol), but it's a pivotal one, nevertheless. We've talked about it for some weeks.

I have visions of going on my own – we've had the conversation about what to do if one of us is indisposed, without coming to real resolution – and I left it to him. 'Look, we'll do it. It's not Stockport is it? [he doesn't look at upcoming fixtures then] I'll revise in the car. I'm desperate to go and the book needs me there. It's just a question of convincing myself.'

And convince himself he does. And yes, he does revise in the car while listening to Tyler, the Creator. He's like Stephen Hawking, if Stephen Hawking only wanted to pass a maths exam so he could leave home sooner.

The Wrexham story is a bundle of contradictions. They're a real club, third-oldest professional club in the world or something, but they've never played in the top flight and when they tumbled out of the Football League in 2008, few tears were shed and there were few fans to shed them.

Now, since Ryan Reynolds and Rob McElhenney bought the club for £2m in 2021, Wrexham are a jet-propelled phenomenon seeking the third consecutive promotion that will leave clubs such as Boro behind, possibly forever. Oscar thinks they'll get it; I don't. The foundations are solid, but they now have the added propulsion of Hollywood. On one level, it's a sham, since the money-spinning documentary series *Welcome to Wrexham* was a major part of the deal. But so was legally turning Wrexham into a city for no obvious reason in 2022, shortly before Reynolds and McElhenney were given the freedom of the place. Locals loved being a town so much that Wrexham FC were informally nicknamed 'Town'. Legal elevation into a city doesn't actually make Wrexham a city.

Oscar expected more, not a shabby small-time club shop, not a stadium with empty seats to spare (and not just in the away section) and not, in the Racecourse, a town centre ground that betrays its National League scars more vividly than Hollywood can paper over. Good for them. That's their foundation. These flaws are, of course, the things I revel in and the programme is a proper programme. They have, to use that awful term, kept it real amidst a glitz that will be kept well hidden this evening. There's nothing to sneer about here.

Mercifully, Wrexham is not Barnsley. The stewards in the fate-temptingly christened Wrexham Lager Stand are xenodochial, the food is sensibly priced and Oscar can't quite believe how scrumptious his £3.50 Wrexham AFC-branded steak-and-ale pie is. And, unlike Barnsley, we 248 travellers are close to both the pitch and the home fans. Better still, unlike the unfortunate Wrexham-supporting souls in the Fourth Wall Stand, we're snug and dry.

Everyone's up for this, even Drackers, who doesn't come away too often. He's sporting a splendid tartan duffle coat and looking for all the world like a designer Paddington. The inevitable 'sheep-shagging bastards' chant tickles someone who hadn't heard it before (i.e. Oscar). 'We're going to win this, Dad, I know we are.' Like Kate Bush – I took tea with her in Harrods one afternoon; impeccable table manners – Oscar knows that something good is going to happen. I know better, not least since no visitors have won here since Tranmere last March. My prediction is in hope, his is in expectation. And the bad news is that there's no Luther, waylaid by a knee injury nobody noticed him suffering at Barnsley.

Something is happening and, yes Kate Bush, it's something good. Starting a league game for the first time since August, Sweens skies an early chance, but Boro are wonderful. They push, they press, their interplay is whiplash, and bedraggled Wrexham don't know what's hit them. The opener is inevitable, although it's a gift from goalkeeper Arthur Okonkwo. Pidge takes the ball out of defence and passes down the middle to Dan Kemp. Kempino finds Robbo, whose shot is spilled back to Kemp, who rattles in his fourth goal in four League One matches right in front of us. That's Boro's fifth away league goal of the season. 'It's too early,' says the bloke in front of me, a doomster after my own heart. I remind him of the games where there wasn't even an early shot, let alone an early goal, but he has a point.

Murphy Cooper kicks long, Reidy plays a neat one-two with Louis Appéré and blasts home a second under the wretched Okonkwo. Reidy charges to us, does the best knee slide I've ever seen and pumps his chest. A crazed Oscar is leaping about and, when I look back, everyone is smiling or shaking their head in disbelief or joy or both. At the break, Boro are two to the good and so wholly dominant it could have been four. Without question it's the best half I've seen from Boro, perhaps the best half I ever will see from Boro. They are monsters to a man, but Dan Kemp is unplayable. How could I have doubted him, but how could he have played like he did until, ooh, December?

'What's going on?' asks Oscar, as if Marvin Gaye were a Boro fan. For the first and regrettably, I fear, the last time, he hasn't looked at his phone for an entire half. He dare not do so in the second. 'Wrexham are either going to come at us from the restart or crumble,' he predicts.

In near synchronicity with Oscar's psyche, the Wrexham PA plays 4-Non Blondes' 'What's Up?' and then 'Things Can Only Get Better'. Good work Wrexham. I do wish them well, I think.

James McClean is singled out for special abuse by the Boro fans and Oscar joins in without knowing why, so I explain that I admire McClean's refusal to bow to poppy orthodoxy and why there's a certain residual resentment against the British Army in some parts of Northern Ireland. I also have to explain that the IRA were murdering sectarian gangsters, so it's complicated. Tricky letting kids make their own choices isn't it?

Wrexham introduce Steve Fletcher and Paul Mullin at the break – off goes Ollie Palmer who, unlike Mullin, wasn't masked in *Deadpool & Wolverine* – and they pull one back when Ollie Rathbone's drive is flying well wide until Dan Scarr palms it into Mullin's path. Mullin can't miss and in fact doesn't. The Boro team charge after the referee to point out the criminal act. Thomas Kirk had a perfect view, but he will not be turned.

What now, with 40 minutes left? The clock starts to move very slowly indeed. Wrexham swarm forwards. None of we 248 are smiling now.

Then, the miracle. Eli King overlaps down the right and squares for Dan Kemp. He spots Jake Young, who's craftily dropped off Ryan Barnett. Young seems to have got the ball lost in his long, lovely legs (handsome boy is our Jake), but his swivel takes out Barnett and he pokes in the third. It feels a tad tacky to use the orgasm analogy – I nearly used it on Saturday, to be honest – but, Christ, it's not far off. We high-five everyone in front of us. The smiles are back and we even chorus 'Ryan Reynolds, she's cheating on you', whatever that means.

Wrexham lay siege and miss chances. Dan Phillips is lucky to receive only a yellow card, Pidge seems to handle in the area and it's all gone quiet over here. 'My heart, my heart,' squeals Oscar as Scarr puts in another cross despite the limpet-like attention of Lewis Freestone. 'This is unbearable, I need to meditate.' He has, it must be noted, never meditated in his life.

A Sweens block is so unbelievable that it wouldn't make a Ryan Reynolds film, and Murphy Cooper makes a fine save from Jack Marriott, before, during the seven added minutes, Max Cleworth heads in Elliot Lee's free kick. 2-3.

We're catatonic now, and when Marriott sets Lee free inside the area, we know the equaliser is upon us. Instead, Cooper rushes out, makes himself enormous and blocks with his face. It's a jaw-dropping save – literally, since Lee fair whacked it – from another planet, a planet populated by a race of superhuman Pat Jenningses.

It's still unbearable, but when Mullin skies a pottable chance at the death and Cooper lingers over the subsequent goal kick while grinning at us like a cheeky goblin, we know it's over. Let's say this very slowly: Boro. Have. Won. At. Wrexham. As Irene Cara had it, what a feeling.

As I've said, I respect those who think football is a pointless, meaningless excuse for not engaging with real life, that it destroys relationships and distracts us from what's really important, etc. But ultimately they're wrong. They misunderstand what it can be to be human. Boro might lose to Exeter this Saturday, but tonight they have given us memories that will last forever. It's brought pure, life-enhancing joy. How can that not matter?

I look around. It's the Rapture. Like every Boro traveller, Oscar and I are utterly spent. We're hoarse, out of breath and we're clinging to each other while we jump about, evoking random passing gods. This moment, after Guiseley, after Bolton, after Cambridge, after Wigan (both times), this shared experience is what I'd quixotically hoped this season would be, but a moment like this can never be planned or predicted. There is nobody in the world I'd rather have gone through tonight with than Oscar and I know he'll reciprocate as the years roll on. Life simply cannot get better than this. It's priceless.

He's talking about baseball in his *Underworld* novel, but Don DeLillo gets it: 'A man takes his kid to a game and 30 years later this is what they talk about when the poor old mutt's wasting away in the hospital.' That's it! That's what I want and that's what I want Oscar to want in time. As I'm slipping into the big sleep, I want him to whisper to me, 'That night in Wrexham in 2025 was really something, wasn't it, Dad?'

A woman kisses me (no tongues, but she is about 70), strangers hug, acquaintances high-five, a burly man looks to the heavens in supplication and so many people are shaking their heads in joy, there's almost a draught. Everyone is shouting, screaming in fact, as are Oscar and I, two grunts grunting. The noise is cacophonous, but I can hear my own blood.

Tonight matters to the players, who stand applauding us and themselves. It matters to Revs, who does his fist-pumps with unbridled, cathartic glee and who will linger for minute after minute, looking at us, shaking his head in wonder. It matters to me, who, after snatching a little sleep, will wake up tomorrow with a big black bruise on my thumb after clapping too keenly. It matters to Oscar, who can't stop grinning and shouting and sending screaming voicemails to his friends. It matters to the bloke who takes his top off in joy and twirls it around his head, and it matters to every travelling Boro fan. It matters so much. And, to repeat myself because I can't get the words out quickly enough, it's what being a human being can be.

As we finally file down the steps, 20 delirious minutes after the final whistle, the Wrexham stewards understand too. They're smiling at us, benign witnesses to our joy. A pretty one says 'well done' to me as if I'd scored the winner myself, and a tattooed hunk in a hi-vis jacket shakes my hand. I wish this moment could last forever.

'The game doesn't change the way you sleep or wash your face or chew your food,' continues Don DeLillo. 'It changes nothing but your life.'

Outside, Oscar exposes his Boro hoodie and we slalom through the disappointed Wrexham fans. I'm not wholly comfortable him doing this but it's edge-free, they're good people, even after finally losing at home. In the middle of the blocked-off road there are Wrexham fans doing television interviews. Adrenaline pumping, fuelled by the evening of his life, Oscar sneaks in front of the camera, displays his Boro logo and, as the camera continues to roll, shouts a solo chant of 'Revell again, Revell again, olé olé'. Some Wrexham fans smile, some don't, but he's oblivious. I'll explain why he might have put himself in danger, but not for a few days. He might have come down by then. 'Getting in front of the camera was my moment of the year,' he says, unable to get his own words out properly because he's laughing so much. God, I love him.

It's a painless, contented journey home as our exhausted bodies gradually reset themselves. We listen to the managers' post-match pressers. Revs's heart is bursting as much as ours but, like Darrell Clarke on Saturday, Wrexham's Phil Parkinson will attribute defeat to his team's ineptitude. Neither credit Boro. That's wrong and extraordinarily disrespectful, but it's fine too. Let us stay under the radar. It's nice and warm here. Somewhere around Daventry, with the M1 almost empty, Oscar points to the moon and sighs. 'I'll never forget tonight, Dad.'

Pie Chart

1. Wrexham
2. Northampton Town
3. Peterborough United
4. Lincoln City
5. Leyton Orient
6. Norwich City
7. Burton Albion
8. Mansfield Town
9. Wigan Athletic
10. Stevenage
11. Exeter City
12. Blackpool
13. Barnsley
14. Huddersfield Town
15. Rotherham United

February – Is That Really You, Vadaine Oliver?

1 February 2025
Stevenage 4 Exeter City 1

My prediction: 3-1
His prediction: 2-1

The days are starting to get longer, which invariably makes me sad. It's reverse Seasonal Affective Disorder, I reckon. Perhaps Lana Del Rey understood with 'Summertime Sadness', although I'm taking the song title too literally and I'm told such a thing doesn't exist. I've always had it. I don't like the heat, the light, the never-endingness of the days and the noisy chav neighbours in their garden, but I suspect it's really my yearly mourning for the end of the football season, although it's only February. Sad indeed.

Anyway, as we know from our lonely lives overflowing with thwarted opportunities, optimism is the real killer and we were so, so, so optimistic tootling back from Wrexham. That night is gone now, in the calendar if not our lives. Could things only get worse? They could. Today is a morning kick-off as part of Sky's Pretending to Care About the EFL campaign. The television nation might not be wholly agog for Stevenage vs Exeter City, as they weren't for Exeter City vs Stevenage a lifetime ago.

What do we eat? Nobody does breakfast at the Lamex and I'm rarely ready for solids of a morning. We both settle on a non-frankfurter hot dog at the ground. 'Great' isn't the word. It really isn't.

Taye wanders off while the team are doing the pre-match huddle in front of us, which bodes ill, but surely the match will make things better. Since Exeter were so dominant in the morning kick-off at their place, it should confirm whether Boro's three in a row is chimera or real progress. We seem to have an answer after less than a minute.

Preying on makeshift full-back Nick Freeman, Exeter break down the left. Debutant Brentford loanee Tony Yogane threads it through for Ilmari Niskanen, who squares past the onrushing Murphy Cooper. Eli King blocks Josh Magennis's shot with his leg. Then he blocks Ed Francis's follow-up with his arm. Magennis tucks in the spot kick.

There goes our optimism, especially since Boro haven't overturned a deficit all season. The East Terrace is deflated but livid, but I'm seemingly alone in thinking it was a penalty; arm to ball, albeit some of the arm was over some of the chest. Perhaps Wrexham, Barnsley and Orient were one medium-sized blip. 'There are 89 minutes left, Dad,' counsels wise Oscar, neither deflated nor livid.

What we hadn't bargained for is Exeter, so demonic in Devon, being so hopeless in Hertfordshire. Boro are ahead after 12 minutes and it's all courtesy of Cheick Diabate, the worst of the bad visiting bunch who will send the 279 surprisingly supportive travellers home in bad spirits. First, he gives Eli King almost instant redemption by weakly passing to him from the edge of the Exeter area. King plays a one-two with Louis Appéré and slots his first Boro goal past Joe Whitworth. Then, in the area itself, Diabate dithers. Dan Kemp robs him and shoots against the post and Alex Hartridge. Robbo taps in.

That's it already, although Oscar giggles when the fourth official's board doesn't work and super-quick Drackers chirps, 'The referee isn't indicating ...' But Boro don't let any light in. Exeter had conceded six at home in midweek and Oscar reckons 'we can get six here too'. Unusually, there is no fear on the East Terrace. A Kemp spin around Diabate is – I exaggerate not – world class and occasions a sharp, joyful intake of collective breath.

A fabulous new chant debuts and it's about Appéré: 'Is it "a-pair" or "ah-pah-ray"? Nobody knows his fucking name.' Without question, it's the best football chant ever. What love we have for him, although I've been pronouncing him 'a-parry' to rhyme with 'barry' and he's still without a league goal. I hope he's honoured.

On the touchline, Exeter manager Gary Caldwell, P45 under consideration were their next game not an FA Cup tie against Nottingham Forest, is having histrionics that culminate in a yellow card. Afterwards, he'll throw his players under the bus (not the really lovely Berrys team bus with its deeply tinted windows, which even Oscar swoons over) and say 'self-inflicted' a lot without mentioning Boro.

Weak defending from Ryan Woods spawns number three. Reidy takes it up and finds Dan Kemp, who cuts in, blasts it at Hartridge and scores his fourth goal in four league games from the rebound. Again, what has happened to him? If this is Revs's doing, it's the achievement of his managerial career.

And for the first time since Barrow were hit for five on a gleeful night in December 2022, Boro score four league goals when Robbo Roberts outjumps two defenders shod in weighted-down boots to head Cooper's kick to Reidy, who cuts in and crosses for Robbo himself to guide in his first brace since October 2022.

Today was nothing like the madness of Wrexham – did that really happen? Did we really see it? – but it's four consecutive victories (let's include the Vertu to enhance the point). There are many 'first since …' here. Always a good sign.

Whatever you do, Oscar, don't look at the table, I order as we drive home listening to the new Weeknd album. He doesn't. At least not until the other games have finished.

'Okay, we're 11th with a game in hand over of most the nine teams above us. Win that and we're a point off the play-offs. Can we Dad, can we?' The game in hand is at Birmingham though.

It's not been perfect. Appéré needs a goal, Sweens seemed weirdly distracted and Exeter were lamentable from first to last, but nobody's complaining. Think back to Revs's lunchtime fist-pumps. He was grinning like he'd won the Lottery again and he tapped his big old heart when we sang 'Revell again, olé olé' at him. He believes. Does this mean we should?

3 February 2025
Transfer Deadline Day 2

Hurrah! It's transfer deadline day, or Neil Metcalfe Day as we now call it around these parts. The great man from *The*

FEBRUARY – IS THAT REALLY YOU, VADAINE OLIVER?

Comet is on his laptop at a frankly bonkers 7.49am, when he unsurprisingly reveals 'absolutely nowt happening'. Elsewhere, injury-prone Nathan Thompson is out for MK Dons' season after, er, injuring himself at Harrogate, and Wycombe striker Brandon Hanlan arrived last Friday for the rest of the season to a massed shrugging of shoulders.

12.19pm: 'Still not a sausage from Boro.'

1.23pm: Boro still sausage-free, but Pauline Metcalfe, Neil's mum, has been in touch to check on her boy. Hi Pauline! That's nice, but Pauline has no transfer news either, although Dean Bouzanis very quietly returned to Reading after Christmas.

3.59pm: 'Ten hours I've been sat here now and not one rumour … still only another seven hours to go … in fact it's so quiet I'm going to put the bin out.' Hang on in there Neil. We're rootin' for ya.

5:13pm: 'Let's have a recap … I've taken the bin out, my mam has wanted to know what I've had for my dinner and there's been about 10 transfers in the entirety of League One. And to be fair, that has made today seem a lot more exciting than it actually has been. Six hours to go.' Boro were scheduled to have a presser for tomorrow's Vertu quarter-final. That's been cancelled, so Neil can't even leave the house.

6.01pm: Neil tells us Vadaine Oliver has joined Shrewsbury Town, where we're going before the month is out, but he's going syntax-manglingly stir-crazy. 'Might not turn out to be smoke, but there might be some steam or clouds rolling in from the horizon. Again, purely a gut feeling and not based in fact at the minute.' You okay, hon?

8.50pm: 'Did ask the club if they could give me any lead … radio silence.' Perhaps Neil could ask the club what's happening vis-à-vis Dan Butler and Luther, or why there were photographs of Jake Forster-Caskey in training before Christmas, but not a word since …

9.16pm: 'Kyle Edwards in from Oxford' and there's a photograph to prove it. Neil is delighted. I'm delighted for Neil, although he must instantly crank out a piece, explaining Edwards is a quality winger who played in the Premier League for West Bromwich Albion, but looks worryingly injury-prone.

But wait! Neil has noticed something: 'Anyone else spot the photo was in daylight?' That's right, while Neil was putting his bin out, telling us Norwich have loaned Ken Aboh to Colchester and chatting to his lovely mam, the deal was already done and the club hadn't told him. 'That's the funniest thing he's ever written,' says Oscar, who, in truth, is more excited about possibly seeing Vadaine

Oliver again. 'Doesn't seem very fair,' reflects Oscar. 'Do the club not like him?'

> 10.58pm: Neil goes to bed. At least I assume he does. For all I know, his private life is a blur of frenzied post-11pm activity. If not, I hope he's asleep by 11.02pm as he must be quite tired. He's at the Lamex tomorrow, of course, but 'warning you all now, I'm doing NOWT on Wednesday and Thursday'. We love you, Neil Metcalfe.

4 February 2025
Stevenage 0 Birmingham City 1 –
Vertu Trophy

My prediction: 3-2
His prediction: 1-0

'I'm in such a happy mood,' announces Oscar. This is uncharted territory. He hasn't delayed our departure, nor has he moaned about acquiring a team sheet. I wonder what it is. Perhaps 'it' is a person. 'There are so many things I don't tell you,' he smiles. Our relationship is shifting. It's shifted since we began this journey (the one in July, not tonight's on the A602); we're more equal, he's stumbling into manhood and he's working out who he is. Overwhelmingly, I'm liking what I'm seeing. I fall a little more in love with him each day. But you never quite know how things will pan out, do you?

And Boro are two games from Wembley. We agree not to discuss the potential semi-final, which would be against Peterborough United or Cheltenham Town, but we can't avoid admitting we're hoping Boro meet Steve Evans and Rotherham in the final we are in no way fantasising about, after having in no way looked up that appearing in that final would mean the postponement of the trip to Wycombe.

Oscar and I will always have those magical nights at Burton and Orient, but somehow the Vertu Trophy hasn't quite grabbed the attention of the Stevenage public, so the East Terrace is closed, which we decide is a huge mistake until we see how few Boro fans have bothered. Yet, the visitors are Birmingham City, who arrive in their defiantly unspecial Birmingham International team bus accompanied by five coachloads of fans. They have sold out the 1,267-capacity South Stand (why does this sold-out number keep changing?) and their fans are everywhere, including a gang of four blokes right behind us.

We have the best seats in the house on the very first row above the tunnel (with unusually expert timing, I pounced mere minutes after they went on sale), we'll hear Scott Cuthbert bellowing in Scottish ('lock him up Robbo!'), we'll chide Birmingham manager Chris Davies for excessive whingeing and we'll share chicken 'goujons' and chips. Great. Let's do this.

Neil Banfield has a footballistic chat with Scott Wright, who he coached at Rangers, as, more intriguingly, does Revs. I'd like to talk to those Birmingham guys behind us, to be honest, but I'm sat next to Arthur. He's about eight, has an awful lot to say for himself and at one point he'll tell Oscar off for standing up. Every other minute he taps me on the arm and asks a question, usually relating to the worrying possibility of flares, pitch invasions and what I'll do if Birmingham score. I rather like Arthur. He reminds me of someone when he was about eight.

Charlie Goode and Eli King have somehow got themselves suspended, and with Kane Smith still incapacitated, three kids are on the bench. Oh.

Whereas Boro took the game to Wrexham, here they're timid once again, although Birmingham have picked their reserve team and benched Jay Stansfield and Ethan Laird. Luckily, Taye – in for Murphy Cooper – has rediscovered himself. At one point the referee stops the game so Alex Cochrane can change his boots. Jake Young picks them up and takes them off the pitch. The referee berates Young. Of course he berates Young.

The game pivots around one grisly second-half minute for Elliott List. Krystian Bielik makes a mess of Pidge's long ball, setting Listy free, but he shoots weakly at Bailey Peacock-Farrell. When the ball comes back to Listy, he miskicks completely. It's not quite Listy at Huddersfield, but Boro's moment has passed and Wembley has gone. To nobody's surprise, it gets worse when Sweens weakly heads Peacock-Farrell's kick to Marc Leonard. The impressive midfielder releases the recently introduced pink-booted, £15m-plus (he's worth more than the Lamex, let alone a Boro player) Stansfield, who runs on and puts Birmingham through with ruthless delicacy.

There's no comeback, just a return to traditional habits: a reluctance to press forwards and a lack of urgency. On the bench, Revs and Scotty Cuthbert can't contain their frustration and they put a couple of the kids on, but even with seven added minutes, there's nothing doing. The correct team goes through and Arthur leaves without so much as a goodbye. Rotherham have exited too, but that doesn't matter now.

Oscar's happy mood hasn't quite dissipated. In fact, he's bullish and eloquent. 'I can't be angry, because we were beaten by a better team who shouldn't be in League One. And it doesn't affect our league position at all unless Revs can't get them going at the weekend. If Kyle Edwards is as good as some people say [later Oscar will be disappointed to hear Revs speak of blooding the new man gradually], we can push for the play-offs, but Saturday's a must-not-lose game. By the way, I know you said we'd win this trophy, but I never believed you.'

His realistic enthusiasm has helped banish my own melancholy. Thank you Oscar and thank you Vertu; you might be a – yes – shambles of a trophy but, after Burton and after Orient, you've given us more than we've taken, much more. Onwards! Boldly!

8 February 2025
Charlton Athletic 2 Stevenage 0

My prediction: 1-3
His prediction: 1-2

Will Boro make the play-offs Oscar?

He looks out at the desolate Deptford landscape as our train crawls past Millwall's New Den, slightly startled that people actually live like this. Perhaps he's too cosseted. He scratches his cheek and contemplates: 'If we keep playing like we're playing, there's a chance.'

Ah, yet another morning kick-off, so yet another very good morning to Sky's Pretending to Care About the EFL campaign. Doubtless the viewing figures confirm just how far-sighted it is and just how much the general public prefer Charlton Athletic vs Stevenage to Leyton Orient vs Manchester City.

It's cold. Poor Oscar will never get warm and by the end of the day his face is a not especially fetching Widow Twankey rouge. We're both of a gentle mindset though. Parking at Charlton is tricky and I want to be a little less predictable, so we take the long way round, via the Northern Line and the overground. It's the season's longest trip through London and Oscar has his Boro shirt on display, but there's no one to engage with.

At London Bridge we're joined by a gaggle of youthful Boro fans. They have beer, they sing their songs, they bang on the toilet doors like it's 1985, but the travelling public seem unfamiliar with Jamie Reid. Ergo, they are unconcerned that he 'makes the Boro sing'.

Charlton featured in the *Domesday Book* and, comedy drum roll, very little has changed since then. It's an inconsequential London suburb, but I like the football club. They're proper, whatever 'proper' means. Since Athletic are all Charlton has going for it, they bring people together like Barnsley seem to think they do. They are a club with tradition, a reasonably progressive outlook and, much to Oscar's surprise, a fine Premier League stadium that used to hold a whopping 75,000. 'A bit like Wembley,' he suggests optimistically, although I preferred it when there was more faded grandeur. They've never been able to fill it for long periods, even when their record appearance maker Sam Bartram and their record goalscorer Derek Hales were starring in different decades.

And speaking of Derek Hales, he's responsible for the finest footballer profile I've seen. It appeared in a Charlton programme. Here's a sample. This is why programmes are important:

PETS: None

NICKNAME AT CLUB: don't have one.

FAVOURITE BRITISH PLAYER AND WHY: none

FAVOURITE FOREIGN PLAYER AND WHY: none

FAVOURITE BRITISH SIDE: none

BEST-EVER BRITISH SIDE: none

BEST-EVER INTERNATIONAL XI: none.

FAVOURITE AWAY GROUND: don't have one

FAVOURITE STADIUM IN WHICH YOU HAVE PLAYED: none in particular

BEST GOAL SEEN SCORED: don't have a favourite

MOST MEMORABLE MATCH: I don't have one

BIGGEST DISAPPOINTMENT: being treated unfairly

MISCELLANEOUS DISLIKES: tolerating boring people

BEST FILM SEEN THIS YEAR: I don't go to the cinema

SUPERSTITIONS: none

IF YOU WEREN'T A FOOTBALLER WHAT WOULD YOU BE: don't know

BEST YOUNGSTER TO WATCH: none

WHICH PERSON IN THE WORLD WOULD YOU LIKE TO MEET: no one in particular

ADVICE TO YOUNGSTERS: don't think the game is all honey.

'I've never heard of Derek Hales, Dad, but he's a lot like you,' contends Oscar, possibly correctly. Should we meet, I'd like to think Derek and I would become fast friends, passing whole afternoons and evenings in silence.

And if Oscar gave out awards for Club Shop of the Year, Charlton's would be vying with Wigan for the gong. Like, say, Barnsley's, it's large for League One. Unlike, say, Barnsley's, it's rammed. There are teabags (£8 for 25), a fetching snow globe (£8.50), an umbrella (£10) and, best of all, if you purchase a duvet, they'll throw in some curtains too. There's a programme too, although nothing inside could compare to Derek Hales's innermost thoughts. Instead, as if to remind us what bigger, wealthier clubs than Boro, clubs with perhaps more legitimate aspirations to the play-offs, are capable of, the programme parades Charlton's new loan signings: Alex Gilbert and Tom McIntyre, who have played in this season's Championship for Middlesbrough and Portsmouth, respectively.

It's dark and dreary, but nothing can dispel our bubbling, our optimism, our bonhomie. And everyone in The Valley is so nice, even the food vendors (a fine-enough Pukka, but it's not yet midday), who wish us a pleasant day.

We must talk, it seems. 'The book, Dad?' Yes Oscar, the book. We do talk about it intermittently. I deploy it sparingly, chiefly when he grumbles about securing team sheets and examining away coaches. I don't mention passing his bedroom and hearing him say, 'My Dad's writing a book and I'm the lead character in it,' to one of his friends.

'I don't think I'm going to read it.'

Why not, Oscar?

'I don't know, I'm a bit scared actually.'

Okay, we'll come back to that. If my father had written a book about me when I was 14, I'd have been scared too. I genuinely don't mind; for him this is for much later.

The early kick-off meant Boro stayed around the corner overnight. Hopefully, Sky has compensated Phil Wallace, since overnight stays before Charlton games are not in the Boro budget. New signings Brandon Hanlan and Kyle Edwards, both keenly proselytised for by Neil Banfield, are on the bench as a sort of Break In Case of Emergency failsafe. Sweens is dropped after giving Brimingham their goal on Tuesday and his peculiar performance against Exeter.

For 43 minutes it's (sort of) okay, against a team who are superior, but not Wycombe/Birmingham superior. We're high above the players, so we compare their baldness: Murphy Cooper's is incipient, Eli King's more pronounced. Then Josh Edwards's miscontrol lets in Louis Appéré, who runs through alone, but, confidence on the floor, he's too scared to shoot, much to the disgust of Dan Kemp. The game pivots. Red-shirted Charlton breeze upfield and score when the excellent Conor Coventry (not sure why West Ham let him go, but what do I know?) crosses low and Matty Godden nips in between Lewis Freestone and Pidge to poke in. 'Fuck off,' snaps Oscar, whose mood is darkening with each passing minute. I pretend not to hear.

Moments after half-time, the unmarked Godden, Boro's old boy bête rouge, heads on a hoof forwards. Charlie Goode lets Tyreece Campbell through to rattle a drive against the bar. It bounces out almost to the 18-yard line. No Boro defender reacts and Luke Berry does the evil rest, via an admittedly mellifluous volley.

We've gone back in time, if only to a few weeks ago. The Boro chants aren't working. Dan Kemp is not 'on fire', Jamie Reid is not 'making the Boro sing' and Jordan Roberts is certainly not 'fucking dynamite'. Charlton sneakily remove the ballboys from behind Murphy Cooper's goal, so he must run 50 yards and take 30 seconds to collect the ball for each goal kick.

Later Revs will argue there was 'not enough character' and, directly citing Appéré's craven effort (Jake Young was in the warm-up but not the 18), 'not enough courage'.

And there's effort. I know it's a lower league cliché that these are young guys with young families they need to provide for. Moreover, they're on short-term contracts and, while they're on good money now, they may be delivering your Uber Eats in a decade's time. They don't have the option of not trying and I've never really thought about lack of effort from Boro, although Bruno Andrade exuded a rather unconcerned air. This has been gnawing at me for a while now. We love Reidy, of course we do. We remember the Torquay-supporting trio we met at last season's Carabao Cup tie at Exeter who'd turned up just to see their former player. Increasingly frequently these days, though, I look at him, remember his behaviour against Guiseley and think, 'Are you giving absolutely everything here, Jamie Reid?'

When Revs makes a quadruple substitution that will have no effect, there's general disgruntlement that Reidy isn't removed, adding to the similar general disgruntlement when he started in the first place.

Kyle Edwards, whose 'Promotion Ting' hip-hop track of 2020 as Edwardo was accomplished in an Xzibit's 'Paparazzi' way, isn't among the quartet but, glass partly broken in this desperate emergency, Brandon Hanlan is. He has the aura of a slightly more mobile Tyreece Simpson, but let's reserve judgement, and not being able to oust Richard Kone at Wycombe is hardly the mark of a failure. Louis Thompson has gone off the boil and Listy is again a passenger rather than a driver. Later, Edwards gets 25 minutes; he has comedy green boots and a comedy coiffure, but he puts in the only cross of the second half. He could be a hero, but we could all be heroes, albeit just for one day. Perhaps.

At the death, Charlton spend the best part of ten minutes in Boro's right-hand corner. Boro just can't get the ball away, surrendering throw-ins and corners aplenty as Charlton toy with their inferiors. At least it's at the other end from us. 'It's the most humiliating ten minutes of football I've ever seen Boro play,' thunders Oscar. Those grisly minutes encapsulate a lunchtime to suck out our souls.

When we 691 travellers are put out of our abject misery, we can't even bring ourselves to clap the team off. It's been a loveless encounter and neither Oscar nor I can name a Boro man of the match. Oscar's not angry, just disappointed at being once again felled by his optimism. After all the progress of recent weeks, it's so many steps back, but steps back in a way that the Birmingham defeat didn't seem to be. For the first time in weeks, I cannot evaluate an opposition goalkeeper, because he had nothing to do.

We amble back to Charlton station in crushed silence. The two platforms are packed and, from the one opposite us, a ginger, Stella-swigging Charlton fan taunts us. 'Enjoy your big day out, did you?' he grins. We can't even bring ourselves to respond, and so we settle on smiling weakly at him. It's more disarming than we'd intended. The guy gives up, not wanting to intrude on private grief.

Out of character and soon to be out of pocket, I take Oscar for a steak near London Bridge. It cheers us up, but it solves none of our problems. 'This has been a good day out, Dad,' he generously offers, 'apart from the thing we actually went out for.'

Will Boro make the play-offs Oscar?

He pushes his steak around his plate, scratches his cheek and contemplates: 'If we keep playing like we're playing, there's not a chance.'

11 February 2025
Crawley Town 3 Stevenage 1

My prediction: 0-2
His prediction: 1-2

'No way is this place real,' declares Oscar. We've left the car in a company car park as directed by the Crawley Town website. We've wandered through an industrial estate, across a tiny pedestrian bridge and through some shrubbery before arriving at the Broadfield Stadium, where the main attraction seems to be some kids playing on an astroturf rather than, say, a League One encounter.

Oscar has been researching. 'They have a smaller ground than us [this is true: 6,134 to the Lamex's 7,800], the worst goal difference in League One [true also, for now] and I know what I've predicted, but secretly I'm going to be really disappointed if we don't get four here [oh].'

If Stevenage was the first New Town (and it was: 1946), then Crawley was the second (and it was: 1947), but it's not always loved by its residents. 'Endless rows of suburban bleakness that blur into the dark dank countryside, always raining, a slate grey sky hangs over everything,' notes one former resident, Lol Tolhurst. Another, his erstwhile partner in The Cure, Robert

Smith, remembers Crawley as 'grey and uninspiring with an undercurrent of violence. I fucking hated it.'

I went to a mid-range restaurant in Lisbon with Robert Smith once. He was surprisingly amenable when I asked to touch his hair. Felt like thorns.

And it's not going well for Crawley Town. Since early 2022, they have been owned by US cryptocurrency investors WAGMI (as in We're All Gonna Make It, so presumably the owners are 13 years old) United. 'Together, we're going to take Crawley Town to the Premier League,' their website suggests, perhaps over-optimistically. Six managers since the takeover, Crawley are in severe danger of relegation to League Two.

They don't do programmes (bastards). The club shop is even smaller than the Lamex's glorified cabin and ominously the prices of their paltry range are not displayed. They can only manage six substitutes, so if reserve goalkeeper Joe Wollacott gets hurt, they're in even more trouble. Their pies (crispy crust, but insubstantial and fatty) are pricey. Their £3.50 chips are served in a cardboard coffee cup, and they've been taken to court, accused of breaking the Modern Slavery Act by their former kitman, who claims they forced him to work 100 hours a week. Apart from that, it's gong quite well.

Revs retains Reidy, but Appéré is jettisoned in favour of Brandon Hanlan, Kane Smith has recovered from his Wrexham injury (no Luther or Dan Butler, though, and I'm beginning to think Jake Forster-Caskey will never kick a ball again), Sweens gets a start, but there's no real creativity in midfield. What do Boro's players think when they're aboard their Greys coach quietly gliding through the M25's rush-hour hilarity after – I think – no overnight stay, hopefully as a punishment for the Charlton fiasco.

Do they think, 'On this drizzly Tuesday night at a tiny faux stadium I'm going give the best I can and I'm going to turn my career around'? I hope so. I used to know so. Right now, I'm not sure.

The first half isn't a classic ('I could be studying academically,' claims Oscar, preposterously), the chants are half-hearted after the passive-aggressive stewards refuse to allow Boro banners to be put up directly behind the goal, but the team hold their own. Wollacott rushes out and saves bravely from Reidy, while Murphy Cooper flings himself across goal in for-the-cameras mode, to paw aside Harry Forster's screamer.

It's not really happening though. Revs's ill-chosen midfield keeps surrendering possession, and when Panutche Camará's scuffed shot bounces off Pidge, Forster reacts quicker than Kane Smith and shoots past Cooper from the edge of the area.

'Fuck off,' says Oscar. I can't be bothered to pretend or not pretend I've heard. But almost immediately Boro are level. Sweens, of all people, runs some 50 yards with the ball before forcing Wollacott into a flying tip-over. Dan Kemp lofts the corner over and Brandon Hanlan heads in firmly, right in front of us. It looked like Sweens to me as they both leapt together, but Sweens points to the striker. 'We're going to win this, Dad,' reckons Oscar. I concur. Class will tell, but when Dion Conroy takes Wollacott's goal kicks by rolling the ball across the area, no Boro player can rouse themselves to intervene.

Class doesn't tell. Revs has a nightmare on the bench and there will be no more Boro opportunities, other than a Pidge header looping on to the bar, chiefly so we can discover that not every ball hitting a bar is a beautiful noise. Rather than Reidy or Robbo, neither of whom look especially engaged, Revs withdraws the very much engaged Hanlan in favour of Louis Appéré, whose timidity now knows no bounds. All momentum is lost. 'Why not Reidy,' shouts someone as the Revs Out faction reconvenes. Then Revs makes no more changes until it's too late.

Three minutes from the end, after Pidge's fabulous block has foiled substitute Tyreece John-Jules, Reidy lazily surrenders possession from a Boro throw. Rushian Hepburn-Murphy (his parents are Audrey Hepburn and Audie Murphy) hurtles past Kane Smith. Murphy Cooper brilliantly stops him, but the loose ball falls to another substitute, Armando Quitirna, who taps in.

Revs seems caught in the headlights, incapable of making a decision, but both Scott Cuthbert and Neil Banfield seem similarly incapable of staging an intervention. By the time the cavalry arrives, the battle is over. Kyle Edwards gets minimal gametime and Oscar is having a conversation with the man next to him. For reasons unclear, they are both shouting at the top of their voices.

'I love Revs, but why is he starting Reidy?' asks Oscar.

'I don't know. I love Revs too, but why did he take Hanlan off?'

'I don't know.'

A friend of the man joins in: 'That's it. I'm not coming back until Revell goes. He's totally out of his depth.'

He turns to the pitch and, as Jordan Roberts jogs gently in the vague vicinity of the ball, bellows 'FUCKING RUN, ROBERTS ...' before joining the mass exodus with one last parting shot: 'And if fucking Jamie Reid starts on Saturday, I'm going to burn down the Lamex.' Charmed, I'm sure.

FEBRUARY – IS THAT REALLY YOU, VADAINE OLIVER?

There's time for another substitute to score another goal when Lewis Freestone's idiotic cross-field pass finds Kamari Doyle in his own half, deeper than the centre circle. He ambles through the purple Boro shirts to the edge of the area, from where he beats Cooper, without whom Crawley would have had a hatful. The goalkeeper is Boro's star performer by whatever a country mile is.

It's a disgraceful performance on any level. It's similar to Charlton, but Charlton were good, while Boro have made Crawley look good. If Wrexham post-game was the Rapture, this is a circle of hell. The few of us who are left of Boro's 374-strong away support mill about, bitter and disconsolate. There are no fist-pumps, no smiles, no love whatsoever, just a few half-hearted claps from the players, who make sure they're out of earshot of the suggestions being made to them. Were the days of joy so few weeks ago? What's happened? Is the real Dan Kemp the one who the opposition find unplayable or the one who Boro shouldn't be playing right now? Why sign Kyle Edwards if he's not going to play? Where's Jake Young? Where's Harvey White?

Oscar is incandescent again, but he does deliver the line, 'That's our worst performance … since Saturday,' quite well. It's a long time since I've felt guilty for bringing him. It's hardly been the most arduous journey and we'll be in bed before midnight, but, but, but … I want him to remember this season forever but not in an 'I remember the night my father made me go to be humiliated in Crawley; that's one of the many reasons we no longer speak' type way when he's 45.

The walk back to the company car park takes us through the Crawley fans and their mascot, ahem, Reggie the Red, greeting them as they leave the ground in celebration. As he often does, the not-always-streetwise Oscar declaims loudly about the defeat '3-1! To a non-league club! How could this happen to a team that won against Wrexham!' and so on, at both length and volume.

A voice in front of us chirps up. 'Ooh Dad, do I detect saltiness?' It's a girl about Oscar's age, and when they veer to our right, I catch her face. I can't help noticing that he can't help noticing she's very pretty.

'Some people just can't take a defeat,' she continues, high horse straddled as she strides on. She will not be turning around to face us. Nor will her father.

'Enjoy your journey back to non-league,' Oscar adds helpfully, chest puffed out.

'And you're going back to school tomorrow,' snarls the expertly goaded, humourless father. Is he like this at home? I suspect so.

'Yes he is,' I declare triumphantly. Because, well, yes he is. 'First period is history.'

'At least it's not a school in Crawley,' concludes Oscar. Touché! The father quickens their pace and harrumphs off into the darkness, but I can just about see his daughter's face. She's smiling. At least we've won something tonight.

We're too distraught to listen to Revs's post-match presser on the way home, so we save it for the morning's journey to first-period history. After he admits last night was 'unacceptable', Revs has another nightmare, suggesting he withdrew goalscorer Hanlan because he was tired. 'No he wasn't!' shouts Oscar, and Hanlan's anguished reaction when Appéré lumbered on supports Oscar rather than Revs. 'This isn't how we play,' Revs adds. Oh, but it is. Not all the time, but too often.

'Saturday!' shouts Oscar, reeling off the poor performances, his now red face contrasting with the white shirt of his school uniform. 'Exeter away! Rotherham! Cambridge! Guiseley! Huddersfield!'

We haven't spoken of the play-offs tonight. We will never speak of them again.

15 February 2025
Stevenage 1 Peterborough United 1

My prediction: 3-1
His prediction: 2-1

The days are getting even longer now. It's still cold but the skies are blue and over the horizon I can see my own encroaching black cloud of summer misery, caused by long nights, no football, hot heat, too-long school holidays (I hated them when I was actually at school), no football, noise, no football and almost everyone else being banging on about sunlight being natural melatonin or whatever it is. Because we've hit such a massive full stop (unless the p***-o*** miracle happens), my feelings of looming despairing dread are more acute than ever. Aren't you supposed to talk to someone? Doctors would laugh, family have no sympathy, but if I had money I'd pay. And Oscar? He doesn't need this nonsense. Still, at least the floodlights are on from kick-off today.

'Let's put it right on Saturday,' commanded Boro's Twitter after the Crawley horror, more in hope than expectation. We're restless today. 'Going to Stevenage games is ruining my social life,' muses Oscar, although by 'social life' he means sitting at home playing on the computer. 'I'm really not that excited about going to Shrewsbury next week, you know.'

Vadaine Oliver might be playing.

'I can't wait to go to Shrewsbury next week.'

Peterborough United were responsible for the last-seconds defeat back when we had hope. But we're denied the Kwame Poku reunion as their best player hasn't kicked a ball since the first week in December. Since then, his team have won just twice, a most unlikely relegation is beginning to beckon and with it surely the end to the fourth Peterborough tenure of Darren Ferguson, who pled guilty to a charge of common assault on his then-wife in 2008. And after losing 5-1 at Lincoln the other week, Ferguson waited for a passing bus – possibly their Greys coach, although it's not the actual vehicle that ferried Boro to Charlton and Crawley – to throw his players under. 'This group is without doubt the softest group of players I've had in my whole management career. Sometimes you think you're just wasting your time.' Cheers Dazza.

Surprisingly, Peterborough have sold out the away end, all 1,348 (hmm) spaces, but as is the way when supporters' belief is ebbing away, after Peterborough reveal today's line-up on Twitter, the first response is 'piss off'. More considered reflections wonder why Abraham Odoh is starting and Cian Hayes is on the bench. You can only guess why I'm bothering to mention this.

Meanwhile, there has been no conflagration in the vicinity of the Lamex, because Reidy has been benched, along with Sweens and Dan Phillips. Louis Appéré doesn't even make the 18, but Kyle Edwards and Brandon Hanlan start, so that's not too far off what might be needed.

To add insult to ennui, we're late, so we're not as close to the middle of the East Terrace as usual and our tiny hands are frozen. Today's encounter is an anti-discrimination game, hence the rather fetching rainbow ball and Pride flags as the teams appear, so predictably the match has to be stopped following some discriminatory chanting from the East Terrace. When the game begins again, Drackers has to threaten prosecution. Neither me nor Oscar heard anything and no Peterborough player seems to be complaining ('Going "wanker, wanker, wanker" at opposition players isn't discriminatory is it, Dad?' Oscar asks, casually dropping in the swearword), but obviously someone did, possibly the linesman, who's wearing gloves.

It's a funny game. Kyle Edwards begins well, but fades. Brandon Hanlan holds the ball up like Tyreece Simpson was meant to and he does shoot on occasion, which differentiates them, but he's not very, um, precise. Early days for both, though, early days.

Peterborough aren't great, but there have been worse visitors to the Lamex this year, although the tireless Tayo Edun stands out. The fourth official's board isn't working again, but for once Drackers misses his gag. Boro ease ahead when Robbo holds it up for Edwards, who plays a cute ball into Eli King. King wisely squares it to Dan Kemp, who lets fly as the defence backs off. Goalkeeper Jed Steer is desperately slow to react and the ball bobbles in. Not pretty, but it'll certainly do.

At Crawley, a Boro goal led to Boro's demise. History can indeed repeat itself. Robbo's horrendously lazy pass falls to Odoh, who cuts in and finds Malik Mothersille, who lays it into the path of Cian Hayes – told you – who gets the better of the already booked Lewis Freestone and smashes home. It could be worse, but today Revs times his substitutions properly, Charlie Goode runs back half the length of the pitch to make a flying but legal tackle and Peterborough are happy enough with a point. We're not, and another game there to be won has been drawn. Revs says the same thing, but he calls Robbo's pass for Peterborough's goal 'really, really sloppy ... we give the ball away like it doesn't matter ... we need to deal with this and I will', uses the phrase 'not acceptable' yet again and he looks and sounds more bereft than is his usually Micawber-esque mien.

Again, we don't clap the players off, but this time it's because we're cold and downcast. On the way home we're sufficiently at ease with what's happened to talk about the game. 'Is it acceptable to draw at home to a team next to the relegation places?' asks Oscar. I don't know, I really don't.

Haphazard fixture scheduling and waterlogged pitches have prevented Broxbourne Borough Under-15s from playing for a fortnight. Tomorrow, they will lose at home to a team a division below them in a cup. It's a headline-making shock, but they're well beaten. Oscar's handling is solid enough – balls stick – but he's not wholly blameless for the four goals conceded. For the first time since he was a lachrymose under-10, he has an on-field rant at assorted team-mates, none of whom blame him for his concessions. They made up at half-time.

18 February 2025
Stevenage 0 Burton Albion 1

My prediction: 2-0
His prediction: 2-1

It's the fifth Tuesday night game in five weeks, but we're content. Not mentioning the p***-o*** has altered our dynamic. I don't actually know what altering the dynamic means, but if I say it and move on, it may sound like I do. Oscar's feeling a tad peaky, although he's not without hypochondriacal tendencies and his condition doesn't prevent him from tucking into his Burger King fare with relish (although not mayonnaise, boom boom).

Once again, he raises the topic of him not reading *Before You Go*; I'm not sure what he's trying to tell me. Once again, I say I don't mind. Once again, I really don't. No matter, for now. He's unusually keen for Jamie Reid to start, since, according to Oscar, Reidy was revitalised after being dropped following the Northampton torpor. I'm not so sure.

Oscar's right. Reidy starts, replacing Kyle Edwards, thus solidifying Boro's crackpot policy of buying players and not starting them. If what Revs says much later about protecting the winger from playing two games a week is correct, then maybe he shouldn't have been acquired in the first place. Oh, and Terence Vancooten is starting for Burton, as is Dan Sweeney's brother Ryan. There's a little 'oh Terence Vancooten' chant, which makes him smile, but subtly. No longer a lost cause, Burton are revitalised under new manager Gary Bowyer, but they're still in deep trouble and half the away end is cordoned off, since they'll only bring a Boro-esque 117 fans.

All our favourite people are here. I can officially announce that we're a gang now, even if nobody else knows they're in it. The cheery guy Oscar lovingly calls SOBF (it stands for ... oh, I've forgotten now), who always waves at us, although we've never spoken. Mrs Chatty, who's worried about her favourite, Luther, whom she last saw hobbling around the Lamex on crutches. The fascinating character that is Mr Loud, because at some point he will loudly berate the hapless linesman, mostly for giving a 'soft' decision; we've mumbled pleasantries in passing. A second man to whom we have never spoken, but Oscar has christened Reverend Richard. From a distance, if you squint, he looks like Richard Coles and, in appropriately Biblical fashion, hollers 'it's a miracle' whenever an opposition player manages to haul himself off the ground after faking injury. They're the best of people. I hope they'd still be the best of people if we actually knew them.

'I feel so good about today, Dad,' says Oscar, who reveals he's wearing thermals. Me too, although obviously not the thermals. I can see how Oscar is going to look as a man now: good posture, my thick hair, slightly currant bun face, his mother's cheekbones and, if he maintains his proportions, long legs, the legacy of an unremembered generation.

In truth, though, there's a quotidian feel to this, beyond the lack of away fans. Most of the hospitality boxes are in unoccupied darkness, like North Korea outside Pyongyang. The crowd is paltry, Drackers seems subdued and even the players' pre-match huddle passes by almost unnoticed and unacknowledged. Worst of all, Neil Banfield isn't wearing shorts. The ravens have truly left the tower. I begin to feel uneasy.

That's nothing compared to how I feel 20 minutes in. Burton are all over Boro, powering forwards at will. They have space, they have pace and the overlapping Udoka Godwin-Malife is making Lewis Freestone look like the centre-back playing out of position he actually is. In one scary minute Burton hit the crossbar twice, first when the excellent Charlie Webster crosses and Kane Smith – who will have a grim evening before hobbling off once again – allows JJ McKiernan's header to smack it so hard the rebound drops outside the six yard box. Second, when Webster crosses again and rural Icelander Jón Daði Böðvarsson nips in ahead of the slumbering Charlie Goode. This time, the ball bounces down on to the line and, defying the laws of physics, doesn't hit Murphy Cooper and trickle in, before Rumarn Burrell totally miskicks with the goal a-gaping. Oscar's jaw drops, the East Terrace turns nasty, singling out Reidy and the hapless Freestone for lack of ability and/or effort. And those were just the closest in a series of clear Burton chances.

Yes, I'm repeating myself from last Tuesday, but it's a disgraceful performance on any level. The defence are on different planets, all of them inhospitable. The midfield are lumbering and poor Brandon Hanlan, marooned up front, will manage to bring one expert save from Max Crocombe, but must already be investigating whether Wycombe could possibly recall him early.

Mrs Chatty is still berating the East Terrace for not supporting Boro correctly – she will not have them criticising the players, any more than she will have swearing – when, seconds before half-time, Burton score with a slinky move. Goode fails to track the onrushing Burrell, who squares for Webster. Lewis Freestone makes a non-challenge type of challenge and Webster plonks the ball past Cooper with a justified level of insouciance.

Boro are booed off. 'Can't we support Liverpool, Dad? I just want us to win.' Again, I feel uneasy roping him into this. What if he has Boro PTSD and hates me for the rest of his life? I know it's life-lessons and all that and he'll have his heart broken by people he's closer to than Jamie Reid, but the boy is struggling. I want to put my arm around him, but he doesn't allow that to happen now. Neil Metcalfe declares, 'Just awful. I have seen better quality in a Temu delivery,' which at least gives Oscar the opportunity to explain what a Temu delivery might be.

Paralysed again, Revs makes no half-time changes, but ten minutes into the second half Terence Vancooten has the worst minute of his career. First Reidy waltzes past him (hallelujah!) and tumbles in the penalty area. Penalty. How we laugh. If that was a penalty, I'm a leg of ham. Better still, we can all sing 'Terence is a Boro fan'. Life was bad. Now life is good. That's life.

Dan Kemp should score the penalty. Boro should go on to win and it's hello again Vadaine Oliver. Except Dan Kemp doesn't score the penalty. He doesn't even take it. Reidy does. Reidy fires high and wide. Very high and very wide. That, too, is life. Fuck.

We're still taking this in when an admirably resurgent Reidy, this time impersonating the Jamie Reid of old, bursts through. TVC crudely upends him and is sent off. That 'Terence is a Boro fan' chant happens again and there are 35 minutes to overcome ten men.

Even so, on an evening that has turned very cold in more ways than one, there's a different barrel to be scraped. It's true both me and Oscar didn't hear anything awful on Saturday when the game was halted. The game isn't halted tonight, but we're closer to the centre and now we hear that awful chant about fucking the Pope and fucking the IRA and, may God help us all, another in support of decency's bogeyman, the Luton-supporting (perhaps Boro don't 'hate the fucking Luton' after all) jailbird Steven Yaxley-Lennon, (nom-de-twat: 'Tommy Robinson'), who's been convicted of assault, passport fraud, mortgage fraud, football hooliganism, cocaine possession, stalking and contempt of court. I can't see who's doing the chanting and while it's not mass and it's slightly apologetic, it's there.

What do Boro's non-white players, seven out of tonight's 18, think? What do any Catholics think? My fantasy of Boro fielding an openly gay player seems silly now – we don't deserve one – and while the funny chants about Louis Appéré and TVC are just minutes away, they feel worlds apart. From what we can hear, the chanters seem to be kids, so somebody's grooming them. Oscar shakes his head. Me too, and if I feel bad about exposing him to Stevenage's football sometimes, I feel even more grubby having exposed him to some of the people of this lovely town, a town where Labour won the seat in 2024 as the Conservatives smashed Reform and where there was an active Militant cell in the 80s.

The comeback doesn't happen. It was never going to happen. As was the sad case in Burton, goalkeeper Crocombe seems to be afflicted by a series of plagues for which the only remedy is for his team-mates to sprint to the touchline to receive instructions from Gary Bowyer and for Crocombe to take goal kicks very slowly until a yellow card (one of two for Burton time-wasting) speeds him up a little. 'It's a miracle!' shouts Reverend Richard as Crocombe rises.

Edwards is given 15 minutes and looks dangerous, but calm, cool and collected Burton deserve everything they leave with in their Ellisons coach. It's not one of Ellisons' Premier League beasts, but Oscar refuses to go into the car park to peruse. We're a long way from him asking whether a bus will be an Ellisons, even though the answer this time is actually 'yes'. Boro are booed off yet again, with the venom coming from all three sides as the travellers celebrate as loudly as we did at Orient and Barnsley.

'You do know that when you mention the team buses in the book, people will just turn over the page, don't you, Dad?'

I do not know that, no. Moreover, I refuse to know it. Meanwhile, Tyreece Simpson seemingly scores for Colchester at Notts County, but the messy goal involves defender Zak Johnson, goalkeeper Alex Bass, and some ricochets, so it's hard to tell. Revs accepts it was right and proper that the team were booed off and speaks about naivety, but I'm not sure. Not for the first time, I don't know where this is heading. I've started looking down the table again.

22 February 2025
Shrewsbury Town 0 Stevenage 1

My prediction: 0-2
His prediction: 1-4

On balance, being fallen out of love with is worse than falling out of love. Unless you've done something stupid or venal or sanctity-busting, you wake up each morning wondering why you hack at frost rather than embracing sunshine. You hope for a positive sign, be it as prosaic as a cuddle or a kind word, knowing it'll never come, but hoping it might. It governs your life, slowly undermining everything you thought was okay about yourself.

That's how Oscar and I feel as we schlep up the M25, M1, M6 and M54 to Shrewsbury. Boro have fallen out of love with us. We're still in love with them, but we're getting only disdain and indifference in return. We've not been unfaithful, we've treated them with respect and passion. In return, we've been cold-shouldered, as they've succumbed to Charlton, to Crawley and to Burton. We think we deserve better, but it's out of our hands.

That said, because we no longer mention the p***-o***, we're more zen than usual. I can't help but remember that in the autumn I'd oh-so-casually but fate-temptingly floated the idea of the car breaking down on the way to Shrewsbury. Like Michael Scott in the US version of *The Office*, I'm not superstitious, but I am a little stitious, so I had my car serviced in the week with this very prospect in mind. We don't even buy treats for the journey. Instead, Oscar ferrets out some salt'n'vinegar rice cakes and we're off, soundtracked by Kendrick Lamar (him) and Irmin Schmidt (me, but he doesn't listen).

I'm not even that excited by the prospect of a new ground, my third and last of the season. But by some curious osmosis, things start to go right for us. We like the look of Shrewsbury, although our Wrexham friend James McClean called it a 'cesspit full of inbreds' after a fiery derby last month, and the local Shropshire council has just cut 540 of its 3,500 posts to stave off bankruptcy after spending on social care increased from 58 per cent to 74 per cent of its budget since 2020.

There's a parking space a five minute walk away. I'd been to Gay Meadow a few times – famously there was a man in a coracle who'd collect spare balls on matchdays when Colin Griffin or Jake King lamped one into the Severn – but not the Croud Meadow, which I couldn't pronounce, even if I knew who or what a Croud is. I assume it's the Croud who are 'a global full-service media agency that drives growth for brands through reinvention', since they claim to have offices in London, New York, Atlanta, Dubai and, er, Shrewsbury. I prefer Gay to be honest ... Outside there's a sort of fan park and that feeling of resignation you can almost smell when a club seems as certain of demotion as Shrewsbury Town do right now.

The club shop suggests a club going out of business. As Manic Street Preachers (and a conversation with Nicky Wire is balm for anyone's soul) once said, 'Everything must go.' In practice, this means everything is reduced, from the ice-scraper mitten to the dog coat, once £20, now just £6, tempting even to the dogless. One thing that isn't reduced is a Land Rover, marooned outside the Croud turnstiles next to a reminder that Shrewsbury Town are an 'official place provider' for Keele University. The Land Rover costs just £75,000 from Hatfields, Shrewsbury Town's 'official vehicle partner'. Official really is the word.

Inside, there are non-Pukka steak-and-ale pies with more steak than usual, which Oscar is delighted with. While we're blinded by the sun – for the first time in months floodlights aren't required, which lowers my morale further – the Croud is splendidly trim, although we're devilishly tilted away from the action.

Better still, after much speculation on the journey north-west, Vadaine Oliver – a footballer I was certain I'd never see again – is actually starting for Shrewsbury. Even more unlikely than our paths crossing again, he'd scored last week with an unstoppable header into an empty goal from two centimetres. It was his first league goal for anyone (except that own goal he scored against Boro at Port Vale last season) since his memorable brace for Bradford against Salford on 1 January 2023, although some present that afternoon said his first was a Theo Vassell own goal and the second was certainly a tap-in. We know he won't be on anything resembling a roll, but the excellent programme gives him a double-page spread and credits him with 94 goals in 486 career appearances, so we may be being harsh. Then we remember last season. As I've said before, he always tried hard ...

There's more. Still injured, Luther has done a TikTok where, instead of talking about property, he's asked for his followers to send him questions on football. Oscar's favourite: 'Is Dan Butler dead?'

Both Brandon Hanlan and Kyle Edwards start. Reidy is on the bench and by kick-off Oscar is so upbeat he's predicting a 4-1 victory, because 'we'll score four and they'll score one', he adds helpfully.

He's wrong, but after 90 minutes a very Boro thing has happened. For the first time since Burton visited the Lamex in 2014, Stevenage have won 1-0, without having a shot on target. What to say? Shrewsbury aren't competent by any stretch of the imagination. Dressed as a highlighter for the afternoon, Murphy Cooper makes himself big to block Aaron Pierre before, just eight minutes in, Robbo's hopeful cross-field bobbler ends up at the feet of the restored Harvey White, who, 25 yards out, rolls the ball towards Kyle Edwards, only for Pierre to nip in to obligingly turn it past Jamal Blackman.

From there, it's comedy all the way. Sweens – scary in the first half, colossus in the second – allows George Lloyd to sprint past him. Cooper brilliantly touches his curler on to the post, but John Marquis somehow puts the follow-up wide. How we laugh, again.

Before half-time, the move of the match finds Dan Kemp, smoking again if not quite on fire, hitting the post after a whiplash one-two with Robbo, but for all that the home team are poor and have no luck, the home fans never stop being rowdy, no matter how much we keep chuckling.

We laugh even more when Vadaine Oliver – so reassuringly inept that at one point Misser Marquis bawls him out – is hooked at half-time. We still love you, Vadaine. Honestly.

We're in loose-limbed hysterics when Harrison Biggins belies Shrewsbury's lack of attacking thrust to rattle Cooper's post from outside the area late on. That's it. No vile chanting, just three points and by the end Dan Phillips is exorcising the ghosts of Charlton when he takes the ball to the corner flag and a platoon of defenders can't get it off him. It's the sort of routine, mostly drama-free away victory I've been craving. That's what teams aspiring to the p***-o*** do. Not that Boro are, of course.

On the whistle, the team and then Revs come over to greet the 194 of us. Yet again, the joy on his face as he does the three fist-pumps after we've rattled the steel barriers to seduce him is infectious. We love him and maybe he hadn't fallen out of love with us after all, maybe the team hadn't too. We bounce out of the Croud and, to celebrate, we stock up with snacks at the Marks & Spencer Food Hall. 'Not just prices, but Marks & Spencer prices', as the advertising slogan probably has it.

It's a serene journey home and Oscar explains that fish'n'chip shops tend not to sell vinegar, preferring instead something called non-brewed condiment. That's why it's in unmarked plastic bottles. I genuinely never knew. It's a Trading Standards thing.

We listen to Steve Evans after another Rotherham defeat – I don't think anyone at Boro would seriously take him back now, although the prospect keeps getting raised on the East Terrace – and we listen to Shrewsbury boss Gareth Ainsworth. As he gives proper answers, I've always liked him and here he understandably laments losing to a team who had no shots on target, but he's oddly at peace. He apologises to Town fans and promises (literally, as in 'I promise ...') special times, even if Shrewsbury are relegated, as they will be. 'Oh God, he's so nice, I feel so guilty ...' says Oscar. 'I've never felt guilty about a Boro win before. Isn't he brilliant?'

Tomorrow, rather like Shrewsbury goalkeeper Jamal Blackman, Oscar will have little to do when Broxbourne Borough Under-15s travel to Hertford Town. It's an actual stadium, with stands and a dugout – rather than the unkempt school field that is their home pitch – so it's everyone's favourite game of the season. Morale is restored after last week's meltdown, the boys win 5-1 and they haven't played better all season. It's been a good weekend.

Pie Chart

1. Wrexham
2. Shrewsbury Town
3. Northampton Town
4. Peterborough United
5. Lincoln City
6. Charlton Athletic
7. Leyton Orient
8. Crawley Town
9. Norwich City
10. Burton Albion
11. Mansfield Town
12. Wigan Athletic
13. Stevenage
14. Exeter City
15. Blackpool
16. Barnsley
17. Huddersfield Town
18. Rotherham United

March – 'Why Are All Our Strikers Awful?'

1 March 2025
Stevenage 1 Huddersfield Town 2

My prediction: 3-1
His prediction: 2-1

I thought the cheekiness of Saturday's victory would tide us over the first week in five without midweek action. I was wrong.

On Tuesday, there's a statement on the club's website: 'Stevenage Football Club is appalled and deeply disappointed to report that a vile, racist message was sent to one of our players via social media following a recent match.'

No, no, no. It strongly implies the racist keyboardist is a Boro fan. The police have been informed, which is right and good. Things must take their course and hopefully they will, but it's profoundly depressing. We love the Lamex, we love the East Terrace, we love our silly and funny little chants ('nobody knows his fucking name …'), we love the first ten minutes of the second half where there's drum-led, eternally hopeful chanting, and we love the weary resignation when things go awry, as they often must. We love our little club. We despise this though. Everyone knows who the abused player is, but he'd rather it was dealt with quietly, in-house. His call.

But whatever was said at the Peterborough game, which we didn't hear, and the anti-Catholic, pro-'Tommy Robinson' chants at the Burton game, which we most certainly did, suggests a nascent trend. Assuming it is a Boro fan, then these people are amongst us. What if it's one of the Burton 13? What if I've said something mildly disparaging about the performance of a non-white player in passing? Did my loose lips embolden them? Perhaps we've exchanged friendly words with the racists in the food queues, in the toilets, in the stands and outside grounds. Perhaps we've sat next to them, stood next to them. Racists don't have a Swastika tattooed across their foreheads. They look a bit like me, they look a bit like Oscar, and Boro don't have enough non-white fans.

To wring my hands further, I may not necessarily be a liberal, but I have the liberal problem of being unable to understand why other people are not overwhelmingly liberal. Yes, the racists are cowards, knuckle draggers and simpletons led by grifters, but Oscar and I are going nowhere. They should leave.

'Wasn't this book supposed to be about love and stuff, Dad?' asks Oscar.

It was, Oscar, it was.

Ah, the Boro accounts (to May 2004) have arrived. They show a £700,000 year-on-year loss, but not too much debt and there are healthy cash reserves. That said, Boro had their highest crowds ever in the accounts' timeframe, although this year's have dipped. There is slightly more television money, but it won't cover income lost by the Sky/EFL schedule tampering. Birmingham, Bolton and, yes, Huddersfield, are just some of the League One clubs

Boro cannot compete with. These are the facts of life and Phil Wallace understands them, as must we. It's not a question of choosing never to forget who Boro are, it's a question of never being able to forget who Boro are. And that's absolutely fine.

This grim backdrop makes us both restless. We can't park in Fairlands opposite the ground off the A602 because a fair has invaded ('Just one bolt not fixed properly and dozens are dead,' declares drama queen Oscar), the bright sun darkens my mood and for the first time there's an end-of-season feel, although not for Huddersfield.

We're on the East Terrace early. Should it happen, I want to make sure I properly hear the racist chanting and get a look at who's doing it. Mr Loud's here, Reverend Richard's here and Mrs Chatty's here. She tells us she'd waited outside to console Terence Vancooten after the Burton game and remind him he's still loved around here. I tell her I'd seen her having a ball at Shrewsbury.

'I wasn't having a good time,' she insists. 'That victory doesn't count because Boro won with an own goal. I want to win properly.' Ah …

Easily superior when Boro visited West Yorkshire in the List Miss game, Huddersfield kick off in fifth, chiefly a result of their sturdy away record. Rightly, Revs persists with the same XI who started at Shrewsbury and there is more good news: Dan Butler isn't dead (Luther never did answer that one), he's on the bench, and before the game he comes over to the East Terrace, clapping, grinning and flashing a thumbs-up sign without a care in the world. He just loves playing. Oscar moves to high-five Boro Bear but Boro Bear turns away. He didn't mean it Oscar. 'Mug. I won't forget this.' The human mascot is in a wheelchair and Pidge – who else – takes control, bending down every

MARCH – 'WHY ARE ALL OUR STRIKERS AWFUL?'

so often to check his charge is okay. At half-time there will be a gymnastics display by a group of autistic dancers, there will no offensive chanting and things feel back on a footing of basic decency. 'I feel good about this one now,' says Oscar before kick-off. 'We'll win this.' It's a sliver of footballistic happiness.

Alas, by their very nature, slivers tend to be slender. Huddersfield start like an express train and they're ahead after two minutes, via the sloppiest of goals.

Sweens loses concentration and lets Callum Marshall through. Nick Freeman shows why he isn't really a defender as Ruben Roosken bamboozles him and leads him on a chase across the area, before crossing for Marshall to poke home.

'We've still got this,' reckons Oscar, and he's right. Boro buck up and before 12 minutes have ticked by, it's 1-1 when Brandon Hanlan latches on to a Louis Thompson hoof forwards. He's far too strong for the feeble Nigel Lonwijk and wallops the hardest-struck goal of the season past Lee Nicholls. For a moment he looks like a scorer. You never know ...

Huddersfield are superior, but Boro are giving as good as they get and should have gone ahead when Dan Kemp side-foots Kyle Edwards's cross wide of an open goal. 'I love Kyle Edwards,' purrs Oscar. 'Watch Revs take him off soon.'

The momentum evaporates with Kemp's miss and Huddersfield win it after another 12 minutes when Antony Evans slings over a corner. Sweens loses Lonwijk, who redeems himself with a downwards header past Murphy Cooper. When Huddersfield almost score a third, Mrs Chatty – the ultimate non-swearer – lets out the opening 'f' of a swear word. Oscar finds this hilarious.

I tell Mrs Chatty I'm shocked. 'I've shocked myself ...' she chuckles.

The second half is a breezy affair. Edwards is withdrawn after an hour, in favour of Dan Butler, who will have little chance to shine despite Revs switching to three centre-backs. Cooper pulls off a wondrous double save from Marshall and Joe Hodge. 'Best goalkeeper in League One,' shouts Oscar, and it's hard to argue. Marshall hits the outside of the post, Lee Nicholls saves at point-blank range from substitute Reidy, who heads against the bar in added time. It's been a hugely enjoyable game. Boro may have deserved a point, but it's still another avoidable defeat and, as Oscar points out, 'a valiant effort, but not good enough. I'd rather see a game where Boro win without having a shot than that.'

Afterwards, Revs berates the goals – 'didn't get tackles in for the first; lost a man for the second' – so surely Charlie Goode will start on Tuesday at Cambridge, but Revs also highlights the last seconds where Eli King and Lewis Freestone dither by the touchline 18 yards out rather than cross: 'We'll have to look at this.' That moment was Boro at their worst, and 1,205 noisy Huddersfield fans head north, as happy as people returning to Huddersfield can be.

Oscar refuses to peruse Huddersfield's team bus, a rather fetching Eavesway with brothel-style strip lighting around the ceiling, if executive coaches actually have ceilings.

'I've thought about that conversation we had after the Burton game,' says Oscar. 'And I've decided you should take every reference to team buses out. It'll be a better book.'

I'll think about it,' Oscar.

'I won't think about it.

The following day, Broxbourne Borough Under-15s will also lose to a better team, 4-0. The boys defend doggedly and barely break out of their own half, but morale is good. Oscar moans about the pitch with an 'I was the man of the match' caveat. He probably was.

4 March 2025
Cambridge United 0 Stevenage 1

My prediction: 0-2
His prediction: 0-1

Oscar has been on the internet. I'm not sure this is always a good thing, but he's found someone who's put some mathematical analysis through some computer programme (I asked for sources; Oscar had no idea, but the analyst seems about 15 and grins like Bruce Dickinson, so he must be completely legitimate) to calculate the chances of each League One club making the p***-o***. According to the young Srinivasa Ramanujan disciple, Boro's percentage chance of reaching said p***-o*** is 0.07 per cent. It's 0.03 per cent to make the final and 0.02 per cent to win that final. You've been checking the table haven't you Oscar, when we agreed not to?

'I have, Dad. Sorry, but y'know …'

The amazing mathematician Srinivasa Ramanujan spent five years of his short life in Cambridge, which of course is where we're heading this evening. For all Oscar's internet frolics, he's used the phrase 'nothing to play for' more than once since Saturday, but there is something to play for, there always is.

Orient notwithstanding, it's the closest Boro will get to a local derby despite Cambridge's programme columnist, a man who uses a Nelson Mandela quote as his banner headline as if he's penning Myanmar's first post-Tatmadaw constitution, sniffily declaring 'other fixtures have a better claim'. This seems to be because 'our fans are not particularly fond of their stewards'. Leyton Orient are geographically nearer to the Lamex, but Cambridge is always more fun and the journey up the A10, as the sun sets in a cloudless sky is so heart-stoppingly beautiful that, unprompted, Oscar takes a photograph. That's beautiful too.

That's not all. Oscar's Cambridge-supporting friend Frankie has informed him that Cambridge have the tallest free-standing floodlights in the Football League. Frankie missed the game at the Lamex because his dad was working, but he's here tonight and he's recommended the double cheeseburger, although, perhaps revealingly, Frankie and his father actually eat at a pub pre-match. I've only met Frankie's father once, but living in the North London Arsenal/Spurs heartland, he's raised his son as a Cambridge fan. Hats off.

I have a soft spot for Cambridge. They're firmly town rather than gown, their Abbey Stadium is on the main road to Newmarket in a residential area, their kit's a classic, away supporters have to walk through a field by a trickle of a river to reach their section, and in Jamie Murray they had a footballer with a tattoo long before footballers had tattoos.

Frankie also describes the Cambridge club shop as a caravan. He's not wrong, although Portakabin would be slightly fairer. Inside, it's heroically bonkers. There's a hand-made wooden clock down from £20 to £10; a four-pack of Abbey Gold, which is a lager; underwear; three golf balls for a feisty £9; and Lycra gear. There's a programme too. A rip-off, I ungallantly pronounce, when handing over my £4. 'Yes it is,' says the smiley assistant, far more gracious than me. 'But so many don't do programmes these days.' She wins, I deservedly lose. She knows me better than I know myself.

Inside that £4 programme there's a feature on the suspended James Gibbons, whose dancefloor favourite would be Ronan Keating's 'Love Is a Rollercoaster'. I'm on the lorry that was driving Ronan Keating through the trees in the Hollywood Hills as he filmed the video. Not sure James Gibbons would be impressed, but he might be.

Lower league football can be an awkward marriage of the well-meaning and the incompetent. Cambridge exude both. We're in good time as Oscar wants to try to see Frankie, who should be in the home supporters' area next to us on the divided terrace. But Cambridge have opened just one gate and that's not enough tonight. There will only be 739 of us, down from last season's 1,259 when we roared on a 2-1 victory from a stand behind the goal, which will be sparsely populated by Cambridge fans this evening.

The stewards are frisking everyone, presumably for the flares that always seem to turn up when Boro face Cambridge. Some Boro fans are picked off and arrested. It's like crossing the 38th Parallel, albeit without the worry of some addled squaddie from Arkansas running across no-man's land to defect. Inside eventually, the queue for the food is 30 minutes long and there are just two servers, who multitask as cooks and money takers. It's painfully slow, and as the queue outside builds up, so does our food line.

The rarely sighted Drackers is ahead of us in the queue. Once again, he looks the part: tonight, it's a splendid half-length, slightly checked overcoat. He could be the dandy bookmaker who's backed competing factions in a British gangster film.

And what happens when we reach the front to order our Frankie-sanctioned double cheeseburger – except it's not a double it's a single – with fries and a drink (Diet Coke for him, Bovril for me) for an okay-ish £10 each? It transpires the servers are mother and son and they're both sweating buckets next to the cooking food, but they're patient, ever so friendly and they're funny. I tell you, my mind's a see-saw.

I've always liked the Abbey or the Cledara Abbey as it now pretends it's called. Cledara is a Spanish company founded as long ago as 2018 by Cristina Vila, 'an entrepreneur at heart, a dreamer and a doer', according to the website. 'Our mission,' they trill, 'is to improve your relationship with software.' Oh goody. I'm rather more taken with Petrest, who advertise all the way across the stand opposite us: 'we're here to help you give a loving farewell to your family's biggest fan'.

Inside, we say hello to Mrs Chatty, who's clapping and bobbing in the less packed area, and we head for the halfway line, next to where Frankie and his father may or may not be stood. It's absolute bedlam. Surprisingly, Cambridge have let the Boro drum in, there are dozens and dozens of people we've never seen before and the chants are loud and lusty but not vile.

Oscar Snapchats Frankie: You've deffo heard us?
Frankie Snapchats Oscar: Nah.

I like Revs's team for tonight, although Dan Kemp's out. 'Why do you like him so much,' asks Oscar. 'He had three good games in a row and that's it. I always see a bigger picture than you.' Lewis Freestone and Harvey White join Kempino on the bench, alongside the unfortunate Kyle Edwards. Eli King, Dans Butler (yay!) and Phillips, plus Reidy Reid all start. That must be a better team than Cambridge, who a fortnight ago splendidly sacked Garry Monk and appointed two former managers in one day: Neil Harris and Mark Bonner (remember him?) as head coach and director of football, respectively.

Just after I'm hugged by a man with swivelling eyes who I don't know, Oscar nudges me. There's a girl next to us who's phenomenally, heroically drunk. She joins in the chanting, hands clapping in exaggerated semaphore and between chants she slumps on the barrier, eyes lolling, before vaping and swigging from the vodka bottle she's smuggled through the far-from-effective-afer-all border guards.

We're about to move out of her vomit range when there's a massive surge to our left. In a move of either hopeless ineptitude or far-sighted enlightenment to ease the crush, the stewards allow the Boro fans to break through the crowd control tape. The keener ones are scaling the segregation fence in order to share the internationally recognised hand signal for masturbation with our hosts.

Oscar nudges me again. Amidst all this mayhem, there's a glam mum who's brought several boys with her, slightly younger than Oscar. He's outraged by the fact she's using Instagram.

'Nobody over 19 should be allowed to use Instagram,' he splutters, incandescent. His irony-free generational outrage has stoked him into spying and he reports back on what he sees. 'She took a picture of them from behind when they set off and now she's said it's a stitch-up because there's no wine.'

She sounds great to me, but she's also having a fierce debate with one of them – her actual son presumably – who wants to throw himself into the more raucous throng than, say, hang out with mom. He wins, and as shop steward he takes his friends with him.

All this periphery has obscured a fiercely competitive first half, albeit with no shots from either side. 'Man, this is a tough watch,' sighs Neil Metcalfe at the peak of his powers on *The Comet* blog. 'Trying to work out if I've seen a worse half of football than this, ever. I'm not sure I have. If a tree falls over in a forest and there's no one there to see it, would it be more exciting than this? It probably would.' We're having a high-tension blast though.

'Teams back out,' notes Neil Metcalfe. 'Not sure that's a good thing.' Boro take control after the restart. Jamie Reid, who's having the game of his season (we've missed loving him), skips down the right and crosses low after Jubril Okedina falls asleep. It deflects off Michael Morrison to Brandon Hanlan, who shoots and turns away in celebration. 0-1! Ah, no. What Hanlan doesn't see is Nathan Bishop fingertipping it on to the post and away.

Robbo – another lost soul having a stormer – heads the subsequent corner into Bishop and pokes the rebound wide. Then it does happen. Dan Butler heads on Cooper's goal kick. Robbo outmuscles Liam Bennett, Morrison makes a hash of his clearing header and Eli King bursts out of nowhere to head down for Reidy.

There's a lot to do. Reidy's on the left touchline some 30 yards out, but he drives for the penalty area, leaves a

MARCH – 'WHY ARE ALL OUR STRIKERS AWFUL?'

trail of golden-shirted defenders behind him and from the D plants a screamer into the top corner.

What a goal, what a moment. Nobody here feels like there's nothing to play for. We have the perfect view of Reidy's redemption. Glam mum isn't so happy though. She claps half-heartedly as everyone around her revels in their catharsis. According to Oscar, she's been texting her charges to get out of the ultras' crush (Boro don't really have ultras, but give me a little rope) and they're replying they can't escape. When the flares are lit (great searching again, steward men and women) and the smoke covers the television gantry above us, she goes full-on lioness and dives into the noisiest section to protect her cubs and yanks them out, glam very much intact. 'Impressive,' admits Oscar. The boys stick with her for the rest of the game. I'm impressed too, and when she looks back, I flash her my finest parental-empathy smile. She scowls back. Why, it's as if I'm the sort of father who allows their offspring to read a stranger's Instagram posts.

From there, stewards attempt snatch-and-grab raids, close to where the flares might have been lit, but they're easily repelled. It's like Italy invading Abyssinia without the mustard gas. On the pitch, it's the plainest of sailing. Eli King strokes one wide, the unmarked Robbo falls over when Reidy crosses for him and Brandon Hanlan runs through alone, only to shoot wide. That said, the colossus that is Dan Phillips might again have been sent off for a reckless lunge and, just as he did at Shrewsbury, he does some added-time ball retaining by the corner flag, but the evening passes without Murphy Cooper being called upon. And Revs's substitutions are masterful: Harvey White for a tiring King late on and Jake Young for Reidy later still, just to further disrupt the game.

On the whistle, we do the chanting stuff while waiting for a visitation from Revs. When he comes over, the grin is huge. You don't have to look too deeply to see the little boy who joined Cambridge as a seven-year-old and made his professional debut for them ten years later. We just stand there shouting at him – 'Revell again, Revell again, olé olé' – and for a moment he looks like he's going to weep with joy. After the fist-pumps, he lingers with us shouters until there's nobody else left on the pitch. Then, for the first time this season, he does a second round of fist-pumps. All our hearts explode as one. We're in it together: young-old, male-female, pleasant-awful, rich-poor. We all want the same thing and we feel the same thing. It was surely the same for the Cambridge fans at the Lamex. I hope they felt like we're feeling. Football is incredible sometimes. 'That,' hollers Oscar, 'was amazing.' He'd hoped to meet Frankie for a post-game chat, but Frankie is long gone, although he tells Oscar he stayed until the final whistle.

It's less fun trying to exit the Abbey. The stewards are revenge-crazed, so they only open one exit gate and, backed up by police now, make more successful incursions into the queue as additional assorted Boro fans are plucked out. The police escort we chanting Boro hordes through the dark park to Newmarket Road. 'Wow, a police escort, Dad.' I'm edgy and Oscar chooses this moment to unveil his Boro shirt. 'Have fun for once in your life, Dad,' he splutters, powered by the same adrenaline that took him on to the cameras at Wrexham.

He's correct by default, since the Cambridge fans have left, partly because it took us so long to squeeze out of the Abbey. We listen to Revs and Neil Harris on the way home. Revs seems genuinely taken aback by the away support's love, Neil Harris seems to know just how poor his team is, aside from Nathan Bishop. It only takes us an hour to get home. 'Turned out well, didn't it?' yawns Oscar. 'Nothing to play for? No such thing.'

8 March 2025
Stevenage 1 Mansfield Town 1

My prediction: 3-1
His prediction: 2-1

I have done a bad thing. Still pumped up by Cambridge, before we set off today I secretly examined the League One table. Boro lay in 11th with 12 games remaining. Twelve games means 36 points. If Boro were to take 36 points from those 12 games (Delusional? Nah. Panglossian? Not me bub …) they would finish with 83 points. That's 23 ahead of Huddersfield, who are in the last p***-o*** place right now. Just a thought. I don't mention this to Oscar. Nor do I mention that, yesterday, in honour of the line in the Talking Heads tune 'Once in a Lifetime', I found myself in a hotel car park in Borehamwood, sort of to be confused with Phil Wallace's ex, Boreham Wood. Also there was the gaudily liveried beast that is the team bus of Bundesliga 2 side, 1. FC Nürnberg. Why it was there I cannot say, and they're at Preußen Münster tomorrow …

We take the train because we're transport convention busters and rituals mean nothing to us. It's sunny, so the walk from the station to the ground is lazy and languid. This feels good. Mansfield are the ideal guests. They haven't won in 13 games and only historical goodwill is keeping manager Nigel Clough in situ. I can't help noticing they have Jordan Rhodes, loaned from Blackpool, on the bench. 'Who's he?' asks forgetful Oscar. He nearly scored from Blackpool's bench up there, I remind him. I don't like this at all.

Inside, in contrast to the madness of Cambridge, it's pretty mellow. Mrs Chatty's on the same barrier as us and she's seen Luther – sans crutches – before the game; he can't be far away now. Mr Loud's along the way and, as a card-carrying member of the Revs In faction, is especially noisy, while Reverend Richard is just behind us. Oscar and I will high-five when he hollers his 'it's a miracle', catchphrase.

The sun's horrible but Kyle Edwards is nowhere to be seen. Hmmm, the club don't share this information but he's only on a short-term deal with a view to getting fit, theoretically allowing another club to hijack him for next season. After all, he's a Championship player. It's not much of a game, although Caylan Vickers seems to have Nick Freeman's number early on. Brandon Hanlan is grappled repeatedly by Deji Oshilaja, but referee Greg Rollason is not for the whistling.

In the last seconds of the first half, Murphy Cooper launches a kick forwards. Robbo heads it on, Hanlan cutely finds Dan Kemp, who crosses for Reidy to tap home. Mansfield are poor, dispirited and sloppy in possession, so that should be that.

Alas, this is Boro and, as we know, that is rarely that. Boro continue to dominate, but the referee saves Mansfield in one shape-shifting minute. First, Stephen McLaughlin (scorer of Mansfield's FA Cup winner) not so much handles Kemp's cross in the area as picks it up and autographs it. I don't even bother to appeal so I can watch Mr Rollason – who has a perfect, unobstructed view – point to the spot. He points for a goal kick.

MARCH – 'WHY ARE ALL OUR STRIKERS AWFUL?'

Seconds later, Jordan Roberts powers through the centre, outpaces the defence and is crudely upended by last man Baily Cargill. Not wanting to tempt fate, this time I join in the 'off, off, off' chants. Cargill receives a yellow. Now I start to feel uneasy, even more so when Louis Thompson canters forwards and finds Kemp, who hits it first time against the post.

Unmarked after good work by fellow substitute Will Evans, Jordan Rhodes tucks in the inevitable equaliser with the ruthlessness of a Sigurimi director. He'd certainly have made a better job of it than Kadri Hazbiu, the Party of Labour of Albania Politburo's only football fan.

That really is that now. Revs's substitutions are baffling from the moment midfielder Harvey White replaces striker Jordan Roberts just after Rhodes's goal. Striker Jake Young doesn't appear until the 94th minute and fellow striker Louis Appéré not at all. Bizarre. With someone else to blame (i.e. the referee), we applaud the players, but before he boards the still-handsome Sharpes of Nottingham team bus, the admirable Nigel Clough is unequivocal: 'Baily should have been sent off, it was a red card all day long.' Fair man. Good man. Mansfield fans are disgruntled when they should be relieved: '12 men and we still can't win,' tweets one of the 712 boisterous visitors.

Revs blames a lack of intensity and the referee: 'I defy anyone to say the referee hasn't cost us the game, the decisions are completely unacceptable … he hasn't refereed the game anywhere near the level it should have been', and 'a really, really poor goal to concede'. Our mood is enlightened by the news from Cumbria that Aaron Pressley has scored for Barrow. Miracles do happen.

Tomorrow, Broxbourne Borough Under-15s will have cause to roll their own eyebrows at a referee as they crash out of another cup. It's a 3-0, where the third goal is a penalty that wasn't. And soon the opposition coach is having to be restrained by his own boy players as he screams 'shut your trap' – a phrase last heard in public when spoken by Sid James circa 1974, probably in an episode of *Bless This House* – at Oscar's coach. Imagine if his team weren't winning ... Oscar makes a terrible misjudgement for the second goal, but he later reacts brilliantly to claw aside a viciously deflected shot. Oh, and Huddersfield have sacked their manager, Michael Duff.

11 March 2025
Birmingham City 2 Stevenage 1

My prediction: 0-0
His prediction: 0-1

The future may not be orange, but the light certainly is. It's gorgeous in downtown Birmingham this evening. 'Look at that, Dad,' coos Oscar, as the dusk sunlight bounces off a giant construction crane. Even now it's almost possible to inhale the Industrial Revolution around St Andrew's, Birmingham City's ramshackle ground since 1906.

It's showing its age, but aren't we all? To enhance the end-of-days feel, there's glass on the floor around the stadium, as if forming a smithereens guard of honour. Industrial Revolution notwithstanding, if it smells a touch 21st-century reeky, that's because the bin men are on strike, like it was 1974 and Trevor Francis still hadn't played for England.

Aston Villa may reside in gangland these days, but their legacy is almost Corinthian. In contrast, City were always the club of the inner-city hardcore. The *Peaky Blinders* characters were fans and the gang's heartland was Small Heath, the club's former name. UB40, a latter-day gang until they fell victim to internecine strife, were fans too. When Ron Atkinson was Villa manager, they would drive to his house in order to answer the call of nature on his drive, and tonight there will be the late Brian Travers's saxophone riff to 'Food for Thought' buried in some musical collage. Kind, generous and funny, Brian was a hard man not to like, and not just because, one summer's day in Jakarta, he bought me the finest room service I've ever gorged upon.

I've not been this way for a few years – Jude Bellingham played; let's just say sometimes greatness is obvious – but there's now what looks suspiciously like a Greggs warehouse opposite the main stand and, since City are sauntering towards the Championship, the buzz is almost palpable. They're getting more fans through the gate than in the latter stages of that man Trevor Francis's playing spell. Like Brian Travers, Trevor Francis was a good guy gone too soon: one lunchtime we talked about his winning goal in the 1979 European Cup Final while watching televised football. 'Not being rude and I am sorry about this, but I like to multitask.' And, like Brian Travers, he was brilliant company, unlike the football we were watching, so banal I can't remember for the life of me who it was. But I remember Trevor Francis.

They won't let us into the club shop. It's hardly overrun but there's a massive queue and they're frisking everyone. As I have a bomb in my pocket, we don't bother. Amidst the hustle and bustle and sheer volume of wandering souls, there is one oasis of calm where a man could go to meditate, safe in the knowledge he would be left in contemplative peace. Welcome, then, to the entrance to the away section. It's like a midnight border crossing between two inconsequential countries. There are more stewards than fans and they're so bored that as Oscar and I stride towards them, they leap forwards as one hi-vis blob, demanding their search rights.

Inside it's more holding cell than concourse. The food is wildly overpriced (not that working class, then) and the £4.50 chips with gravy only come without gravy, and there's no concomitant discount. For a moment I'm tempted to invoke the Trade Descriptions Act, but the staff are so sullen and so hostile that said temptation is resisted. I settle for a £4.80 Pukka, which I spill most of. He goes for a £5 hot dog and the bun splits before he breaks off a piece with his greasy fingers and hands me the mush to sample. Thanks Oscar.

For reasons I can't quite fathom, the cup Oscar supped his pint of Pepsi Max from has 'don't take this home' printed on the side. I'm thwarted once again, this time in my desire to take a sticky plastic cup from ground to car and then from the West Midlands to Hertfordshire. My God, my God, why have you forsaken me?

In the stand, knowing Brimingham haven't lost a home league match all season, we try to reimagine the Wrexham night of wonder, but it doesn't feel the same. Unlike Wrexham, Birmingham are clearly in the wrong division. There's over 25,000 here but the draughty ground is atmospherically flatter than it should be, despite a feeble light show ('It's just someone switching some lights on and off isn't it, Dad?' theorises Oscar) and some rather better, super-smoky fireworks.

Boro have sold just 291 of the 950 allocation. This means we're surrounded by Birmingham fans, so there's a backs to the wall feel and Oscar is doing more posing, waving, pouting and pointing than I'd prefer, but most of our similarly posing, waving, pouting and pointing hosts seem to be his age, rather than the Zulus of yore. Even so, the police are doing the segregating rather than the stewards and one of the more expressive Boro fans is doing his best to get himself arrested. Who's intervening on his behalf? Mrs Chatty.

Deep down, we both quickly realise it's going to be one of those nights, especially since Jordan Roberts is, apparently, injured and, again, Kyle Edwards doesn't even make the bench. Meanwhile, Boro have received an official letter of apology for Saturday's refereeing calamity. So that's alright then.

Just before kick-off, the City fans deliver 'Keep Right On to the End of the Road', football's most weary anthem. Oscar's mood lifts. He decides that 'we can get something here' and defiantly sticks to his prediction.

Jamie Reid, whose day has already seen him dropped from the Northern Ireland squad and will end with him being substituted, has an early screamer turned aside by Ryan Allsop, but it's clear who's superior as both Birmingham wingers get behind Nick Freeman and Dan Butler at will.

Murphy Cooper saves brilliantly at the moneyed feet of Jay Stansfield, whose seven-year deal must surely have some kind of break clause. Birmingham stumble ahead when, following a terrific Stansfield reverse pass, Louis Thompson taps Alfons Sampsted's ankle and another poor – but not obviously terrible – refereeing decision gives Brimingham the penalty, which Kieran Dowell sends to his left as Cooper dives to his own left.

Still, Boro are not out of it at half-time. A minute and four seconds into the second half, they are very much out of it when, following a low corner, substitute Alfie May tees up Paik Seung-ho to beat Cooper at his near post. The argumentative pre-match Boro fan gets himself thrown out, Birmingham fans sing 'you're fucking shit'. We respond with both 'we're fucking shit' and a chant mocking them for never winning the Conference. It's that sort of game and when we try a 'we're gonna win 3-2', nobody really believes and it fizzles out.

Birmingham cruise and Boro look a little likely, although Pidge hobbles off and Dan Phillips gets himself booked again and thus misses the next two games. Brandon Hanlan and Dan Kemp have long-range efforts they might have done better with, but in the fourth minute of added time, substitute Jake Young's exemplary technique enables him to volley a consolation past Allsop. By then many of the Birmingham many and a few of the Boro few have departed.

At the whistle we clap the team off, but it's lacklustre and some people succeed in getting players' shirts, which adds to the air of cynicism. It's been no disgrace, but it has been shoulder-shrugging, where it should have been frenzied.

Outside, where it was once *Fort Apache The Brummie Bronx*, it's sedate. Our car is intact and the traffic home is passable until the M1 is closed just before the M25. We listen to Revs saying the goals Boro gave away were poor, but it was okay overall. Oscar plays PAWSA's version of Stevie V's 'Dirty Cash (Money Talks)' in protest at Brimingham's new-found wealth. I can't bring myself to begrudge them a penny.

15 March 2025
Reading 1 Stevenage 1

My prediction: 1-2
His prediction: 0-1

After all this time, after all these years, I still love going to football matches. It still tickles a pleasure muscle and when I'm at a game I'm at the centre of the world. It was ever thus. Oscar's just about there now.

And yet there's Reading, with their soul-sapping stadium just off the M4, a symbol of Thatcherite hubris (or Thatcherite can-do) under John Madejski, their plodding team, their lack of history, their refusal to do a programme (bastards) and their current rogue owners.

I quite liked their previous inner-city home, Elm Park, especially at night, I always knew Robin Friday wasn't as other footballers and I was intrigued by my Reading fan friend, the late Tom Hibbert, claiming Steve Death's death wasn't what it seemed. I still think he was joking, but I'll never know now.

And there's the journey. I had planned to take us on the supporters' coach, but it was £30 apiece and a ludicrous 11.00am start from Stevenage. By car, it's either just over an hour or well over two. Today it's nearer three as they've shut the M4, so we take the same countryside route every lorry and Addison Lee has also discovered.

Since the Madejski is situated on an industrial estate, there's nowhere to park for free (there must be somewhere, but Sixfields was a once a season miracle), so I pay £8 (off-site, the cheap option), which at least saves time after we leave the M4. Reading are pushing for the p***-o*** so there's a buzz as we powerwalk to the stadium.

They've been through a lot these Reading fans. They deserve a change of fortune and an owner to hold their hands, but at every end of every day this big club by League One standards and bigger still by Boro's are still Reading. They may yet ply their trade in the Championship next season, although on the evidence of the 180 minutes we've seen of them, I doubt it. They might not, though, be plying any trade at all if the EFL cannot force far-from-loved owner Dai Yongge to sell up. I doubt the EFL will follow through. I don't really want them to.

The giant club shop is doing a roaring trade though. We do a quick scout. There are a lot of cufflinks and everything is on sale, but Oscar can't cope with a teeny, tiny pin badge going for £4.50.

Inside, we have varying food experiences. My pie is overcooked-to-burnt, filling-light and costs more than the pin badge. He loves his sausage roll, so much so that he buys a second, pretending he wants me to share his joy. Its greasy filling is unpleasant indeed, but he's unrepentant.

It's cold, windblown, and while the legroom is good, we're too far away from the pitch and too far away from the silent Reading fans. Mrs Chatty comes next to us 'so I can sing' and explains how the coach dropped its cargo outside the ground at 12.30pm, just in time for a Reading fan to call her 'Stevenage scum'. She's not happy and she has no news on Luther's return.

Right now, it seems each game brings less to play for, but Revs is cautious, restoring Jordan Roberts ahead of suspended Dan Phillips. The 343 of us sing, 'your ground's too big for you' regularly, but it's less funny than when we serenaded baffled Birmingham fans at a packed St Andrew's with it. We're distracted throughout the first half. Boro are playing in sky blue, not entirely dissimilar to Reading's royal blue – they've long swapped being quirky Biscuitmen in favour of the dull as Reading itself Royals – and I can't get into the game or follow it properly.

Boro are more than good value for 0-0. But for a comedy Brandon Hanlan miss they would have gone in ahead, although Murphy Cooper is prevented from taking drop-kicks properly by the aggressive Lewis Wing and he saves well from the gifted Chem Campbell, who will surely have decisions to make when he rejoins his parent club, Wolves.

And when Nick Freeman goes down with no opposition player near, the Berkshire boys' bark begins, but he's clearly hurt and cannot continue. Pidge, that man amongst men, loudly and lengthily berates the dozy bench who don't introduce Lewis Freestone quickly enough. 'Pidge is going to be a manager, isn't he, Dad?' suggests Oscar. I do hope so. But not just yet, eh …

Shortly after half-time, Pidge scores. Alas it's for Reading, when he heads in Charlie Savage's vicious corner. We don't actually see it because two giant, late-arriving Boro fans block our view as we let them pass. Shit happens, Pidge.

Then something happens to both of us simultaneously. I'm cold, I'm tired, I've got more problems at home than I can handle and, as I said, little is riding on this for Boro. But when Pidge's header accidentally goes past Murphy Cooper – Oscar feels it too – football casts its magic and shows its capacity to bring passion from the ostensibly mundane. We're both suddenly and properly engaged. Oscar trills his 'we can do this' mantra, we chant with more resolve and Boro inspire us.

Robbo Roberts is that mixture of guile and non-stop effort that makes him such a tricky proposition when he's in his pomp, Dan Kemp is all impish magician, Eli King holds everything together and Jamie Reid deserves more than he's getting. Goalkeeper Joel Pereira – dodgy at the Lamex – saves brilliantly from Eli King, but then Kemp somehow manages to cross from the left on the byline with a defender in attendance. Pidge rises for redemption and Pereira is too slow to react as the header loops in. The madness isn't like it was at Barnsley or Wrexham, but it's there. Mrs Chatty gives Oscar a hug. In my delight, I somehow smash my hand on a seat, take a layer of skin off and there's blood everywhere.

Boro hunt the winner, but the momentum is stalled when mostly excellent referee Lee Swabey retires hurt. The handover duties to the fourth official take so long (and yes, we rattle out the newly literal 'you're not fit to referee' chant with cheery gusto) there are eight minutes of added time, but it's time Boro run out of and Reading cling on.

For some reason the players and Revs don't come too close to swap applause afterwards, but it's a job well done. We enter the traffic hell outside in high spirits, and when five police cars with sirens and flashing lights squeeze through us, the most joyous part of the day comes when they return on the other side of the dual carriageway two minutes later. All hail their Keystone incompetence.

Next morning at 3.55am, I'm woken by a telephone light shone in my gunk-blocked eyes. It's Oscar. 'Come on Dad. You promised …'

So I did. We haul our duvets down to the living room. I make us herbal tea and we watch the season's first Formula 1 Grand Prix from rainy Melbourne. I don't mention that Neil Finn's wife, Sharon, once cooked myself and Neil's parents a meal at their Melbourne home, but that's what I'm remembering. Oscar is beside himself with excitement and, vicariously through him, so am I. 'I can enjoy this more because Boro were so good yesterday,' he says. Sometimes we're really at one. I could do this stuff with him forever.

Later that day, long after we returned to bed, like Boro, Broxbourne Borough Under-15s put in an admirable shift. Like Boro, they suffer a player loss through injury, but unlike Boro they lose. Worse, as he ruefully admits afterwards, the winner is Oscar's fault when he slices a clearance to their striker. As the ball rolls in, he pounds the pitch in frustration. 'But what else could I have done?' I put my arm around him to offer comfort. He lets it linger for a second, shrugs it off and where once he would have wept, now the near-man takes stock. 'I'll do better next week.'

20 March 2025
Speaking Truth to Power (2)

It's an Equinox, the only day of the calendar named after a Jean Michel Jarre album. Better still, I, Oscar and a roomful of Boro fans have been bought a drink by Phil Wallace. Cheers.

Since he really doesn't want to attend Phil Wallace's second fans' forum with the great unwashed, I've bribed Oscar with a Nando's ('I'm very bribeable, you know'). And he's adamant that he won't ask a question, especially after I've rolled my eyes when he half-jokingly suggests, 'What type of car do you drive?'

I'll ask one, partly to provide a public speaking example for Oscar, partly for the book and partly because I really do want to know what diligence was done before cash was splashed on Jake Young, a player the manager won't play, and Kyle Edwards, a player the manager can't play because those rumours of him being injury-riddled are seemingly true. 'Don't be too aggressive though ...' cautions fork-wafting Oscar before wondering if he can prise a dessert out of me. He can.

In the subway heading to the Lamex, we pass the mural and we're accosted by a man on a bike. He's the guy who sells the half-time 50/50 draw tickets on the East Terrace. Needless to say, we buy a ticket every game. Needless to say, we have won precisely £0. I have attempted to bribe him with chips and, in one reckless moment, a chicken 'goujon'. I have suggested he fixes the draw so we can split the winnings. I have told him I am not only dying, but dying in poverty alone and that winning the 50/50 is my last wish. I have threatened to report him to the Boro hierarchy for not selling me a winning ticket. I have threatened to report him to the police for the same heinous crime, and I have theatrically turned my back on him to buy a 50/50 ticket from his companion, as he laughed at me. I have spurned his offer to allow me choose which ticket I buy because he's clearly tricking me with his voodoo. And every time we leave him with our losing ticket, I'm chuckling like a drain. I feel better about the world and so does Oscar. We love this impish gentleman and his cheeky smile. He's the grandfather I might have had if I could remember my own. And now he's bumped into us and dismounted from his bicycle.

'Ah gentlemen, are you going to the Lamex?'

We confirm his surmisations are correct and that is indeed the case.

'I can't. I'm going to work. See you a week on Saturday. I might even let you win, hehehehe ...' Off we trot, happier than ever

It's the same set-up as the pre-season forum, plus the free drink. I go wild and have a pint of Moretti, my first alcohol at the Lamex. Oscar asks for an apple and raspberry J20. Living the dream people, living the dream. Thank you Phil Wallace.

If the younger generation took over the evening at Cambridge, this is for the oldies. Oscar's the youngest by some distance as we sit amongst what's mostly a group of pensioners with time on their hands. Oscar has a grump because, while I mentioned the notices said 5.30, I neglected to also mention that the doors opened at 5.30 and it was a 6.30 start. But we have a seat at a table, we have drinks and Oscar's phone has run out of charge. Happiness abounds for one of us.

Genial Mike Pink, Boro's CEO, does a little walkaround and he stops by to chat with us. 'This is to give transparency,' he insists, transparently. Mike Pink doesn't have to do this, nor does he have to emphasise just how united the dressing room is. Phil Wallace doesn't have to do this either. In fact, I'm not really sure why he has, but it's mostly a good thing. It will prove to be lower league life in minutiae.

Maybe I do know why he's doing it actually. One of my ambitions, unfulfilled at the time of writing, is to become the dictator of a small country. I'd have a firm but fair secret police, I'd reward competence almost as much as loyalty (that was the major difference between Hitler and Stalin: Hitler's inner circle were flibbertigibbet buffoons; Stalin's were supremely able) and I'd have a personality cult that wasn't quite the full Ceaușescu, but more sparkling than, say, Todor Zhivkov's. And, like Phil Wallace, I'd have forums where my subjects mostly told me how great I was, parallel to a little, carefully controlled letting off of steam.

A visit to Reading was another illustration of how having an owner such as Phil Wallace makes sense for Boro. For all his caution, he won't run away, he won't asset strip and he won't bet the club's future on unsustainable short-term success. Boro are lucky to have him. But he's 76 in October and there doesn't seem to be family members in the wings learning the ropes.

Ever eager, little Phil Wallace turns up six minutes early. He has that special sort of skin only very wealthy people are allowed to have. They go to a clinic in Geneva to have a skin change every decade, don't they?

There are the usual platitudes, questions that start 'how happy are you ...', and 'thank you for ...' but there's another thing: for all the Revs reservations, for all the goal drought, Boro are punching above their weight. Deep down everyone in the room knows it.

Phil Wallace reiterates his faith in Revs – the gathering will be about 60-40 in favour of the manager but the In faction is more voluble and less tolerant than the Out – and asks the Who Would You Rather Have? question. It's a crucial point: from Darrell Clarke to Michael Duff, those who looked good in the summer don't seem so seductive now.

To his credit, host Drackers raises the existence of the Revs Out faction. 'It amazes me,' responds Phil Wallace. He sets next season's budget – 'it's how much we're prepared to lose' – but the spending on facilities is now

MARCH – 'WHY ARE ALL OUR STRIKERS AWFUL?'

over, so more money can go into the signings pot. Perhaps. Without going wholly Ceaușescu, I'd rather pay off any debt first and then build. Phil Wallace claims Boro voted against the new Sky deal and then changes his mind to admit Boro said yes. And, worse than anything he can possibly do or say, he confirms there will be no return to printed programmes, essentially because it's too much like hard work. Because I don't want to embarrass Oscar, I resist the temptation to weep loudly and squeal 'in the name of all that is holy, no', but only just. Oscar grins his slyest grin. He knows. I saw it coming, but still …

I ask my question about Young and Edwards. It's not a mood disrupter, and Phil Wallace sidesteps any notions of lax diligence. Revs does fancy Young, but the player didn't have a pre-season so is playing catch up (surely he should have caught up by March, but hey …), his best is yet to come, and Young is still young. And without admitting the nature of Edwards's contract, he accepts Edwards wouldn't be here if he wasn't injury-prone and Boro have to work with it, which proves my point. Kind of.

More platitudes later, Oscar's getting so twitchy that I can almost smell him. He thumps me on the thigh and whispers, 'I've had enough.' He summons Drackers, who it must be noted is wearing a rather fetching tank top, channelling the dad in a 50s US sitcom.

'Phil,' Oscar says in his most polite voice, 'please could you tell me why we've signed four or five strikers and they've all been awful?'

There's an audible gasp. Phil Wallace doesn't really have an answer. He asks Oscar to name them. Oscar does and he doesn't blush at all, a quality not inherited, since I'd have turned the colour of beetroot at his age, although I wouldn't have had the courage to speak in the first place. Pressley, Simpson ... Before Oscar can finish, other tables join in. Someone adds Appéré. Someone else – not me, this is Oscar's show – Vadaine Oliver. Phil Wallace suggests Simpson might still work out and is still young and that Pressley is also still young. Apropos of nothing, he brings up midfielders.

Oscar politely shuts him down. He's got the part about starting questions with the target's name. 'Phil, I explicitly asked about strikers, not midfielders,' with the beyond-his-years assurance born of those nights in Wigan and mornings in Exeter. Phil Wallace shuts it down: 'I'm always happy to take a gamble on a striker.' Drackers asks Oscar for his name and age and says 'keep an eye on this one', possibly with a view to having him shot later. I'm so proud. He's come so far since the first Speaking Truth to Power. He's a different boy now, comfortable in himself with his contact lenses, his fragrances, his teeth-whitening strips, his time-consumingly but bafflingly coiffured hair, his gym body and the clothes he enjoys wearing. He's in a good place.

The mood has changed, thanks to Oscar. The Revs Out faction reveals itself at some length. 'Look,' says Phil Wallace, exasperated now, 'I'm happy with the decision I made. If I wasn't impressed, Revs wouldn't be here.'

Nobody asks about racism or Jake Forster-Caskey, but there is just enough time for someone to say they don't want Boro in the Championship. It's not as daft as it sounds – think Yeovil, think Burton, think Southend, teams who went there, only to come back down, broken – but it's sad. That guy remembers leaving Bramall Lane in 2012 after Boro's only League One p***-o*** attempt ended in defeat and telling his son he was glad their team wouldn't be in the Championship.

'You'd never say that to me, would you, Dad?'

Never, ever. I couldn't trample on our dreams.

Yet that's who Boro are: a well-run small club looking to be more competitive in League One. It's okay, it really is. For now.

Oscar's pleased with himself afterwards. 'Nobody was asking the right questions,' he explains. 'Yours wasn't bad but it wasn't great how it ended. So I thought I'd ask. Someone had to.'

27 March 2025
Leyton Orient 1 Stevenage 0

My prediction: 0-2
His prediction: 0-2

Another trip to Leyton Orient. We'll never fall in love with Orient's ground, although we never thought we'd fall for the Vertu, especially at Orient. But like the Vertu, their ground has changed its name mid-season. The Gaughan Group Stadium has reverted to the name we all know and shrug our shoulders over: Brisbane Road. The extremely terse divorce announcement merely stated that 'Leyton Orient and Gaughan Group have agreed the early termination of its stadium naming rights partnership.' Since there are no lines to read between, 'your go-to experts for heating, plumbing and drainage in South East London and Kent' may have overreached themselves. Or they may not.

We need a reset. As with our Vertu trip, we forget something. This time it *is* my fault. We're already on the Central Line when I realise I've left my phone in the car. I need it to make the notes I'll ignore when I come to write. It's not the end of the world, I can use Oscar's.

'No you can't.'

His face has an ugly hue. He's cross with himself for using that same phone in school and rightly receiving a detention. He doesn't like Orient and Richie 'cream rises to the top' Wellens. He wants to prove a point about my uselessness and there's something at school he's not ready to share yet. He's not for turning. He taps his coat smugly and grins: 'And don't forget I have the tickets in my pocket.'

We schlep back. I sneak out of the underground without paying, retrieve the bloody phone, sneak back into the underground without paying and we're off. Again. Belatedly.

Good job we set off in good time, Oscar. He ignores me and I'm unusually angry with him, but we slowly make up by pondering whether the food for the away fans will equal the banquet offered to the home fans at the Vertu. It's stilted conversation, but he's feeling guilty.

The Leyton underground Tannoy is warning people against phone-snatchers, but we perk up when we see Brisbane Road's feeble floodlights. It's a local derby neither set of fans want to be a local derby, but you work with what you're given.

Maybe there's late-season, mid-table apathy kicking in, but I miss tension. We're going to have to find a way to approach the last few games, refind our mojo and power past the finish line. Let's look at the good things tonight. There's a programme, the cover of which lovingly recreates the design of Orient's 1977/78 vintage, although there's nothing of interest. And there's the food. It's served by the sweetest of sweet-natured souls and it's roughly what the home and away fans were served at the Vertu tie. We rekindle our love affair with pie and mash

Dan 'Sweens' Sweeney: 'alright lads?'

Dan Phillips holding off Ollie Rathbone at Wrexham.

Harvey White: 'a polite young man', tackling Daniel Udoh at Wycombe.

Dan Kemp: Player of the Season, at Shrewsbury Town.

Louis Appéré: 'nobody knows his name'.

Revs after Blackpool's third at the Lamex.

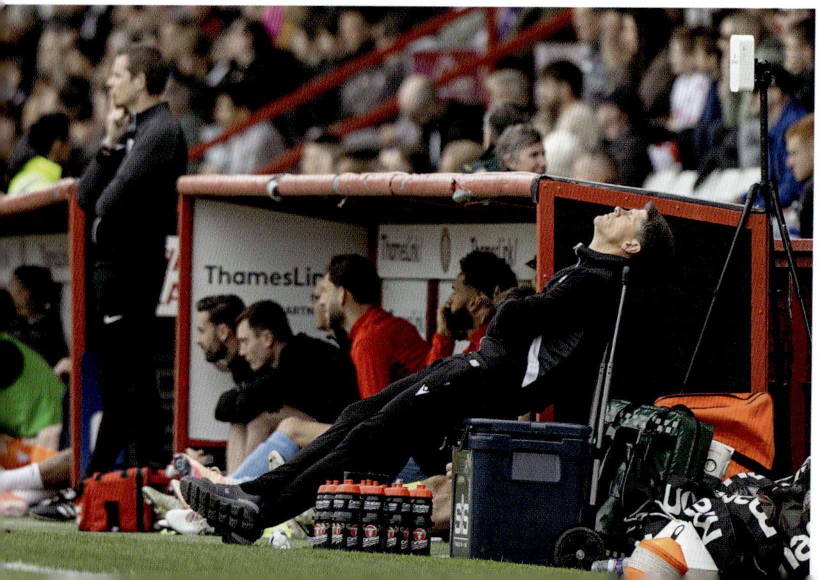

Jordan 'Robbo' Roberts on the end of season lap of honour. He's 'dynamite'.

Jamie 'Reidy' Reid grapples with Blackpool's Oliver Casey. Quinn the Eskimo, he 'makes the Boro sing'.

Aaron Pressley against Gillingham. Goal literally and metaphorically out of shot.

Jamie 'Reidy' Reid's penalty soars into orbit against Burton Albion.

Dan Kemp after scoring at Wrexham.

Jake Young scores at Wrexham.

Birmingham City's Jay Stansfield puts Boro out of the Vertu Trophy.

The end. Celebrating the final goal of the season at Bolton.

MARCH – 'WHY ARE ALL OUR STRIKERS AWFUL?'

and sensibly priced buckets of popcorn. 'It's going up the pie chart,' notes Oscar.

Mrs Chatty comes over for a chat. Since Luther's finally back (Nick Freeman's injury at Reading turns out to have been a serious cruciate one, so we won't be seeing him again until January) and there's so little sign of Kyle Edwards, even Neil Metcalfe – who reckons it's not injury related – is moved to ask why. Mrs Chatty is looking for Luther's mum. We can't see Mr Loud, but we hear Reverend Richard in the distance ('It's a miracle he's made it on time,' chirps Oscar, good humour restored by food) and all is fairly well once more.

The away support has collapsed like the Kerensky government of 1917. There's just the 345 of us for the campaign's least arduous trip, as opposed to 826 last season. Partly that's because as part of their Pretending to Care About the EFL campaign Sky have relegated it to a Thursday night as some kind of punishment beating. This does mean it's the most important game in English football today, I guess, although, again, Sky's viewing figures should make it some kind of tax loss, since the good people of Usk and Uttoxeter may not give a toss.

There's a new breed of Boro traveller too: younger, noisier, more enthusiastic and more tribal. They were at Cambridge too but, since there aren't so many of us here, they're more conspicuous. If their bonds hold, it's going to be a very different experience following Boro over the next decade. Were they doing the awful chanting? I can't say, although there will be nothing to shame Boro tonight.

Sean Clare's playing for Orient, still in his Snoop pigtails and still overflowing with the sheer joy of playing football. 'He's good isn't he?' sighs Oscar, although later Richie Wellens, who may or may not live in those flats adjoining the ground like Russell Slade, one of his predecessors, did, the flats where drying washing gets the best view of the game, will single out Sean for excessive tiredness. We love Sean Clare, don't we Oscar? 'You do. I don't,' he huffs.

Boro lose it as early as the 12th minute, but by then Charlie Goode – who will have a shaky evening – has already had a row with the uncharacteristically nervy Murphy Cooper. Diallang Jaiyesimi lobs a corner in. Cooper punches it out, but only to, inevitably, Sean Clare, who's well outside the area. I reckon he guides it back into the box with craft and precision. Oscar reckons it's a terrible shot. Either way, Charlie Kelman nips in ahead of rusty Luther to head in.

After that, it's a game that sums up the season. In a passage showcasing the very worst of Boro, they attack, play the ball around the edge of the Orient penalty area without anyone daring to shoot, before it goes all the way back to Cooper. Once Orient's early storm has been weathered, Boro are better, but powderpuff. Ludicrously, Oscar has further taken against Dan Kemp: 'He's just bad, he doesn't add anything.' But he does, he's a cavalier in a roundheads collective.

Late on, after Kemp has collected Clare's sloppy back-pass and rolled the ball across the area to nobody, and a couple of half-chances have gone begging, Sweens is introduced as a striker. Orient win and Cooper hasn't made a save.

Oscar's really angry. 'I hate this team. So, so frustrating,' and I concur. Nobody's had a stinker, although I'm beginning to think Brandon Hanlan is another non-striking striker, but yet again Boro are weak up front. Looking at it from a fissiparous point of view,

MARCH – 'WHY ARE ALL OUR STRIKERS AWFUL?'

the Revs In faction argue there are no strikers out there, which is shallow nonsense. The Revs Out faction contend it's simply a question of finding the right striker, but that's far too simplistic, too.

At the forum, Phil Wallace revealed the academy costs £700,000 a year. One sale, such as 16-year-old goalkeeper Elyh Harrison, who moved to Manchester United in 2022 and has already made their bench, will more than pay for it. It's an obvious lower league model of survive and prosper, assuming a club finds and develops a diamond. But, in a rare moment of bizarre logic, Phil Wallace also said he doesn't want young players in the first team as they're not physically strong enough, hence Ryan Doherty travelling to Orient but getting matchday experience rather than a place on the bench. But if you're only looking to sell on, you might miss a first-teamer and there are no academy graduates in today's 18. Doherty, Alfie Thornett, David Hicks and Lenny Brown may be the way ahead. I hope so, but I'm not sure Boro are committed enough. It's the truest of cliches that one of your home-grown own feels better somehow. Love is easier then.

We trudge back to Leyton underground station. We're heading east, but heading west is a bunch of Boro fans making a lot of noise. More unfamiliar faces and they're all drunk. They start pointing at us and laughing at us for supporting Leyton Orient. More disgruntled than ever, Oscar unzips his coat to reveal his Boro shirt. They all apologise. Even Oscar smiles now. It's not been a great night though.

For reasons known only to the fixture compilers, there's no game for Broxbourne Borough Under-15s this Sunday. Last week, Boro were forced to take the international break off. Dan Phillips missed Dwight Yorke's Trinidad & Tobago's CONCACAF Gold Cup qualifier victory in Cuba, but in the return he played 90 minutes and hit the bar in the 4-0 victory that sent them through to the 16-team summer finals in the US. That's great news for Dan, but not so great news for Boro.

The Broxbourne boys did play last Sunday. Playing fine football, even triangles at one point, they won 2-1. The first goal was the peachiest of peaches and Oscar was blameless for the hosts' scrambled consolation. It rained though. Biblical rain, and at one point there were just two Broxbourne parents on the touchline. I didn't mind really. Oscar was more drenched than me and at one point he shouted to the bench that his gloves had no grip, thus alerting the opposition to that very fact. Nice one Oscar. March is about to finish and we still haven't talked about not getting season tickets next season. I'm going to let it go.

MARCH – 'WHY ARE ALL OUR STRIKERS AWFUL?'

Pie Chart

1. Wrexham
2. Reading
3. Shrewsbury Town
4. Northampton Town
5. Peterborough United
6. Lincoln City
7. Cambridge United
8. Birmingham City
9. Leyton Orient
10. Charlton Athletic
11. Crawley Town
12. Norwich City
13. Burton Albion
14. Mansfield Town
15. Wigan Athletic
16. Stevenage
17. Exeter City
18. Blackpool
19. Barnsley
20. Huddersfield Town
21. Rotherham United

April – The Things We Do for Love and a Free Pie

1 April 2025
Stockport County 3 Stevenage 0

My prediction: 0-1
His prediction: 1-2

Oscar has a poorly toe. It's so severe that he has to leave school early. Luckily, it clears up during the walk between school and car. So we're off to Stockport.

Rotherham lost 4-0 at home to Crawley Town on Saturday. That's a hard one for managers to come back from. On Sunday, I'm lolling on the stairs discussing Steve Evans's prospects with Oscar – one of us thinks he'll stay, the other thinks he'll go – when the news of his sacking comes through.

Being a budding narcissist, I think of myself first. Rotherham's visit to the Lamex is the final home game of the season and it was meant to be Steve Evans's first return. I'd already half-written the chapter in my head, about how you can love someone until they leave you; how you can come to terms with that and remember the best days (Dean Campbell's winner at Villa) rather than the worst (an especially grisly home defeat by Bristol Rovers); how you can look upon their subsequent activities,

APRIL – THE THINGS WE DO FOR LOVE AND A FREE PIE

simultaneously hoping they'll fail and sort of wishing they won't; how that when our paths do cross again, as Martha & The Muffins had it in 'About Insomnia': 'In a tunnel, on a bridge or a viaduct/we'll meet just by chance/ And in a moment or maybe just an hour or so/renew our romance.' That won't be happening.

To be honest, we'd just like to thank him for giving Oscar some of the very best moments of his life, for taking a National League-bound Boro to League One and for last season's flirtation with the p***-o***. Every last fan on the East Terrace would have joined us. It's not to be. Another life lesson.

The Revs Out faction is already positing an Evans return, but surely that ship sailed when he fled. According to a terrific piece by Paul Davis in the *Rotherham Advertiser*, Evans seems to have left a similar trail at Rotherham to the one he left at Boro (and Gillingham and possibly others) following the rebuttal of Rotherham's first approach. Davis revealed that 'behind the scenes, there was tension, discontent, dissent … short training sessions, not enough work on shape, little attention to set pieces, a lack of modern tactical thinking, unedifying treatment of young players'. You can still miss someone while knowing they're no longer right for you. Can't you?

Steve Evans being unemployed is a problem for Revs, but it won't fell him. While Rotherham were struggling, there were no suggestions of reconciliation. Now, for all Phil Wallace's seemingly unequivocal backing of Revs, the man who kept Boro in the Football League in 2021/22, secured glorious automatic promotion from League Two in 2022/23 and almost made the League One p***-o*** in 2023/24 is available for work. And while the universal panacea for any football issues is winning, defeat tonight will mean Boro have taken just two points from five games, have scored three goals in this sticky period and haven't scored more than once in a game for 13 matches. The more Boro sink, the larger the large man looms. Tonight, it will take just 54 minutes for the first 'Evans again, Evans again, olé olé' and 'we want our Evans back' chants to be rolled out. Oscar doesn't join in. I don't either, because it won't happen and it would be a retrograde step, but I ask him why not on the way home.

'Because it was only 2-0 and I thought we might get something. I'd have joined in at three.'

This is our season's last long school-night trip. I don't know when we'll do this type of game again and my heart lurches. I love these late nights, coming home on deserted roads. We don't even have to talk. On the way home, we're on the M6 autobahn listening to the pastoral strains of Kraftwerk's 'Motorway' and I tell him how I feel. He looks up at the star-swamped cloudless sky and says softly, 'I know what you mean, Dad. But I hate this song.'

Before the game, we're off the M60 before it's crossed by the Stockport Viaduct, which was built during the 1839/40 season, all 11 million bricks of it, and it's featured in assorted L.S. Lowry paintings. Instead, Oscar is bowled over by Stockport's drive-thru Greggs: 'The best thing I've seen in my life.' We never find the Jaffa Cakes factory just off the A6, but I haven't been to Edgeley Park this century and it's a ground where Boro have taken just one point. It's changed a little, but there's still nothing not to like, unless you're part of a larger away support than Boro's 117 and you're dumped on the open end when it's raining.

APRIL – THE THINGS WE DO FOR LOVE AND A FREE PIE

The terraced housing estate that used to surround the ground is partly cleared, but where it still stands, the streets are narrow and houses, including the one where ex-manager Danny Bergara lived, are 12 feet from the stadium. And, as with Oscar's preference for Boro over Arsenal and Tottenham, everyone who supports Stockport County has spurned the chance to follow Manchester United and Manchester City. Good people, all.

We're in good time, so we investigate the spacious but bland club shop and decide against the £16 dog collar and the £72 coat, but the programme is £3 and full of, er, stuff. We sneak past the stewards into the County fanzone where non-playing players Ben Hinchliffe and Ethan Pye are being interviewed. Their words of wisdom are performed by an animated sign language translator, which makes our inclusive little hearts sing.

We're subjected to the most bonkers search of the season, so Oscar is very politely ordered to run his finger around his waistband, perhaps to check for flares, and roll up his trousers, perhaps to check for legs.

We're hungry travellers, but the food, oh the food: pie (meat and potato for me; jerk chicken for cosmopolitan Oscar), mash and proper northern mushy peas for £7.25. And it's delicious. Couldn't Boro do this, instead of greasy burgers, 'goujons' and claggy chips? We'd eat at the Lamex every game.

Against a backdrop of a sunset to savour (the clocks have changed, to appease a handful of indulgent Scottish farmers), Revs goes for the same starters who lost at Orient and it's a pretty game until the 25th minute when left-footed right-winger Jayden Fevrier gets the better of Dan Butler for the third time and cuts in to shoot. Murphy Cooper dives to his right. The ball hits Pidge, a Stockport player as a teenager, and rolls into goal to Cooper's left.

Again, Boro are unlucky, again they're the better team, but again (sorry to be repetitive, but this repetition has power) I can pass no judgement on County keeper Corey Addai, because he will have no serious work to do.

Boro's second half response never comes. Quietly impressive, Stockport look like scoring every time they attack, Boro never look like actually attacking, apart from Oscar's anti-hero Dan Kemp putting a free header wide. It's two when Tanto Olaofe bests Charlie Goode and crosses low. Kyle Wootton shins it and the ball ricochets in off Luther. The ball of the night, a reverse pass from the excellent Lewis Bate spawns the third. Jack Diamond shimmies through some feeble non-tackles from Dan Phillips and Goode to beat Cooper. Revs's response is to bring on two centre-backs and leave Appéré on the bench. Sweens does join the attack intermittently, but every Boro fan is perplexed by these manoeuvres. Nobody has a rational explanation and Mrs Chatty berates the Boro fans who chant, 'We lose every week.'

On the way home, we hear Revs and Stockport manager Dave Challinor agreeing that Boro were the better team in the first half, but that's no consolation. Oscar selects d4vd's 'Where'd it Go Wrong?' to chronicle our time at Stockport and he's too deflated post-Kraftwerk to moan when the M1 is closed, forcing us to crawl through Dunstable, where a haunted-looking man is using a cashpoint before sneaking back into the casino he'd just left. 'That's the saddest thing I've ever seen,' sighs Oscar. Shall we send a search party for Kyle Edwards?

5 April 2025
Stevenage 3 Crawley Town 1

My prediction: 2-0
His prediction: 1-0

I have done another bad thing. I've looked at the League One table again. Again without telling Oscar. I've looked down this time. With seven games to go, Boro are ten points ahead of upwardly mobile Burton Albion who are in the fourth relegation slot. That there are seven teams between the two of us should ensure Boro are safe, but all of them, apart from Wigan, are in better form. Surely not, but …

Summer has arrived early, which lifts everyone's spirits but mine, and Boro's inspired move of allowing season ticket holders to bring a friend for free has boosted the attendance a little. Let's hope they try it again. I gave Oscar the option to bring one of his friends, but he demurred. This game is just about make or break for Crawley, who are desperate for points. They'll bring a whopping 688 noisy travellers with them, since they sense it's a winnable encounter against an out of form team with seemingly nothing to play for.

Beforehand, we have an unsuccessful, half-hearted reconnaissance for the girl we sparred with at Crawley, but Revs has changed half the outfield starters from Stockport. It's out with the old, in with the mostly older. Dan Butler is dumped after his torrid Tuesday, but so are Reidy, Robbo, Brandon Hanlan and Eli King. Listy starts a league game for the first time since January and the hunt for a goal finds Louis Appéré leading the line. Even in these dark times, Jake Young doesn't make the 18, which, as in the reverse fixture, is one more body than

Crawley can muster. It's Phil Wallace's money, I guess ... Excitingly, the elusive Jake Forster-Caskey was the 19th man in the warm-up. We'll be seeing him before the season's out. Yay!

It's not much of a game so, still yearning after a lost love, the East Terrace serenades the ghost of Steve Evans. We used to sing the one about him being a 'fat Scottish bastard' at the helm of a 'shit football team' with delicious irony. Now there's a new, harder edge. Oscar sings along. I can't bring myself.

When Armando Quitirna skies a shocking effort high and wide park-footballer style, we sing 'say hello to Barnet' before Reverend Richard loudly bellows 'well that was unlucky' with dripping sarcasm. Oscar and I high-five and it happens yet again: by some invisible osmosis, football spins its spell and we're both engaged, both shouting and both up for it.

Then Boro ease ahead with a wonderful, wonderful strike from Harvey White, a swerving, dipping free kick from over 25 yards out. It's a world-class moment and we forgive him for wearing gold-soled boots.

I can't make Harvey White out. He's capable of wonder such as this and his passing can be almost extrasensory, but he frustrates the life out of us. David Pleat was at Tottenham when White almost came through there.

'I often saw him training at Tottenham,' he tells me. 'He's short on pace and power, but he has such a good body shape that he can glide past people. He's a very polite and decent boy, who listens, but he was a self-doubter, not forceful and not inclined to impress himself upon you.

'I saw him at Peterborough when he was on loan to Derby, but while he was there Conor Hourihane wanted to take all the set pieces: sometimes more experienced players resent younger ones. The Spurs loans manager said he was at that game too, although I didn't see him. When I said Harvey had done very well, he told me I was delusional. I was shocked anyone could be so rude to me.

'The Stevenage deal was very last-minute. I thought he signed for the wrong club, and that how Steve Evans's sides played wasn't for him. He could have been more patient, but he was crowded out at Tottenham.'

Was it money as well as game-time?

My understanding was that he was very well looked after contractually at Stevenage in comparison to what he was getting at Tottenham, but when I met his parents at the KFC opposite Stevenage's ground they told me that wasn't true, that he'd moved for more game-time rather than money.

'He'll hit Carl Piergianni nine times out of ten with dead balls, but his passing game needs better players around him. Today, Stevenage have fit runners, but they don't always take their opportunities to get forwards and that must be frustrating for him. He's not a Premier League player because he doesn't dominate games like Bernardo Silva or David Silva. I see him as a Championship player with a more football-esque team.'

Crawley are awful, aren't they? I muse to nobody in particular. Seconds after that, Crawley equalise when Jack Roles crosses high from the right. With one touch, Bradley Ibrahim chests it down. With another he guides it past Murphy Cooper. 'Why did you say that, Dad? It's your fault they've scored. Nobody else's.' This may not be scientifically provable, but Oscar knows he's right and I know he's right. I have cost Boro a goal.

'Oh for flip's sake,' shouts Mrs Chatty, the closest she gets to overt criticism.

'Where's the atmosphere gone?' asks Oscar,

For once, that's not it. When Crawley went ahead in Crawley, Boro equalised only to fall to two late goals. The reverse happens here.

Charlie Goode's 89th-minute long throw is nodded on by Pidge. Reidy flies in at the back post to head past Joe Wollacott, thus becoming the first player to score 25 League One goals for Boro. There's worse to come for the goalkeeper. Robbo surges down the right and crosses deep. It's headed clear, but only as far as Dan Kemp, whose first-time effort squeezes through Wollacott. Poor man. Crawley's journey home will have been hushed, but bus-wise, while they once used Clarkes of London (as seen on *Succession*) and the mysteriously downgraded Kings Ferry, there's no sign of who the coach belongs to, although its windows are very darkly tinted indeed. Most peculiar. Coaches advertise themselves on the road, surely …

Afterwards, Revs does the fist-pumps. Some may say that fist-pumping after a scrappy victory over Crawley where neither goalkeeper made a save of note is over the top. It's absolutely not. We waited for Revs, we did the rumbling sound that summons him, seduces him and sets him grinning. We join in with each pump. Yes, it means nothing in the real world, but football cannot be part of the real world. Of course, it really means something and Boro hoisting themselves over the 50-points barrier will certainly do.

A relieved Revs will suggest that Appéré hasn't been training intensely enough, which is worrying, but Crawley boss Scott Lindsey, newly restored after an ill-fated spell at Milton Keynes Dons, gets stroppy with his in-house interviewer for correctly pointing out that Murphy Cooper had nothing to do. Scott Lindsey is not for Boro. Not ever.

Oscar's been in a lovely mood all day and he's still floating when we get home. There's no Broxbourne Borough Under-15s game yet again tomorrow (the opponents couldn't raise a team), but we have an early start when he wakes me up for the Japanese Grand Prix, which kicks off at 6am. Bleary-eyed, we snuggle under our duvets and watch the dreariest procession I've ever seen. 'I still can't believe that Harvey White goal,' he smiles. 'We've seen some things this season, haven't we, Dad?'

12 April 2025
Wycombe Wanderers 1 Stevenage 0

My prediction: 1-3
His prediction: 0-1

All change, again. We are finally travelling to an away match on the Supporters' Association coach. It's a prospect that fills us both with mounting dread, for reasons neither of us can quite articulate. But go on the coach we must (I made vague promises to the publishers about going to games via car, coach and train, although they've probably forgotten) and how can we talk about lower league love otherwise? I haven't been on a supporters' coach in decades. It's Oscar's first time.

For hopefully the last time, it's yet another morning kick-off in support of Sky's Pretending to Care About the EFL campaign. Later this particular morning, once again two sets of fans will be united in chanting 'fuck Sky TV' and, reminding everyone whose lax governance allows this idiocy to happen, 'fuck the EFL', and once again the viewing figures may contrast unfavourably with those for Manchester City's thrilling 5-2 demolition of Crystal Palace. It's time for the Who Can Possibly Be Gaining From This? question again.

Wheelchairs are loaded, the drum is loaded, the coach is loaded with young, old, singles, couples and we're not the only father/son combination. It's a fairly fine coach, a Chalfont ('we go the extra mile', their website ominously threatens) with a side door and everything, although the seat of the woman in front of me is set only to recline. But hey. It's £25 each and the coach is full, Mrs Chatty is somewhere towards the back and there's as much communal anticipation as a day trip to High Wycombe for a League One match with ostensibly little to play for can possibly bring. More than I'd imagined, actually, much more.

The journey is just under 50 miles, but we're leaving the Lamex at 8.45am. I bow to nobody in terms of needing to arrive at destinations in good time, but I'm bowing now. The coach sets off in the wrong direction, literally going the extra mile.

The view is grand from our elevated position. We talk to the people behind us, about how we despise the racist keyboard warriors amongst us (no evidence for them here), how we're confused about Revs, how we'd like Reading to survive and the whereabouts of Kyle Edwards. Oscar delights everyone by sharing the pie chart he keeps on his phone and in no time we're at Beaconsfield Services, around the corner from High Wycombe. Alas, 'no time' means it's only 9.30. Oscar wolfs down a Greggs steak

APRIL – THE THINGS WE DO FOR LOVE AND A FREE PIE

slice. Guilt-ridden at my lamentably poor parenting, I go hungry.

The team are forced by the kick-off time to stay overnight (again, I do hope Phil Wallace invoices Sky and/or the EFL) and we're so early that we pass the team coach, stationary at the Holiday Inn just off the M4. Let it be known for the record that everyone is as excited at seeing Boro's team coach as myself. Even Oscar cranes his neck.

The closer we get to the ground, the more rowdy the coach gets. Windows are banged upon, chants are chanted and what was a mild hubbub waxes into the genuine noise of anticipation about to be satisfied. Everyone gets it. Everyone loves it. This is lower league life.

When we're parked up and raring to go, it's two hours before kick-off and we're marooned on an industrial estate in High Wycombe.

What to do? Oscar doesn't have a jacket over his Boro shirt, but we wander at will. Naturally, we visit the club shop. It's spacious but unimaginative beyond the £20 sliders and £6.50 dwarf teddy bear. We clap the team off the coach and into a ground for the first time since Huddersfield, another lifetime ago. The players bound into the ground like frisky puppies, except for Dan Phillips, who's far too cool for school and strolls in wearing giant headphones as if he's a Premier League player in a mixed zone.

Robbo cracks a big smile, Pidge is carrying a giant duffel bag, possibly with a body inside (ah, Kyle Edwards, perhaps) and Taye still has lovely hair. We're accosted by some friendly Wycombe fans. We tell them they were the best team to visit the Lamex and they ask how Brandon Hanlan (not allowed to play against his parent club) is doing. It turns out he's doing much the same as he did at Wycombe: effort to spare but very few goals.

Interestingly, despite kicking off in third place, to a man the Wycombe fans are downbeat. Nobody mentions their impressive midweek victory at Huddersfield. Instead, their talk is of the last home game, a 0-0 with doomed Shrewsbury where Wycombe managed an extraordinary 33 shots ('The amount of shots we've had all season,' quips Oscar, the wag) without scoring. A change of manager after Matt Bloomfield was seduced by Luton hasn't helped, but these Wycombe fans – one of them turns out to be Tony Hector, the charming and erudite supporters' representative on Wycombe's board; not I suspect a route Phil Wallace may take, even if it's a sinecure – are tense, nervous and full of trepidation. Just how we like it. We shake hands with them and head in.

On the way, Oscar strokes Boro's Greys coach lovingly, although he doesn't see me noticing, and just to add a little spice, he's called a 'dickhead' by some less friendly Wycombe fans before we reach the turnstiles. That's excellent, unlike the Boro fans who whisper to each other that a flare has been smuggled in.

We've been allocated about a quarter of an end, but that's more than enough. Wycombe don't do programmes (bastards), but they do pie and mash and gravy. By the time I feel hungry enough to partake, they've run out of mash and they won't give me gravy. The steak'n'ale pie is a joy though. Oscar's £6.80 hot dog has raw sectors and the serving woman has tissue paper dangling out of her nostrils. Ooh, sexy and hygienic.

Revs isn't tinkering, although Murphy Cooper has developed another mystery illness, which raises our eyebrows if not our hopes. The truth seems to be that he's signed for a bigger club and, with Boro having nothing to play for in theory, it's mutually agreed that a potential injury won't scupper the deal. This really is how football works. Luther signed a new deal in the week (as did Louis Thompson) and today becomes Boro's top EFL appearance maker, while Pidge notches up his 150th outing. It's all good, we feel good, the Appéré chant sounds good and we can see trees on the hill outside. Adams Park (named after Frank Adams, who gave the club Loakes Park, their sloping town centre home until 1990) is Oscar's last new ground of the season and he's perplexed by one giant stand alongside a tiny terrace and two smaller stands.

Wycombe are paralysed by fear, especially when a scandalously unmarked Richard Kone – a shadow of the striker who climbed into Pidge's head at the Lamex – unaccountably heads a free header wide from inside the six yard box.

It's a very Boro performance. Everyone plays well apart from the toothless Appéré, but yet again there are no chances. Early in the second half, wily 37-year-old substitute Garath (did his parents not know how to spell 'Gareth' or is it a family thing?) McCleary is warming up in front of us. There's some cheery teasing.

Then Taye flaps at a cross and Fred Onyedinma heads in. McCleary runs towards us, knees bent, grinning, gurning and fists pumping. He's greeted with a chorus of 'wanker, wanker, wanker' and then he's invited to turn around. When he does, McCleary discovers the goal has been disallowed, although no Boro player appealed. He trots away, but when he returns to be greeted with the inevitably renewed 'wanker, wanker, wanker', he grins again and gives us a massive clap.

Who couldn't be disarmed? We clap back and all is right with the world. We all love you, Garath McCleary.

We 332 are in fine voice and, yes, it means nothing outside this pleasant space, but it doesn't feel like that. When Pidge rises imperiously to head Harvey White's free kick towards the top corner we're already cheering. Then Will Norris somehow tips it over.

When the 90 minutes are up, it's been a sturdy draw where Boro frustrated Wycombe by dominating midfield and some handsome defensive solidity, Jake Forster-Caskey has made his first appearance in over a year and we spoilers of the promotion party are ready to ride home, heads held high.

Then Adam Reach crosses from the left. Harvey White half clears to Alex Lowry on the edge of the area. Lowry scuffs his shot. Charlie Goode's block ricochets to Caleb Taylor, who in turn is foiled by Pidge, only for the loose ball to roll off Pidge's shoulder and back into the path of Taylor, who pokes in. Jesus. A horrible goal. 'Every fucking time,' shouts Oscar. And the match is over. Was there ever a flare? We'll never know for sure.

Afterwards, Revs trots out the 'we'll look at it' line again, but even he's talking about the summer now and only Shrewsbury and Wigan have scored fewer League One goals.

Not everyone makes the coach back, but there's no noise as we glide along the M40, M25, A1 and A602. 'This hasn't been that bad,' reasons Oscar. 'I could do the coach again.' As Fiddler's Dram almost said, didn't we have a lovely time the day we went to High Wycombe? We did, on balance.

APRIL – THE THINGS WE DO FOR LOVE AND A FREE PIE

18 April 2025
Stevenage 1 Blackpool 3

My prediction: 3-1
His prediction: 2-0

Yet another new lower league table has appeared. This one ranks League One clubs by how much they've paid to agents. Unlike the proper table, Huddersfield are top, which suggests not all agents are value for money. As in the proper league, parsimonious Shrewsbury are bottom, although some of their trickle has gone to Vadaine Oliver's agent and their relegation suggests not spending on agents is a false economy.

Boro are a very respectable 17th, having spent £187,423, although the representatives of Tyreece Simpson, Kyle Edwards, Louis Appéré and Jake Young may perhaps have included some old rope as part of that exchange.

Let's start at the end of today, shall we? Boro have lost 3-1 in a game that, weirdly, they dominated apart from 15 unspeakably dismal minutes during which Rob Apter, last season's League Two Young Player of the Season while on loan at Tranmere, scored the first hat-trick of his career. The most deployed chant from the East Terrace has been the old favourite 'we're fucking shit', and Revs's lengthy post-match presser has ticked all his own boxes: the lack of desire, the absence of clinicality, the giving the ball away too cheaply, the word 'unacceptable', and the need to 'put things right'. No blame is accorded to himself or his staff, although, in an admirable new twist, when the players come in for Sunday training before leaving for Bristol, he's going to force them to watch the horror show all over again.

Blackpool have sped off in their handsome Ellisons coach (a superior Ellisons to Burton but not Premier League superior) with its tiny Blackpool FC Team Coach sign. They're 50 minutes behind their 558 supporters, but all must negotiate their way home through the Good Friday traffic. That's lower league love.

Oscar, who again refused to examine this particular bus, notes that 'when you're dead I'm never going to look at a football team's bus again. I'll tell people it's what you would have wanted.'

But it isn't Oscar.

'Yeah, I know. But nobody else will.'

It's been a miserable, miserable day on every level. Marching on to the East Terrace with the swagger and assurance of a burly bailiff evicting a teenage mother and her baby, I fall flat on my face, phone first. In a bid to protect the team sheet, I fell awkwardly, hurt my wrist and there's blood spurting out of my knee. One man comes to my aid, a sweet lady asks if I'm okay and three blokey blokes behind a barrier chuckle mercilessly. Oscar's face has turned scarlet and he's doubled up with belly-shaking laughter. A kindly steward soon picks me out to ask if I'm okay. I'd like to reply, 'This latest humiliation might perhaps be the breaking point and I'd really like a quiet room where I can sob gently before putting myself to sleep,' but I give him a big smile and a thumbs-up, not least since his concern has soothed my soul. At least I wasn't carrying a coffee.

'I'm worried about the book, Dad,' says Oscar on the way home. 'Things are just petering out aren't they?'

I explain that you can't pick your special season, that it's about love rather than promotion or relegation, that it's lower league life, and that this is something he'll

APRIL – THE THINGS WE DO FOR LOVE AND A FREE PIE

remember for the rest of his life, especially when his incredulity and that sense of 'did we really do that?' kick in. On the A602 before the game, I'd asked him whether he'd rather spend this Friday afternoon at anywhere else than a mid-table League One game. He thinks for a while. 'Not really, no.' That's enough for me.

It starts well enough. Luther receives a framed shirt for becoming Boro's record EFL appearance maker last week (he looks so happy), and while we know we won't be seeing Murphy Cooper in a Boro shirt again, he's here, as is Eli King. Louis Appéré is dumped from the whole 18, the search party hasn't found Kyle Edwards, and Boro are playing in a fetching sky-blue kit to raise money for Bob Wilson's noble Willow Foundation. These are the ties that bind us.

The first half is encapsulated by its last kick when Harvey White kicks the ball out of the ground. Technically that counts as a shot. The referee, Simon Mather, is pernickety and mostly wrong, but he's right to book Dan Kemp for his latest dive, the fourth official's board still doesn't work first time around and Taye's hair is still lovely.

Eleven minutes into the second half the horror begins. First, Harvey White dallies, dithers and is robbed by Lee Evans, who finds Ashley Fletcher (yes, that Ashley Fletcher). That Ashley Fletcher rolls the ball to Apter, who fires smartly past Taye first time. Harvey White pounds the pitch in frustration, showing rather more passion than he had when on the ball.

Then that Ashley Fletcher carries the ball though unimpeded and finds Apter, who takes one touch to steady himself and another to fire smartly past Taye. Finally, goalkeeper Harry Tyrer launches a long kick forwards. Sweens's dreadful attempt to control it reaches, yes, that Ashley Fletcher, who strolls to the byline and crosses low for, yes, Apter to, yes, fire smartly past Taye. Sweens kicks the post rather more competently than he'd dealt with Tyrer's kick. Smart finisher is Apter.

It could have been worse when Sonny Carey beats Taye, only for the ball to hit the underside of the bar and go out rather than in. Boro rally a little. On for Harvey White, Jake Forster-Caskey's very first touch is a free kick that Pidge imperiously nods in. Dan Kemp scores another from a corner, but his first reaction is to look for the linesman who correctly gives offside.

The players slope off, some returning for half-hearted applause. It doesn't matter. But it does.

The Second Photograph

Remember the photograph from the Stevenage website? It's sepia-tinted now, but by magical serendipity there's another photograph on the website, this time to promote the remaining home fixtures. It's from the East Terrace, probably from the Crawley game, although I wouldn't stake my life on it (but what would any of us stake our lives on, eh?). It's arms aloft time. We're on the left. Jacketless. Totally in the moment. Totally oblivious to anything else. Boro-shirted Oscar, mouth agape, fists clinched, looks for all the world like he's just thrown the winning dice at high-stakes blackjack. I'm next to Oscar, still clothed by Mr Fat Bastard, but smiling broadly and pointing. Again, there may be spittle. We really couldn't be any more happy. I wish this moment could last forever, but there are so many moments this season I'd like to last forever. Do we look as intense, as deranged and as ludicrous as we did in the first photograph, from a year ago? Yes we do. I'm so, so proud of us.

21 April 2025
Bristol Rovers 0 Stevenage 1

My prediction: 1-3
His prediction: 0-2

As with downwardly mobile Cambridge, I have a little soft sport for equally downwardly mobile Bristol Rovers. No idea why. Maybe it's the kit. Or the perennial underachievement. I saw them at Eastville as a tot, at Bath in a deluge and occasionally at the Memorial, as quirky as a ground built for rugby union in a housing estate can be. Last season, Chris Martin's freakish late fluke equalised Reidy's early effort, but it wasn't enough to keep Joey Barton in a job.

I dare not tempt fate until we're through the Bolton turnstiles, but I can feel the building emptiness of the end. Oscar is beginning to, too. No matter, we're early, and while I've forgotten my coat, it's so sunny and clement, it doesn't matter. We wander around the fan park. There's a covers band – the, ahem, A-Street Band – who teach us that 'She Sells Sanctuary' can be played sitting down. They're ideal for this moment. Having appointed a new head coach, Iñigo Calderón, with no understanding of League One or experience of management, Rovers were dismal at the Lamex when Calderón made his managerial debut. It's gone downhill since then and they're in deep, deep trouble, although (see also Wycombe and Crawley) they must have fancied facing an out of form mid-table team who have made seven changes in a crucial game. It's the *Silence of the Dans*, for Phillips, Butler, Kemp (out for the rest of the season: another mystery injury) and Sweeney are all non-starters. Jake Forster-Caskey does start, though, for the first time in a year. Ye gods, Kyle Edwards is in at kick-off too.

Unlike last season, Bristol Rovers don't do programmes (bastards) and according to today's tickets, the visitors are 'Stevenage Borough'. The lacklustre club shop (another 'Superstore', no less) is doing scant business, even for £3.50 bars of Rovers chocolate or some admittedly stylish coasters for £4.75.

Last year we stood in the corner shivering in the evening cold, but today we're in the newly erected South Stand, which Rovers started work on in the summer of 2023 without planning permission. The Portakabin toilets are flooded ('fresh water', claims a grinning steward) and ominously there is no menu or price list at the food outlet.

We discover why when we order a steak-and-ale pie apiece, a Pepsi (him) and a Bovril (me) as the sliding glass door drops off the food cabinet. How much will it be? 'Nothing,' smiles the flustered server. 'It's on one of your director's tabs.'

Heavens. We've shown nothing but love this season, and while it's not wholly gone unrequited, sometimes it's separate beds. Sometimes, too, love needs a big gesture to show it isn't just one-way. It's a finite tab but there will be 211 of us and we would have spent about £15. To us, it's a big thing, a kind thing, a thing worthy of thanks. Even more impressively, as far as I can discover Boro don't publicise the gesture on social media. Requited love is surely the best love of all. That nobody else needs to know about it makes it better still. Thank you.

The pie's perfectly fine. 'Does being free count in the pie chart position?' asks Oscar, who, after weeks of internal debate, has moved Leyton Orient's pie and mash upwards. After all, that food joy was nothing

APRIL – THE THINGS WE DO FOR LOVE AND A FREE PIE

to do with Richie Wellens or cream rising to the top. Yes, Oscar, it does; think of your £6.50 cocktail hot dog at Barnsley.

And amongst we travellers is Murphy Cooper, not looking very 'ill' at all. He's with a couple of women (I'm not speculating who they are, chiefly because I have no idea) and a male friend. Naturally, we serenade him with 'Murphy Cooper, we want you to stay'. He smiles up at us and gives us a sheepish little wave, the same sheepish little wave he gives to his soon-to-be-former team-mates when they warm up in front of us and him.

Not for the first time, there's a chant of 'Cheryl give us a wave' to the Hertfordshire policewoman responsible for Boro fans. She's at nearly every game – in uniform of course – and, loving the love she's shown, she gives us a cheery wave back as the Bristol constabulary film us. I hope she's helping to unearth the racist keyboard warriors though.

We're next to some Rovers fans, so they're serenaded with the full repertoire for the nearly departed: 'Say hello to Barnet ... going down with the Cambridge... Bristol City, they're laughing at you ... fucking useless ... that's why you're going down ... we'll never play you again ...' We're having an absolute blast. 'This is the best isn't it, Dad?' says Oscar. The Rovers fans invite us into the car park to discuss matters further.

The trepidatious fan park atmosphere is carried into the ground. Rovers have gone for an odd kind of Boro-copying broke by allowing season ticket holders to bring a friend for free and kids enter for just £1 (a concession not accorded to visiting fans) on an Easter Monday afternoon when they might have expected a bumper crowd anyway. Rovers are so abysmal that £1 feels like a rip-off. At one point, Connor Taylor takes an eternity over a free kick (your time lads, your time) on the left touchline close to the halfway line. His solution is to whack it 20 yards down the same touchline, almost taking the head off Luke Thomas as it flies into touch. After 90 dismal minutes, the nervous enthusiasm initially bolstered by an enormous tifo passed across the main home end, has evolved into venomous booing.

Boro win it in the 12th minute when Listy feeds Reidy, who cuts in, pokes it through Taylor Moore's legs, waltzes around Romaine Sawyers's couldn't-care-less challenge, past sprawled goalkeeper Jed Ward and along the six yard line, before finally smashing it in off Jack Hunt.

The only blot on this merriest of days comes when poor Forster-Caskey lasts just 27 minutes, before a shoulder injury forces him off. He looks heartbroken and we're heartbroken for him. It's the last we'll see of him in a Boro shirt. Kyle Edwards is that rarest of things, a thrilling Boro striker, keen on one-on-ones and, praise the Lord on the day the Pope dies, unafraid to shoot.

Harvey White hits the post with a free kick similar to the one he scored with against Crawley, Jordan Roberts misses a sitter and, to the intense irritation of the home fans, the almost untested Taye and his lovely hair take an eternity over goal kicks. I hate it when goalkeepers do that to Boro, since it undermines the spirit of the game and, frankly, it's cheating, which I despise in any area of life. Naturally, I'm shouting, 'Take time Taye, no rush mate,' to the other end of the pitch this afternoon, although Boro are never in any serious peril. The home fans are broken in a way, even at the lowest moments, we have never come close to this season.

For Boro, it's been a Shrewsbury-style professional performance. Revs delivers his fist-pumps with glee but without the usual intensity and that feels right and correct. We pick our way through the Bristol Rovers fans, angry but not with us. At the car, a couple come up to us and say how much Boro deserved to win and wish us a safe journey home. Oscar and I both say we'd rather Rovers stayed up. It sounds like an exchange of platitudes, but it wasn't. And the Easter Monday traffic isn't so bad.

24 April 2025
Stevenage 0 Birmingham City 1

My prediction: 1-0
His prediction: 2-1

Ah, Thursday night football. It's not even Sky's fault. Rather it's a combination of Birmingham's progress in the Vertu after knocking out Boro and international breaks.

The win at Bristol calmed the Boro naysayers and Birmingham won the League One title some time around September. They need a draw to reach the magic 100-point mark, as Steve Evans predicted they would back in August.

It's warm, sunny, and cheery Birmingham fans are everywhere. Despite City putting out one of those 'do not travel without a ticket' warnings, some have surely infiltrated the vast vistas of empty home seats. None will make themselves known, unlike the Boro fan sporting a Villa shirt on the East Terrace. It causes the stewards no end of consternation and confusion. I'd eject him for being unfunny, but I have no sense of humour.

Oscar's sensing the end of our journey even more. He's hoping we're the only supporters to have attended every game. I know at least one of the Burton 13 has missed a game, so that leaves us and ten possibles. We'll never know. Honestly, we don't need to know.

Oscar has started telling other Boro fans we're 100 per centers and he's making more friends. He'll ignore me for most of tonight because he's deep in Boro-based conversation with a friend of Mrs Chatty. He's found his place here amongst people who care like he does and who have the knowledge he has. As I lean on the barrier, alone but not alone, my heart soars.

The unknowing gang's all here. Mrs Chatty and her daughter are stood behind us. Because we're gentlemen, we'd offered them our places on the barrier. They turned us down. Reverend Richard's there and I'd forgotten just how sweary he is, Mr Loud is making his own noise and SOBF is smiling to himself.

I don't know them, but I love these people; they are kind, decent, committed and witty. Mrs Chatty dances a little jig of delight when I tell her that her beloved Luther is captain for the night – he does the talk at the pre-match huddle too – because Revs has benched Pidge, the first league game he's missed through anything other than suspension or injury since he signed three seasons ago. It's another side of lower league love: we're a small band, connected by nothing but being here. It's our safe space, our happy space, even when the football makes us unhappy.

And there are changes. Kyle Edwards is benched despite only playing 78 minutes since 1 March. One day he may even complete a Boro game, but I doubt it. He won't get a kick tonight and there's a new striking combination of Jamie Reid and Louis Appéré. Neither

APRIL – THE THINGS WE DO FOR LOVE AND A FREE PIE

will score, but we'd already assumed that. Without Pidge, Revs switches to a back five.

It's an evening that brings hope of something to build on. Boro are the better team in the first half, albeit without testing Ryan Allsop, and Birmingham's official total of 1,313 fans are hushed. City leave Jay Stansfield on the bench and we chorus 'we'll never play you again' and a splendid 'where's your binmen gone'. Oscar speculates that the Birmingham fans might have brought their rubbish with them, since the strike that began the evening we spent at St Andrew's is ongoing. I'd imagine the tabloids have already run the Rats as Big as Cats headlines. Assisted by the season's most feeble referee (banging on about referees is undignified, but gullible Lee Swabey has a shocker), Birmingham's players take turns to theatrically tumble to the ground, so it's a stop-start first half, although Robbo, playing his 150th Boro game, almost sweeps one in.

Joyless Birmingham don't look like a team about to reach the 100-point milestone. Their new Championship peers may sleep soundly over the summer. Naturally, Birmingham win it and fortuitously defeat Boro by one goal for the third time this season when Kieran Dowell's no-hope cross hits Listy, bounces once and lands perfectly for unchaperoned £1m-plus substitute Alex Cochrane to bobble his first Birmingham goal, and his first anywhere for two years, past Taye from 25 yards.

Harvey White will almost equalise in the last seconds when his fine long-ranger forces an excellent Allsop save and there's no suggestion of post-match booing. Instead, the appreciation for a feisty performance is heartfelt.

City leave on their Birmingham International bus and Revs is rightly furious – nobody confronted Cochrane and Taye might have got down quicker – but thems the breaks kids. He'll also finally admit Dan Kemp won't be back this season and Murphy Cooper won't be back at all, although he doesn't elaborate. Tonight, though, was a glimpse of who we are and who we can be. The love is still strong.

27 April 2025
Stevenage 1 Rotherham United 1

My prediction: 3-0
His prediction: 2-1

A grumpily terse tweet from Rotherham United blamed Stevenage for moving this fixture to 2pm on Sunday to give Boro extra rest after the Birmingham game in order to prepare for the all-important battle for League One's 13th place. Cue social media: 'tinpot ... joke club ... non-leaguers etc., etc., etc.' avalanche.

First though, Broxbourne Borough Under-15s have their own battle. Without a game for too long, their season will finish with another trip through Harlow's roadworks (nobody's working on them, in fact nobody seems to have worked on them since we last visited; surely their laissez-faire council will be defenestrated imminently), where victory will secure seventh place out of ten in whatever league they compete in. Their hosts are pushing for third, according to Oscar, so there's everything to play for.

The opposition are better and are soon ahead, but the Broxbourne boys dig in. Oscar – ever-present here as well as at Boro – has his finest game of the season and makes a succession of saves until a wonder-strike from the Broxbourne captain secures a point. Oscar is buzzing afterwards, not least since Bolton Sam called a niggly opposition forward 'Tommy Tough Knuckles' after the kid tried some futile teenage mind games. Oscar even tries the faux serene 'I've had several better games actually, Dad' line.

I love his team. It's anchored his life and he's learned and gained so much. Surely, surely, surely, there is no better way to teach a boy about the ups and downs of life, about teamwork, about grappling with worthy and unworthy opponents, about losing and winning and about making mistakes and saving days than being part of a team who've grown up together. Apart from supporting Stevenage. He's sweating like a hog on the A602, but he's brought deodorant.

Our Stevenage race is almost run and today is our season's final home game. As we know, I had hoped Steve Evans would be making his first return to the Lamex with my hometown team, but his dismissal is a reminder of things we can't control. It's sunny, we've stuffed ourselves with Burger King (he'd taken exercise making those morning saves) and the gang who don't know they're a gang (or each other mostly) reconvenes for the last time before the summer. Mr Loud is at his loudest, Reverend Richard is sporting summer attire that includes some splendid shorts, SOBF is smiling beatifically and Mrs Chatty is distressed that she missed Luther being presented with April's Player of the Month Award (I voted for revitalised Reidy; Oscar went for Luther) and she's even more distressed that he's injured today.

There's a new banner, a labour of true love. It's a giant screen-printed picture of Revs at his most handsome, most cult leader and least grey-haired, next to a word he keeps using: 'togetherness'. The banner-bearers struggle to pin it to the East Terrace wall, but it looks terrific, although we can't help thinking mischievously taunting the Revs Out faction is some part of this. Their banner would have showcased another of Revs's regularly used words: 'unacceptable'.

A handful of the 654 Rotherham fans have come dressed as bananas or traffic cones, and the game is a distraction, although Dan Phillips is deployed at right wing-back, Kyle Edwards starts, but he won't finish or kick a ball again for Boro, and young full-back Ellis Bates is on the bench. Moments after last season's 'Taye Ashby-Hammond in goal' chant (to the 'Rocking All Over the World' tune) has been resurrected, Taye stands transfixed as Sam Nombe screws in Joe Powell's low free kick from a physics-defying angle at the far post. It's a combative affair, though, albeit one without chances apart from the open goals that Pelly Ruddock Mpanzu and Liam Kelly obligingly miss.

Horribly, moments after Rotherham scored, there was another announcement about racist/homophobic/misogynistic (why so vague?) chanting. It certainly didn't come from near us in the centre of the East Terrace, so it must have been from the corner close to where Rotherham players jigged and cuddled after scoring. This is getting silly and wearying. The Boro stewards lack assertion, but the poison will drag the club down if there's no confrontation with these people. Perhaps we should police ourselves better. I'd snitch on a racist chanter in a heartbeat. Maybe others would too.

Boro have the best of the second half, but as a sign that Revs is taking things seriously, there are no minutes for Ellis Bates. The ghost of Steve Evans hasn't hovered over anyone; there's a brief desultory Evans chant from

APRIL – THE THINGS WE DO FOR LOVE AND A FREE PIE

the East Terrace midway through the second half and Rotherham fans seem to prefer Evans's less expensive successor Matt Hamshaw anyway. I spent an afternoon with Matt Hamshaw once ... he's smart.

It ends happily. Sweens comes on as a striker and in the 92nd minute, Harvey White collects a Dan Butler throw and curls it upfield. The ball bounces once, goalkeeper Dillon Phillips hesitates and Sweens, oblivious to the prospect of taking a punch in the face, outjumps Phillips and heads in his first goal since September 2023. Oscar doesn't lose himself, but he's pleased, very pleased indeed: 'One, we deserved it; two, what a way to end our season at home.' He's right, it's a fine way to temporarily vacate the Lamex when the season seemed destined to finish with three consecutive home defeats. Boro could have even won it in the smattering of remaining seconds, but Phillips redeemed himself a little when dealing with Harvey White's blockbuster.

Afterwards, Revs will use the word 'togetherness', but he also deploys 'unacceptable', vis-à-vis the first-half performance, which in truth was a little on the harsh side. He also says Boro are 'really close' to moving onwards and upwards and 'just a few bits here and there' are required. If he's right, he's called this season correctly; if he's wrong he's gone next, for Boro won't be two places clear of the drop zone.

The fun hasn't set yet though. There's a lap of honour, after Revs has taken the salute from the away fans who still adore him; that's lovely to see, by the way. The Boro players wander around the pitch and Rotherham head north in their impressively tall Wilfreda Beehive bus, which is possibly the equal of the local, family-owned Gordons in which they used to whizz across the country. Sweens throws his boots into the crowd. Pidge does selfie after selfie, Revs admires the 'togetherness' banner, and Harvey White lingers longer than the rest. The unfortunate Jake Forster-Caskey has one arm in a sling and carries his child with the other, and I don't see a more cute infant than Kane Smith's, although this will be the last we see of him too. There's mutual love and a mutual understanding of what this season has meant and how it's encapsulated lower league life and love. Oscar stands and claps. He doesn't want to shake any player's hand and doesn't want selfies, he just wants to watch. He's putting away childish things, but I can't tell him he's misplaced here.

There's more. Once the lap of honour is over, it's the Player of the Season Awards, run by the splendid folk of the Supporters' Association. These are the people who give time, money and support for no other reason than lower league love. They took us to Wycombe and we had such a good time that perhaps we should have allowed them to take us to other places too. I make a mess of our entry, but they're unspeakably kind about it at the very moment Oscar was getting anxious.

I haven't had a bad word to say about anyone who works for the club. I'm not rose-tinting; to be honest, I wouldn't have minded a little grit in the sugar. From club shop workers to the 50/50 seller, via Drackers, Phil Wallace, Boro Bear, the woman at the main reception on the one occasion we spoke, the Supporters' Association volunteers and those I've forgotten, there isn't a bad word to be said about anyone. Maybe Boro only attract good people. I believe so, I really do.

Once we're in, there's food, and had the kickass chili been eligible for Oscar's pie chart, Boro would have been

APRIL – THE THINGS WE DO FOR LOVE AND A FREE PIE

in the pie p***-o*** at least. Oscar wonders why they can't serve it at games. 'We'd have it every week, wouldn't we?' We would, we would.

The players, management (Neil Banfield swaps his shorts for tracksuit bottoms) and some of their families – Luther brings his mum, partner and child – join us. The whip will have been three-line, but if they're uncomfortable being here, it doesn't show. Dan Butler's first in, just as he's always last off the pitch; nobody loves being a footballer more than Dan Butler. Kyle Edwards exudes coolness, but his short-term contract is up. I guess Boro can't afford to take a chance on him. Even stone-faced Sweens smiles when he's the only player whose name is chanted on entry.

This is mostly an older crowd, enjoying breathing the same air as the players, but not in a weird way. The ceremony is short and sweet. Revs treats us to a brief speech, evokes that night at Wrexham (automatically promoted yesterday: Oscar right, me wrong) and admits for possibly the first time that Boro should have finished higher.

There are three awards. Since Boro don't do teenagers, the management-picked Young Player of the Year award goes to 23-year-old Murphy Cooper, whose speech ('I've enjoyed my season here') further confirms he really ain't comin' back. Drackers knows for sure, so he makes a gallows humour joke, 'Never fall in love with a loan player.' In the cold light of football reality, Drackers is right. But we have. The heart wants what the heart wants. And Drackers mentions Tyreece Simpson and Aaron Pressley, but not in an overly complimentary way. Drackers is a major part of this club and of why we love it. As the public face of Boro, he sets the matchday tone, which takes both skill and goodness, and he's the best-dressed man in the greater Stevenage area. We love him too.

Then the players reveal their Player of the Year. That's not somebody they don't like. Dan Kemp wins it and gives a speech that thanks the fans, before a giggling Drackers hauls him back to remind him of the award he's just won. 'Best dressing room I've ever been in,' chuckles Kempino, only slightly abashed.

And finally the fan-voted Player of the Year award for our wonderful season, the season where we've seen every kick, the one we'll never forget, even when others struggle to remember it. We'd have both voted for Murphy Cooper, so consistent over the whole season, but he's not the player whose brilliance has made us gasp. Mrs Chatty shouts 'Luther' and everyone laughs, but kindly. Pidge is third with 9.7 per cent, Cooper second with 24.7 per cent, and Dan Kemp – the one whose brilliance *has* made us gasp – wins with 52.7 per cent. He thanks the fans again. It's been a very Stevenage FC event: brisk, well-organised, low-key and life-affirming. Love was all around.

It's an intriguing choice. Dan Kemp is a queen bee in a hive of worker ants (n.b. nature comparison may not be exact) and in some games he's been unplayable. It took a while for him to get going and I'd have liked his imperial period to have lasted longer, but I was wrong about him at the first fans' forum, and again I'm sorry. I wish I'd been more wrong about Louis Appéré. Lewis Freestone? That jury's been out all season and shows no signs of returning a verdict.

May – Is That All There Is? Yes

3 May 2025
Bolton Wanderers 1 Stevenage 1

My prediction: 0-3
His prediction: 1-3

This is it, then. This is where our journey finishes, at a retail park in Horwich, a small town just north of Bolton best known for hosting Loyalist terrorist Johnny 'Mad Dog' Adair, who lived on the Chorley New Road in 2003. Exiled from Belfast during an internecine Loyalist feud, Mad Dog brought some of his cuddly chums with him. Naturally they were christened the Bolton Wanderers.

Oscar's been talking about one last push since the Rotherham game. He doesn't want this to end any more than I do. We pack a greatest hits of this season's snacks: Toffifee, salt and vinegar rice cakes, Haribos, the Wagon Wheels with jam, a McDonald's breakfast (I know, I know), a giant latte for me and a medium chai tea latte for him. We'll both go to the gym tomorrow.

We make a vow and seal a pact not to talk about the end until the actual end. On the way up, as if to bid us farewell, we see a selection of team buses, mostly travelling to Sunday's games: Tottenham's on its way south from the Ellisons depot in St Helens, Liverpool's off to Chelsea, and Newcastle's trekking to Brighton. 'Just think, I was ten metres away from Mo Salah,' coos Oscar. There's no need to tell him Liverpool fly and meet the coach at the airport.

Speaking of aircraft, just south of Bolton we spot a low-flying private plane descending into some local airfield. I remember my friend John Bauldie, who perished in that awful helicopter crash that also took his friend and Chelsea vice-chairman Matthew Harding. They both loved Bob Dylan, but John loved Bolton Wanderers, Matthew loved Chelsea so much that he invested over £25 million and they flew to the game when their teams met at Burnden Park in 1996. I spoke at John's funeral, but it's easy to speak at funerals when you've a lot to say. I don't want to forget him whenever I visit the stadium he never saw: the Reebok, the Macron, the University Of Bolton (Bolton has a university? How John would have scoffed) and now the sniggeringly named Toughsheet, from which Oscar will message Bolton Sam 'hilarious' toughsheet-related witticisms throughout the day.

Whatever it's called, John would have liked the new stadium, especially how it looms into view from the M61 like a giant, well-designed spaceship. John would have been less enamoured with a team who looked p***-o*** certainties until taking one point from their last five games.

I don't mention John to Oscar. He's sad enough anyway. We're early again – I had actual nightmares about car trouble – and it's warm enough for Oscar to be without a coat. It's safe enough for him to walk round the Toughsheet in his Boro shirt muttering, 'What's the point if I don't get hassled?' too. Even I'm sporting my Boro polo shirt. Last day of the season and all that.

The programme seller tells us to hang on to ours (as if I wouldn't) since he's heard grim rumours that Bolton are going programme-free next season (potential bastards), a season for which, just to remind us of the chasm between Bolton and Boro, they've already sold 15,000 season tickets. I hope he's wrong. He hopes he's wrong. He probably won't be wrong.

The club shop is cavernous and bustling and we cause accidental mayhem. I knock down a display of faux vintage footballs, Oscar blocks the route of a livid wheelchair user and we both laugh at the thinnest, most gaudy jackets (think Timmy Mallett at the peak of his powers), which have been reduced from £40 to £18, presumably in the wake of sales approximating zero. It's a brilliant shop, as Timmy Mallett might say. I spent a spirit-boosting hour with him talking about his beloved Oxford United. He's not what you think, although I'm presuming to think what you're thinking here.

Through the turnstiles to complete our 100 per cent, we quietly note what we've done. We're content, relieved, proud and distraught. Inside, we each have the same Holland's peppered steak pie. It's not short on pepper, but it's long on clag. 'I'm never doing a pie chart again,' says Oscar. 'No point if it's incomplete.' My heart breaks a little more.

The Supporters' Association coach broke down a mile or so from the ground. It's fancy dress day for some of the travellers, so a motley crew of clowns, knights, bananas, prisoners, Mexicans, Homer Simpsons, plus Mrs Chatty in a Super Mario Brothers costume spilled on to the M61 hard shoulder. None of them miss the match and now they all have another war story to tell. I never discover whether the coach was fixed in time for departure. They could be still be marooned in Horwich for all I know.

The coach party has just arrived when there's a loud and explosive concourse chant: 'Luton away. Luton away. Olé, olé.' Luton have been relegated. We're going there next year. I'm trying to savour the last moments of our season, but we're already looking to the future. 'What's Luton like, Dad?' Well …

The game is a tension-free delight. Bolton add to the gaiety when John McAtee and Aaron Collins miss sitters in the first minutes and Taye makes himself big and saves when the hungry Hungarian Szabolcs Schön seems certain to score. It's Pidge's birthday and we hope for a birthday goal for him. Instead, he gets a yellow birthday card. Looking to the future again, Pidge is replaced late on by Ellis Bates, a pale but composed academy teenage full-back. We'd like to love him next season.

Ever-smiley PC Cheryl makes herself visible. She loves the attention and, in turn, some of the 308 travellers are more than a little bit in love with her. 'Why is she always here, Dad? What does she do?' Well, she aids morale, she's a recognisable police presence, and when the coach broke down, she rounded up a couple of police vans to ferry the disabled fans to the ground.

It's turning chilly, so before goalkeeper Luke Southwood saves well from resurgent Reidy, I offer Oscar my hoodie. 'I have too much pride. I'd rather die,' which I interpret as a no.

Neil Metcalfe argues that the game is 'absolutely terrible' quality-wise, but 'such fun', and he's right. Alas, it's Taye's fault when Bolton sneak ahead after

MAY – IS THAT ALL THERE IS? YES

a near-post effort from Josh Dacres-Cogley squirms under a goalkeeper who surely can't wait for next season.

The goal changes things a little. 'We can't lose the last game of the season,' mutters Oscar. We can't and we don't. With 15 minutes of the season remaining, Dan Butler crosses deep. Luther cushions a serene header at the back post and Jake Young volleys home Boro's final goal of the campaign in some style. Dan Phillips almost breaks his goal duck when he fires over late on, but nobody cares too much and Boro have completed the third most successful campaign in their history, finishing 14th, scoring fewer goals than everyone but Wigan and Shrewsbury, while conceding fewer than only Wigan and the top six.

The Bolton Trotters trot off on a disconsolate lap of 'appreciation' rather than honour, before the dozens of the 20,000 crowd who remain. We swap more enthusiastic applause with the players, Neil Banfield removes his headwear and takes a very theatrical bow, and on the way out we hug a few of our friends. Since we won't be seeing any of them over the summer, we wish them a happy one with all our hearts. 'That's it then, Dad.'

We walk to the car in silence, bereft yet fulfilled. I've been dreading the emptiness of this final journey, but so has Oscar. There's a magical twist once we have again enjoyed the magnificent, complete 20-something-minute version of Kraftwerk's 'Autobahn' as we cruise down the M6. 'Again, Dad? This is the worst music ever. What's wrong with you?' But he's smiling now, as for the last time wir fahrn, fahrn, fahrn auf der Autobahn. Then, just before we pass Stoke, unprompted, he starts talking about our year.

'I love being with these Boro fans, Dad. This book isn't about us [he really hasn't been sneaking a peek, then], it's about them. We're telling their stories, aren't we? We've had lows this season, but the highs have been incredible. I won't say I've loved every second, but it's not far off. Norwich seems so far away now, but I'll remember this season for ever.'

I think he senses me welling up. He saves us.

'Let's talk about our highlights. One at a time, first you, then me …'

And out those highlights pour. We spark off each other with different aspects of Wrexham, of being two of the Burton 13 and of the Cambridge mayhem. I remember things he's forgotten such as golf putting in Peterborough city centre and he remembers things I've let slip, such as Crawley Girl. 'She'll never read this,' he smiles. 'She'll never know she's in a book.'

In fact, I'm so wrapped up in our reveries that I accidentally take the M6 toll on an evening when the M6 itself is empty. To finish this particular journey and the season, I take us on a detour past the empty Lamex. What do we do Oscar? Salute from the A602? Go into the car park?

'No, Dad. Drive slowly so we can take in our little ground for one last time. Then speed up, but we mustn't look back. It's gone now.'

The End

It's a week or so after Bolton and we're in a café in Cheshunt. I'm having lime and soda, he's having a J2O and bacon waffles with maple syrup. It's slightly awkward, a little like Julia and Winston meeting again at the end of

MAY – IS THAT ALL THERE IS? YES

1984, albeit without the betrayal and torture. He's here to award marks to every Boro player. I'm here to prise some feelings out of him. As ever, he surprises me.

'Our season had its ups and downs,' he muses. 'It took a lot of time out of my life but I enjoyed it. It's such a cool thing to have done and I'll never forget it.'

It's very hard to say 'what about me?' without seeming overly needy, but, er, what about me?

'Well, after spending 500 hours in the car with you, you've not entirely been as bad as I thought you would be. I now know you can't drive properly, but this year has strengthened our relationship overall. Why have you done this though? Even if you're too lazy to learn to cook, you took me to soft play (or so you keep saying, since I can't remember), you've driven me to and from school most days, we played football in a basketball cage for whole summers, you've taken me to football training, we've seen all the *Star Wars* films, we've been to a *Star Wars* convention when I dressed up, we've had holidays, we've been around a nuclear power station and around Wembley Stadium and you let me get you into golf. And now this, which, for me as well as you, probably tops everything. You care much more about things than you let on, though, even when those things don't count.'

He's on a roll now. I think he's prepared his speech.

'I have, yeah, but only because you asked me a week ago. There is something I have learned though. We've met so many people – not just Mrs Chatty, Reverend Richard, Mr Loud or SOBF – and in our own little way we've become part of a community. All these people are so different, but we have one thing in common, one thing that brings us together, I'll never figure out how and why, because its different for all of us, but that doesn't matter. It just is.'

And me? I've seen thousands of football matches and, while I've seen some rubbish (so much rubbish), I've loved being at every single one. That fine man Martin Tyler once told me with a certain pathos that his life had been 'a football life'. I see what he means, although I'm on a much less elevated level.

More important things have happened than, say, Burton Albion vs Stevenage on a Saturday morning in August: births, deaths, loves, break-ups, hurt and pain, joy and pleasure, assorted catastrophes, assorted triumphs. That's real life, unlike fantasising about when Aaron Pressley might score. I'm older, wiser and more broken because of real life, but nothing has brought more untrammelled pleasure than football and it momentarily turns me into the kid I probably never was. I may have pushed my mortality too often, but for one last time, when I die, I'd like to be full of poor-quality pie and holding my programme, if programmes still exist. I'd like the programme saved afterwards, ideally by Oscar.

If we do this again, it'll be when Oscar asks. I'd love that. Then I'll be with him every step of the way and he can drive. This season has been the end of something – it's the last stop before he goes – but the wider implications have already started to drop with him.

For Oscar, this stupid, crazy, but utterly, utterly magical year is the real beginning of him becoming a man. He's still talking about not reading the book right now, and that's just fine, it really is. But he will read it one day; one day quite soon, I reckon. I hope he returns to it in 20 years, when he's made his own mistakes and secured his own triumphs. I know he'll get it, but I hope, too, he'll remember the little details and remember them with elegiac affection and no little amazement. I hope too that he'll know that this really was for him. And I hope, more than anything, that he'll know how much he was loved. Before he goes and after he's gone.

Oscar's Final Pie Chart

1. Wrexham: own-brand emblem pie.
2. Stockport County: jerk chicken pie with mash.
3. Leyton Orient: pie and mash.
4. Reading: sausage roll.
5. Shrewsbury Town: steak-and-ale pie.
6. Northampton Town: Pukka.
7. Peterborough United: Pukka.
8. Lincoln City: Lincolnshire sausage.
9. Cambridge United: cheeseburger and chips.
10. Bristol Rovers: free.
11. Birmingham City: hot dog.
12. Charlton Athletic: Pukka.
13. Crawley Town: own-brand pie.
14. Norwich City: steak-and-ale pie
15. Bolton Wanderers: peppered steak pie.
16. Wycombe Wanderers: partly raw hot dog.
17. Burton Albion: hot dog
18. Mansfield Town: cool looking, but dry pie.
19. Wigan Athletic: own-brand pie.
20. Stevenage: chicken 'goujons' and chips.
21. Exeter City: sausage roll.
22. Barnsley: £6.50 cocktail hot dog.
23. Blackpool: filling-free pie.
24. Huddersfield Town: pie with worst-ever pastry.
25. Rotherham United: pie that split open and burned me. Too horrible to finish.

Appendix 1

Best and Worst Moments

My Best Moments of 2024/25

1. 'Is it "a-pair" or "ah-pah-ray"? Nobody knows his fucking name.'

2. Wrexham away. Every second of it.

3. Being two of the Burton 13.

4. Oscar asking Phil Wallace questions at the second fans' forum.

5. Walking through the turnstiles at Bolton. We'd done it.

Oscar's Best Moments of 2024/25

1. Getting in front of the television cameras at Wrexham.

2. Fish'n'chips at Blackpool.

3. The ball hitting the bar at Orient in the Vertu.

4. The celebrations at Cambridge.

5. Garath McCleary and the non-goal at Wycombe.

BEST AND WORST MOMENTS

My Worst Moments of 2024/25

1. Kwame Poku's winner at Peterborough.

2. Racist trolls and chanters.

3. Guiseley.

4. Listy's miss at Huddersfield.

5. Leaving Bolton. It was over.

Oscar's Worst Moments of 2024/25

1. Losing to Birmingham three times in one season, each by a single goal.

2. My pie falling apart at Rotherham.

3. Kwame Poku's winner at Peterborough and the downwards spiral it sent us on.

4. The morning kick-off at Exeter. Thank you Sky. Thank you EFL.

5. The absolute humiliation of the last ten minutes at Charlton.

Appendix 2

The Players

Ken Aboh 1(6) apps, 1 goal, 2 yellows
- Me: 3/10. Norwich City loanee. Full of pace and vim. Didn't get a chance. Looked a little slight. Just ten minutes game time after being reloaned to Colchester. Contracted to Norwich until 2027.
- Him: 3/10. Too little involvement. Didn't seem too bad, but we didn't see enough of him.

Louis Appéré 9(11) apps, 1 goal, 1 yellow
- Me: 4/10. Initially looked the part. Rarely looked like scoring. No league goals.
- Him: 4/10. Signs of quality, but couldn't find the finishing touch; a pattern in our team.

Taye Ashby-Hammond 14 apps
- Me: 3/10. Derailed by pre-season injury. Moments of brilliance, lovely hair, but he went backwards.
- Him: 4/10. Lost his form after being replaced

by a better goalkeeper. Hope he gets the chance to come back.

Ellis Bates 0(1) app
- Me: 5/10. The future.
- Him: 2/10. Only played five minutes. Hope to see him again.

Dean Bouzanis 1 app
- Me: 2/10. Reading loanee. Always a third-choice. Kept a clean sheet though. Returned to Reading before signing short-term deal with Charlton, who released him in May.
- Him: 2/10. Kept a clean sheet. Seems like a fun guy.

Lenny Brown 0(2) apps
- Me: 3/10. Looked comfortable, but no first-team sniff after November.
- Him: 2/10. I don't really remember him, but I hope he grows next season.

Dan Butler 34(4) apps, 6 yellows
- Me: 7/10. Infectiously enthusiastic, always an overlapping threat, tendency to drift inside.
- Him: 6/10. Maybe a little below par. I still don't know why he warms up every half-time.

Murphy Cooper 40 apps, 2 yellows

- Me: 8/10. QPR loanee. Brave, assured, almost howler-free, too good for League One. Returned to QPR.
- Him: 9/10. A brilliant season. He'll get a Championship chance because of this.

Ryan Doherty 1(2) apps

- Me: 6/10. Right now, the pick of the kids. Unfazed when used, unused sub too often.
- Him: 3/10. The best of the academy players. Hope he keeps developing.

Kyle Edwards 5(3) apps

- Me: 5/10. A thrilling revelation, rendered ineffective by lack of game time. Most peculiar.
- Him: 5/10. Positive signs but injured, injured, injured and now released.

Makise Evans 0(2) apps

- Me: 2/10. Seemed on the cusp of a breakthrough last season. Loaned out three times this, before being released.
- Him: 2/10. I don't remember him much. I wish him well though.

Jake Forster-Caskey 1(2) apps

- Me: 1/10. A calendar year out injured. A few

minutes playing. Injured again. Released. We'll miss him.

- Him: 2/10. Looked good in his three appearances, but …

Nick Freeman 20(17) apps, 1 yellow

- Me: 6/10. Often played out of position, although it didn't always show. Elusive.
- Him: 5/10. I have no idea how to rank him. A very odd season.

Lewis Freestone 27(6) apps, 1 goal, 8 yellows

- Me: 6/10. Not a left-back. Rapidly evolving as a centre-back. Concentration sometimes drifts.
- Him: 6/10. Forced to play out of position for over half a season. Had to adapt, so props.

Charlie Goode 20(4) apps, 1 goal, 6 yellows

- Me: 7/10. Season ruined by injury at Exeter. Solid and Boro's best tackler.
- Him: 5/10. Bang average. Very disappointing him and Pidge still hasn't quite worked out.

Brandon Hanlan 12(4) apps, 2 goals

- Me: 3/10. Wycombe Wanderers loanee. Brilliant striker's goal against Huddersfield. Didn't build on it. Shot-shy. Returned to Wycombe, to be released.

- Him: 2/10. He does have talent, but it just didn't click for him.

Luther James-Wildin 31(2) apps, 4 yellows
- Me: 8/10. A mainstay of the Revs Revolution. Tighter than ever in defence, dangerous when overlapping.
- Him: 7/10. I really enjoyed watching him. So consistent.

Dan Kemp 40(8) apps, 11 goals, 6 yellows
- Me: 7/10. Magnificent in his golden spell. Golden spell too short.
- Him: 7/10. We would have had far fewer points without him.

Eli King 19(14) apps, 1 goal, 4 yellows
- Me: 7/10. Cardiff City loanee. Cultured and rugged, but struggled to dominate. Returned to Cardiff, where he's contracted until 2026.
- Him: 5/10. The gaffer seemed to hate him. He should have had more minutes.

Elliott List 19(25) apps, 4 goals, 3 yellows
- Me: 5/10. Fleeting glimpses of the old pace and power. That miss at Huddersfield …
- Him: 6/10. Four goals isn't good enough, but he still has some quality.

THE PLAYERS

Dan Phillips 32(14) apps, 12 yellows

- Me: 8/10. Great thighs, great at breaking up attacks, great at the dark arts. Less than great at scoring.
- Him: 7/10. Vital in our midfield and I always enjoyed him getting booked.

Carl Piergianni 48(1) apps, 3 goals, 12 yellows

- Me: 8/10. Still the leader. Slightly more mistakes and slightly fewer goals than of late, but, oh, some of his blocks …
- Him: 7/10. Very solid and he truly leads the team. Consistent but not outstanding.

Aaron Pressley 2(5) apps, 1 yellow

- Me: 1/10. Effort never in doubt. Everything else though …
- Him: 2/10. We love him so much, but he's just not so good.

Jamie Reid 36(9) apps, 9 goals, 2 yellows

- Me: 6/10. Injury-delayed start, unfathomable mid-season dip, strong ending.
- Him: 6/10. Never as good as his great half-season, but by the end he showed signs of real quality.

Jordan Roberts 43(5) apps, 4 goals, 8 yellows

- Me: 6/10. Sometimes a hive of industry, sometimes slothful, always mercurial, too often unlucky.
- Him: 6/10. I've never understood his work rate. He clearly has the skill and with a bit more luck would have had more assists.

Tyreece Simpson 10(15) apps, 2 goals, 1 yellow

- Me: 2/10. Unlimited effort, limited everything else. But Boro should have known that when they signed him.
- Him: 1/10. Not that he never scored, more that he never seemed likely to score.

Kane Smith 20(2) apps, 2 yellows

- Me: 4/10. Too little game time, too little progression in that game time. We'll miss him.
- Him: 5/10. Never a liability, but never got going. Released, sadly.

Dan Sweeney 16(8) apps, 1 goal, 4 yellows

- Me: 6/10. Another injury victim. Some shoddy moments, but Boro look better when he plays.
- Him: 6/10. Still stresses me out every time he's on the ball, but not too many major mistakes. Still a good partner for Pidge.

Ben Thompson 1(2) apps

- Me: 1/10. Revs didn't fancy him, so he found love at Bromley.
- Him: 2/10. Three games and off he went.

Louis Thompson 37(7) apps, 2 goals, 12 yellows, 1 red

- Me: 6/10. Too many yellows, too few goals, but on his (several) days, he was a colossus.
- Him: 7/10. One of the few consistent starters. Worked well with Phillips.

Nathan Thompson 18(2) apps, 3 yellows

- Me: 5/10. He'd looked formidable, so there was no happiness when he left. But it was the right thing to do.
- Him: 3/10. Didn't play enough and left too early.

Harvey White 31(19) apps, 3 goals, 7 yellows

- Me: 6/10. Brilliant and awful, sometimes within the same move. What to do?
- Him: 6/10. A banger of a free kick against Crawley. Played his part, but never dominant.

Jake Young 17(19) apps, 4 goals, 1 yellow

- Me: 6/10. Dazzling and woeful. Needs a proper striking partner, game time and consistency.
- Him: 4/10. Our record signing, but given so

few minutes, he's not worth the money at the moment ...

Alex Revell 55 games, 2 yellows, 1 red

- Me: 7/10. He didn't solve the problems in the last third and bought mostly poorly, but Boro never looked like being relegated. The football has evolved post-Evans. When it worked, it was wonderful.

- Him: 7/10. Did what he was brought in to do. No more but no less.

Acknowledgements

Thank you to Pitch Publishing, to Stevenage FC (a club who really do attract the best and kindest souls), to Oscar's friends, Cambridge Frankie and Bolton Sam (may you never fall out of lower league love), to David Pleat and to Michelle and Jessica: it's for you two, too.

Bibliography

Aizlewood, J, *Playing at Home* (London, Orion, 1998)

Astley, R, *Never* (London, Macmillan, 2024)

DeLillo, D, *Underworld* (New York, Scribner, 1997)

Harrison, P, *Inside the Hermit Kingdom* (Chichester, Pitch, 2024)

Herbert, I, *Tinseltown* (London, Headline, 2023)

O'Farrell, J, *An Utterly Impartial History of Britain: Or 2000 Years of Upper Class Idiots In Charge* (London: Doubleday, 2007)

Orwell, G, *1984* (London, Secker & Warburg, 1949)

Price, S, *Curepedia: An A–Z of The Cure* (London, White Rabbit, 2023)

Tolhurst, L, *Cured: The Tale of Two Imaginary Boys* (London, Quercus, 2016)